BORN
to be
HANGED

BORN
to be
HANGED

THE EPIC STORY OF THE
GENTLEMEN PIRATES WHO RAIDED THE
SOUTH SEAS, RESCUED A PRINCESS, AND
STOLE A FORTUNE

KEITH THOMSON

Little, Brown and Company
New York · Boston · London

Little, Brown and Company
Hachette Book Group
1290 Avenue of the Americas, New York, NY 10104
littlebrown.com

First Edition: May 2022

Little, Brown and Company is a division of Hachette Book Group, Inc. The Little, Brown name and logo are trademarks of Hachette Book Group, Inc.

The publisher is not responsible for websites (or their content) that are not owned by the publisher.

The Hachette Speakers Bureau provides a wide range of authors for speaking events. To find out more, go to hachettespeakersbureau.com or call (866) 376-6591.

Map by Jeffrey L. Ward
Additional illustration credits located on pages 357–59.

ISBN 9780316703611
LCCN 2021948136

Printing 1, 2022

LSC-C

Printed in the United States of America

For Trouser

Contents

Part I
The Sacred Hunger of Gold

Part II
The South Seas

Part III
Straits

Contents

Landed at Dartmouth,
England, March 26, 1682

Antigua, January 30, 1682

January 18, 1682

New Spain

Petit-Goâve

Port Royal

North Sea

Nevis

Barbados,
January 28, 1682

Golfo de Nicoya,
May 6–29, 1681

Area of detail

Panama

I. Taboga, April 24–May 13, 1680

Golfo Dolce, June 6–28, 1681

I. Coiba, May 22–June 6, 1680

I. Gorgona, June 17–July 25, 1680

Equator

Galápagos

I. La Plata, August 10–17, 1680
August 12–16, 1681

Guayaquil

South
America

Paita

April 4, 1681

Ilo, October 28–November 3, 1680,
March 28–29, 1681

Arica, January 30–31, 1681

Sept. 19, 1680

Sept. 21,
1681

Tropic of Capricorn

Nov. 23, 1680

Huasco, March 12, 1681

Coquimbo, December 3–7, 1680

Nov. 26, 1680

Feb. 23, 1681

Mar. 1, 1681

I. Juan Fernandez,
Dec. 25, 1680–Jan. 12, 1681

South Sea

I. Duque de York
October 12–November 5 1681

Strait of
Magellan

November 13, 1681

Drake Passage

November 21, 1681

500   1,000   1,500

Miles at Tropic of Capricorn

© 2022 Jeffrey L. Ward

The South Sea Adventure

Cape Verde Is.

January 12, 1682

Atlantic Ocean

Equator

December 31, 1681

December 25, 1681

Tropic of Capricorn

December 15, 1681

Africa

20°N

10°N

0°

10°S

20°S

30°S

N
W · E
S

North Sea

San Blas Islands:
arrived March 23, 1680

Portobelo

0   30
Miles

Chepo

Isthmus of Darien

Isle of Pines:
April 3, 1680

Golden Island:
April 5, 1680

40°S

Panama

Isla Chepillo

April 23

Perico

Taboga

Otoque

Santa Maria River
(Rio Tuira)
April 6, 1680

Golden Cap village
(Meteti):
arrived April 7, 1680
departed April 9, 1680

50°S

*Bay of
Panama*

departed
April 20, 1680

Point
San Lorenzo

Boca Chica

60°S

*Gulf of
San Miguel*

Santa Maria:
arrived April 15, 1680,
departed April 17, 1680

South Sea

Part I

The Sacred Hunger
of Gold

1

The Princess

ER NAME IS lost to time. What is known is that she was one of the Indigenous Kuna people in Panama's Darien province. A description of her can be culled from the journals of European soldiers and adventurers who met her and her sisters and straightaway proposed marriage: "lively and sparkling" gray eyes, "long, black, lank, coarse, strong hair," and dark, "copper-colour'd" skin streaked with red paint in the Kuna fashion. She wore a thick golden nose ring and, sometimes, multicolored beads roped around her lean, "well-featured" body. Her father was a regional Kuna chieftain, her grandfather the de facto king of the Kuna, and, in the spring of 1680, she was a sex slave, having been snatched from her father's palace by Spanish soldiers and taken to their garrison.

The circumstances of her subjugation were not unusual. The Spaniards, who controlled most of the New World at the time, took the position that enslaving the Indigenous peoples was a beneficent act. As an official Spanish historian explained in a sixteenth-century essay, the "naturally inferior" Native populations benefited from Spanish tutelage as well as from conversion to Christianity, objectives that were easier to achieve if the would-be converts were first enslaved.

The Spaniards' self-professed altruism was called into question, though, by their treatment of the enslaved Natives, a typical example being a woman in the colony of Hispaniola who, one morning, told her Spanish overseer that she needed time off from the mine to care for her newborn, whereupon the overseer took the baby in his arms, smashed its skull apart against a rock, and declared the problem solved. The issue was not merely that the conquistadors placed a higher value on gold than on human life, but, as the Incan leader Manco Inca put it, "Even if the snows of the Andes turned to gold, still they would not be satisfied."

In 1501, when the Spaniards discovered Panama (insofar as land already inhabited for millennia by Indigenous peoples can be discovered), the Natives might have appeared relatively fortunate, because the Spanish effort was led by Rodrigo de Bastidas, regarded as the kindest and most humane of the conquistadors. In a seminal history of the Spanish conquest, Bastidas was described as a "gentleman" with "the unique distinction of acting like a human being in his dealings with the natives of America." Yet just a year after his arrival in Panama, when two of his ships were sinking, Bastidas and his men rescued their gold and pearls while leaving their chained-up Kuna slaves to drown.

This was just the prelude. Over the following two centuries, Panama's Indigenous peoples were devastated by enslavement, genocide, and European diseases. At its most harmonious, the Spanish-Kuna relationship was that of cats and mice. Many of the Kuna fled into the farthest reaches of the Darien province, five thousand square miles of mountainous jungle on Panama's eastern border. Others left Panama altogether, settling in the San Blas Islands, an archipelago just off the country's Atlantic coast.

On April 3, 1680, on Golden Island, a tiny slab of coral, sand, and palm trees at the eastern end of that archipelago, the princess's grandfather devised a plan to rescue her. His Spanish name, Andreas, was a relic of his own time as a Spanish slave. Since his escape from the Spaniards, he had become the leader of the Kuna community in the San Blas Islands as well as a regional chief paramount, what the Europeans thought of as a king, his dominion extending well into the Darien. At his disposal was an army of warriors, many of whom may have been among the finest archers in the world. One English visitor told of eight-year-old Kuna boys able not merely to hit canes standing on end twenty paces away but, unfailingly, to split them in two.

Were Andreas to send his men to the Spanish garrison to rescue his granddaughter, however, they would be quickly torn apart by Spanish gunfire, against which they had no defense. But he saw a way to enlist a supplemental force whose firepower was as good as, if not better than, the Spaniards': pirates.

An English pirate

His scouts had brought word that a company of 366 buccaneers — Caribbean-based pirates who preyed on Spanish ships and towns — had just landed at the Isle of Pines, a few miles north of Golden Island.

Mostly Englishmen, the buccaneers had banded together in Jamaica in December of 1679 to raid the Spanish port city of Portobelo, on Panama's northern coast. The raid netted them a good deal of silver, but the most valuable prize would prove to be mail that merchants in Spain had intended for Spanish colonists. Again and again in their letters, the merchants lamented the vulnerability of Spanish settlements on the South Sea, as the southern Pacific Ocean was then known. The near impossibility of circumnavigating South America meant that English pirates rarely, if ever, sailed into the region. But the narrow Darien Isthmus (between Panama's Atlantic and Pacific coasts), the merchants warned, could "open a door into the South Seas."

Accordingly, the buccaneers circulated a new expedition plan through Caribbean taverns, brothels, and other pirate haunts. All comers were to rendezvous on the Isle of Pines, where they would leave their ships and then go by canoe to the Darien Isthmus, cross the isthmus on foot, and raid Panama City (then known simply as Panama), the repository for much of the gold, silver, and gems the Spaniards were extracting from Central and South America.

But before they could advance to the isthmus, the buccaneers needed a Native guide. Without one, they knew, they had little chance of surviving in the Darien, much less of finding Panama. The last company of buccaneers to raid Panama — 1,200 men under the command of the legendary Captain Henry Morgan, nearly a decade earlier — had grown so hungry during the crossing that they'd eaten their leather sacks after first fighting one another over portions.

Andreas canoed from Golden Island to the Isle of Pines in hope that the buccaneers would choose him as their guide. His pitch was documented by first-time buccaneer Basil Ringrose, a gifted mathematician and navigator, fluent in Latin and French as well as his native English. Unlike his shipmates, mostly ne'er-do-wells and scoundrels whose curricula vitae made them sought after only by hangmen, Ringrose had had his pick of employment opportunities in the West Indies. But only piracy offered the twenty-seven-year-old an escape from the poverty and drudgery that had dogged him for most of his life.

Hoping to trade fruit and venison for axes and hatchets, a number of Kuna men and women had preceded Andreas to the Isle of Pines, canoeing up to the seven buccaneer ships anchored in the crescent bay and astounding Ringrose: "The men here go naked as having only a sharp or hollow tip, made either of gold or silver, or bark, into which they thrust their privy members; the which tip they fasten with a string about their middle," he wrote in his journal in a loose, frilly cursive that contrasted starkly with the maps he often drew beneath the entries — rigid technical renderings shaded with precise crosshatching. The handwriting offered a hint of the romantic spirit that had lured the staid, ruler-straight Englishman into his current company. "They wear an ornament in their noses," he added, "a golden or silver plate, in shape like unto a half-moon; which when they drink, they hold up with one hand, meanwhile they lift the cup with the other."

Most of the Kuna had dark copper skin and black hair, but there were a few who stood out, appearing, in the words of Ringrose, "fairer than the fairest of Europe, with hair as white as the finest flax." Lionel Wafer, a buccaneer surgeon with whom Ringrose would become fast friends, noted that these albino "Indians" (the buccaneers' term for almost all the Indigenous peoples in the New World) had skin "much like that of a white horse" and "their bodies are beset all over, more or less, with a fine short milk-white down, which adds to the whiteness of their skins." Indeed albinism was — and still is — 150 times more common among the Kuna than the rest of the world's population, and the tribe considered it fortuitous based on a pair of unusual beliefs: first, that lunar eclipses were caused by a celestial dragon trying to eat the moon; second, that albinos possessed superior night vision. Therefore, given the Kuna people's renown as archers, their albinos aiming arrows at the night sky was enough to scare the dragon off.

Including Ringrose and Wafer, seven of the buccaneers assembled on the Isle of Pines were either keeping journals or would later write about their experiences. Those combined accounts paint an impressive portrait of Andreas in his mantle of pure gold, with a gravitas in keeping with his advanced age — "No less than an hundred years of age," wrote one of the buccaneer captains, Bartholomew Sharp. In all likelihood, Andreas was closer to sixty. (On a perhaps not unrelated note, seamen at the time often consumed more than a gallon of beer or a pint of rum per day, and Sharp, as will be seen, did a good deal to perpetuate the popular image of pirates with a bottle of rum in hand at all times.)

In Spanish, which the buccaneers' interpreter spoke fluently, Andreas offered to guide them first to Santa Maria (today, El Real de Santa María, in the Darien's Pinogana District), where his granddaughter was being held, and then, if they were unsatisfied with the plunder there, on to Panama. But Santa Maria might be more than satisfactory. In addition to exclusive access to the richest gold mines in Central America, the settlement boasted a massive gold-panning and sluicing works. During each

December-to-April dry season, Natives enslaved by the Spaniards panned gold dust that had washed down from the mountains during the rainy season, collecting a reported eighteen to twenty thousand pounds. Andreas would let the buccaneers keep it all if they rescued his granddaughter.

The buccaneers discussed his proposal before putting it to a vote: pirate crews were democracies ahead of their time, with egalitarian practices born both of their disdain for classism and their prior experiences at sea with whip-happy captains on exceedingly hierarchical European naval and merchant ships. Andreas more than met their criteria for a guide. Not only did he know the Darien, he was also Kuna: over the previous decade and a half, a shared hatred of the Spaniards had fostered an unofficial alliance between the Kuna and the largely mercenary population of buccaneers. Even better, as a monarch enlisting them to battle the Spaniards, Andreas elevated the buccaneers, arguably, to the status of "privateers" — a shortened term for private men-of-war, namely, the captains and crews of private ships who were given legitimate government-issued licenses to plunder vessels of other sovereign nations. (The term *buccaneer* originated in the second half of the seventeenth century, when English and French colonial governors began issuing such licenses — also known as commissions, or letters of marque — to the boar and bull hunters on Hispaniola and Tortuga known as *boucaniers*. The name is derived by most accounts from *boucan*, a French term — in turn adapted from Brazil's Indigenous Tupi people — for the wooden grill the hunters favored for cooking meat, though other sources trace *buccaneer* to the French verb *boucaner*, meaning "to hang around with lowlives" as well as "to imitate a foul tempered billy goat.")

Like their predecessors (most of whom were English, French, or Dutch), the buccaneers gathered on the Isle of Pines sought to be part of their nations' sides in proxy wars with Spain waged by privateers. Following a spate of peace treaties negotiated among the European powers in the 1670s, however, legitimate privateering commissions had largely ceased. Still, any sort of commission, no matter how flimsy, would be useful to the buccaneers in case they wound up in court, where, lacking a legal raison d'être, they would be judged to be simply pirates, the meaning of which hadn't changed since *peiratēs* in ancient Greek (and *pirata* in Latin): sea robbers who plundered indiscriminately. As pirates — rather than privateers — they would hang.

At the moment, the only credential in their possession was a license they'd purchased in Petit-Goâve (part of French Hispaniola) that permitted them to cut logwood trees in certain parts of the Spanish Main, the New World territory controlled by Spain. Although the license was expired, they believed the doctored expiration date would survive scrutiny in court. But whereas logwood might have explained their presence in Portobelo, on the Caribbean coast, they would require the world's most sympathetic jury to buy the defense that they had trekked sixty miles across the Darien Isthmus to Santa Maria to cut it — only to find themselves under attack from a Spanish garrison and forced to return fire in self-defense. An actual letter of marque — or just about anything official that Andreas could give them — would be much sturdier.

But even lacking a commission — or a princess to rescue — the buccaneers would have been enticed by the eighteen to twenty thousand pounds of gold. At the going rate per ounce of fifteen Spanish *pesos de ocho reales* — the silver eight-real coins known as "pieces of eight" — such a haul would net the group a total of more than four million pieces of eight, or nearly twelve thousand pieces of eight per man, at a time when a plantation worker or a sailor earned just a hundred pieces of eight in a year. That would be enough for each buccaneer to buy his own plantation or to commission a new high-end two-hundred-ton Dutch ship and still have four thousand pieces of eight left in his sea chest (or, in fact, two chests, thanks to the size of the coins, which measured an inch and a half in diameter, about the size of a casino poker chip).

The biggest obstacle was the Spanish garrison in Santa Maria, which was manned, according to Andreas, by four hundred soldiers. Those soldiers would be firing a hail of musket balls at the buccaneers as they advanced — or, more likely, as they limped out of the jungle following nine or ten days of arduous trekking through swampland and mountainous, dense-to-the-point-of-impenetrable jungle. (On account of the same obstacles, the isthmus today constitutes the "Darien Gap," the lone break in the 19,000-mile Pan-American Highway stretching from Alaska to Argentina.) Although Kuna archers could provide cover for the buccaneers' advance, upon reaching the garrison the attackers would still need to climb the tall barricades while taking fire from directly overhead. And even if they somehow made it over the walls, how could they possibly get the better of an entrenched, larger, and better-rested Spanish complement? The plan was madness.

Nevertheless, the buccaneers put it to a vote. The result — and an analysis thereof — comes from another of the company's diarists, the jocular New Englander John Cox:

That which often spurs men on to the undertaking of the most difficult adventures, is the sacred hunger of gold; and 'twas gold was the bait that tempted a pack of merry boys of us... being all souldiers of fortune... to list ourselves in the service of one of the rich West Indian monarchs, the emperour of Darien.

2

The Golden Swordsman

BASIL RINGROSE NOW had three choices. First, he could join the Santa Maria expedition. Second, he could opt out in favor of a saner venture; it would be only a matter of time before he caught on with another of the buccaneer crews that routinely stopped in the San Blas Islands for provisions and ship maintenance. Third was the sensible option, the one that took into account his nascent awareness of this band of buccaneers' utter disregard for risk— perhaps even a pathological affinity for danger: he could write off his brief involvement with them and return home to London. Although he frequently committed hundreds of words at a time to his journal, he wrote nothing about his decision. That was also typical of him: he was his own least favorite topic. Among the most intimate personal revelations in his journal were that he had been to Calais once, that he could speak Latin, and that he liked strawberries.

Historical records, however, may shed light on his thoughts that day on the Isle of Pines. Prior to March of 1680, when the buccaneers came together in the San Blas Islands and he first took quill to journal, the lone evidence of Basil Ringrose's existence is a parish registry record of the christening of "Basill Ringrose" on January 28, 1653, in London's Church of St. Martin-in-the-Fields. Neither his name nor any permutation thereof appears in the rolls of English academic institutions whose curriculum included either Latin or advanced arithmetic.

Probably his family could not afford to send him to such places. Two years after Basil's birth, his father, Richard Ringrose, was listed as "poore" in the local rate book, a record of property valuations for the purposes of taxation. The same source listed Richard in arrears in 1656–57, after which he and his young family left High Street, Westminster. Probate court records reveal that Richard was a "sword cutler" — he made swords — as well as the proprietor of the Golden Sword, a small shop nestled on Charing Cross Road alongside two taverns, a vintner, and stables. Although just two hundred square feet, the shop was "very plentifully furnished and provided with all manner and sorts of swords, daggers and rapiers." It is no stretch to imagine Basil there as a small boy, regarding the pristine blades on display, all aglow in the reflection of the forge's molten bronze, and picturing himself someday slashing and clanging his way to wealth and glory.

As an adolescent, when it came time for him to apprentice for his father, Basil seems to have weighed wielding a sword by profession against barely eking out a living making swords and selling them to bolder men. In 1672, Richard took on as apprentice a boy who was not his son, and Basil went to sea, finding work as a supercargo, the heroic overtone of which is misleading. Derived from the Spanish word for "purser," *sobrecargo,* a supercargo is the person on board a merchant vessel who oversees the sale of the cargo and keeps the accounts. Rather than a sword, Ringrose wielded an abacus. According to the probate court records, he undertook several voyages "to parts beyond the seas" in that capacity. It paid decently, but far less in the best year than buccaneers spent in a single night in the rum houses of Port Royal, Jamaica.

While back in London at some point between 1672 and 1677, Ringrose married a woman about whom nothing is known except her first name, Goodith, and that she was from the countryside. In 1677, the couple had a son, Jonathan, who was baptized in the same Westminster chapel where Basil himself had been christened twenty-five years earlier. Basil's journal contains no mention of either Goodith or Jonathan, which, in combination with another christening record, raises the possibility that the marriage was troubled: on March 11, 1681, an infant named Basil Ringrose was baptized. But the man listed as the father, the senior Basil Ringrose, had been out of the country for at least thirteen months. Since children were typically baptized within eight days of their births, if Basil senior was indeed Basil junior's father, Goodith's pregnancy would qualify as the longest in history.

Ringrose's turn to piracy may also have been influenced by a book he read, *The History of the Bucaniers of America,* which offered a survey of piracy in the New World through surgeon Alexandre Exquemelin's account of his own sea-roving experiences, including his participation in the 1671 sack of Panama. Never before had readers been privy to a first-person account of piracy, which stands to reason: After all, what criminal publishes a record of his crimes? The book was an instant sensation in several languages; printers were unable to keep up with demand. Single-handedly, Exquemelin ignited Europe's fascination with pirates. In the process, he blazed a path to adventure for educated young men such as Ringrose and Wafer, who, at just twenty years old, had established himself as a surgeon in Port Royal at a tremendously opportune time, given the wealth of the residents, their propensity for drinking rum as if it were water, and the near certainty that each new arrival from Europe would contract at least one tropical malady. Wafer's life was laid out before him like a golden path. But to a born adventurer, the predictability of such a path makes it a dead end.

One other Exquemelin disciple on the Isle of Pines was twenty-eight-year-old William Dampier, a world-class naturalist with an especially anomalous background for a pirate: a member of the gentry, he was married and owned an English country estate, in Dorset. Like Wafer, Dampier had signed on for the Portobelo expedition, which netted the fleet a good deal of adventure — including a harrowing four-day jungle march and a dramatic raid yielding one hundred pieces of eight per man.

Joining the Santa Maria expedition now offered Ringrose his own once-in-a-lifetime opportunity for adventure. An augury of its success was the commitment of so many illustrious buccaneers, including Bartholomew Sharp, who, at thirty, had already been pirating for fourteen years, developing a sixth sense for prizes and a reputation as an even better navigator and battle tactician than he was a drinker. Captain Richard Sawkins, too, was famous in buccaneer circles, as much for his plunder of the Spanish as for his narrow escapes from the English. In fact, to join the expedition, Sawkins had escaped from an English jail in Port Royal, then overpowered the lieutenant at the helm of his old brigantine and reclaimed her from navy custody. Such daring and gumption had won the twentysomething Sawkins admirers among buccaneers twice his age. Finally, there were the veterans, Captain Peter Harris and the fleet's admiral, John Coxon (not to be confused with the aforementioned crewman John Cox), partners in the famous 1677 surprise attack on the Spanish city of Santa Marta, in modern-day Colombia.

Of course, buccaneer luminaries tended to flame out, or get snuffed out, either dying in action or being captured and executed. Not for nothing was the unofficial pirate motto "A merry life and a short one." It was this idea of a merry life that seems ultimately to have compelled Ringrose to join the expedition to Santa Maria. Given the respect for risk that set him apart from his fellow buccaneers, however, he had reason to hope that his life would not be short.

3

The Gap

THE EXPEDITION COMMENCED at sunrise on April 5, 1680, as Andreas, five other Kuna, and 331 buccaneers shoved off from Golden Island in dugout canoes, leaving behind two English buccaneer captains — Alleston and Mackett — and thirty-three other men to guard the ships. Three-quarters of a mile ahead, the Darien Isthmus loomed like a low-lying thunderhead. As the canoes drew closer to it, the scene sharpened into pale sand and a forest so densely contoured that it more closely resembled a giant reptile than any sort of verdure, an effect augmented by the sweaty jungle air.

Once the buccaneers had landed and hauled their canoes onto the beach, the rumble of the surf gave way to an incessant scream that was the fusion of humming insects, high-pitched chirping of birds, and bloodcurdling shrieks of some sort of animal. It was as though the jungle were warning the buccaneers away. They were told by their guides to avoid "adders," i.e., snakes. Of particular concern was the fer-de-lance (head of the lance), a highly venomous pit viper named for its manner of attack. The fer-de-lance could be identified by its brownish-gray scales, dark streaks, and triangles, all of which blended in with the forest floor. The woods similarly camouflaged the blue-black jungle scorpions and the bark-colored tarantulas known as Panama Blondes. Fortunately, the most lethal of all the Darien's creatures, the dart frog, was easy to spot. But if a buccaneer touched one of the tiny strawberry-red amphibians, he could expect respiratory paralysis within seconds and then, just as quickly, death. For this reason, Native peoples dipped their arrowheads and dart tips in the frog's poison, hence its name.

In spite of Andreas's stewardship, another potential problem on a long march was men straying and getting lost. Consequently, the buccaneers divided into seven units, each bearing its commander's colors. Sharp, Sawkins, and Captain Edmond Cooke each led a division, and Harris and Coxon led two apiece. Coxon's companies each carried the unadorned blood-red pennant widely used at the time to signify to the crewmen of an enemy vessel that no quarter would be given — which is to say that they would not be taken prisoner and afforded room and board but rather killed. The infamous Jolly Roger, the black flag emblazoned with a white skull and crossbones, would not debut until early in the eighteenth century, but one of its early pictorial forebears distinguished Cooke's company: a muscular arm brandishing a cutlass, rendered against a backdrop of horizontal red and yellow stripes.

Andreas led the way through a jungle consisting mainly of mangroves, tall and cylindrical Panama trees, and *Manicaria* palms, whose fronds stretch upward, giving the plants an unmistakable resemblance to feather dusters. The buccaneers were preoccupied with dodging the low-hanging branches and vines, some as thick as arms, all the while hacking shrubs, ferns, and undergrowth out of the way. Their bodies were protected only by coarse shirts, baggy linen or canvas breeches that hung to the knees, and, on their heads, either kerchiefs or hats with brims cut longer in the front, like modern baseball caps. In addition to providing shade, the head coverings held the men's long hair in place. To keep their hair from falling into their eyes — and from catching in the rigging while at sea — some of them gathered it into pony-tails, while others resorted to smearing in a bit of tar.

On their feet, some wore raw cowhide or pigskin shoes, and others wore nothing. None of them, it should be noted, wore boots — ever. The iconic over-the-knee riding boots were not worn by pirates until the early twentieth century, on movie sets. Similarly, none of the buccaneers had colorful tattoos, although a few had crude drawings rendered in "dye" — often nothing more than gunpowder mixed with spit — that was deposited beneath the skin using knives or sail needles. Wafer wrote that one of his first patients on the expedition, an old buccaneer named Bullman, "desired me once to get out of his cheek one of these imprinted pictures." Wafer didn't describe the image, but typical of the era were initials, crosses consisting simply of a pair of inter-secting lines, and, on the more elaborate end, sword-wielding stick figures. Whatever was on Bullman's face, Wafer couldn't remove it despite "much scarifying and fetching off a great part of the skin."

True to popular conception, the buccaneers carried cutlasses, short swords with broad, slightly curved single-edged blades. Each man was also armed with a pistol or two as well as a *fusil bou-canier,* or buccaneer's gun, a rugged flintlock musket with a barrel nearly five feet long and a wooden butt suitable for use as a club. In buccaneers' practiced hands, muskets were magic wands, and they were treated as such. The rules that buccaneers agreed to for each expedition — known as the articles of agreement, or *chasse-partie* (French for "division of the hunt") — often specified that any man who failed to keep his weapons clean and combat-ready would lose his share of the booty as well as face a punishment determined by his captain and shipmates. And God help the man whose hammer failed to rotate on account of a rusty mainspring while he was supposed to be providing cover fire for shipmates attempting to board an enemy vessel.

None of the buccaneers could use their guns now, though. As reported in an anonymous chronicle of the expedition, they had been instructed that "no man, on the loss of life, should fier a gunn in the woodes, least some Indian rogues or other should betray us, by runing afore to acquaint the Spaniards." For reasons that will become clear, the anonymous chronicler was almost certainly seaman Edward Povey, an Englishman whose writing skills, though wanting, would be enough to save him from the gallows.

Of greater value than weapons during the march were the provisions: three or four doughboys (cakes of fried flour weighing half a pound apiece), which each man carried in his satchel, and tobacco, typically stored in a pouch fashioned from a pelican beak. The Kuna would procure water and additional food along the way. Or at least that was the plan.

Before long, the trees thinned, revealing themselves to have been just a small skirt of woods rimming a bay. All of a sudden, rather than contending with pit vipers, the buccaneers were taking a long walk on a beach, for nearly a league (from the Latin *leuga*, a measurement of the distance one could walk in an hour, approximately 3.45 miles), by Ringrose's reckoning.

The beach brought them to a wooded valley bisected by a path perfect for marching, and seven miles later, at two in the afternoon, they reached the day's objective, a largely dry riverbed where they would make camp. In it, they found stones that sparkled with gold, an auspicious sign to men who traditionally saw good luck foretold by as little as an albatross flying overhead or a ship that was free of bananas, which were thought to jinx navigators.

Ringrose was among those with sufficient energy and industriousness to build a hut to sleep in. The day's march had been easy by Darien standards, particularly for the Coxon, Sharp, and Cooke crews, who two months earlier had marched sixty arduous miles over three nights to raid Portobelo. But among the newer recruits, many of whom had lately walked no farther than to get another beer from the galley, some were so exhausted that they opted to bunk on the ground despite the threat of rain and a Kuna warning of "monstrous adders" (anacondas in the Darien are known to measure up to forty feet long and weigh more than a thousand pounds).

When night fell, as if switched on by the sunset, overwhelming sounds blared from the jungle, among them insects chirping far louder than any insect the buccaneers had heard before and terrifying shrieks that resembled those of the most disturbed inmates in the most torturous asylum. In fact, the shrieks emanated from howler monkeys. Not much larger than cats, they possess a cavernous larynx and a specialized, unusually large hyoid bone (in the neck, supporting the tongue) that together act as a natural microphone, allowing the monkeys' territorial claims to carry three miles.

Having had enough of the Darien, four of the buccaneers turned back to Golden Island, reducing the already diminutive force to 327 and raising fears of further attrition in the days ahead.

* * *

On April 6, the second day of the expedition, the buccaneers did not enter the Darien jungle so much as they were swallowed by it — instantly cut off from the rest of the world by a throbbing, fecund darkness. Sixty feet overhead, branches, leaves, and vines grappled with one another in a competition for sunlight, forming a veritable ceiling. Every so often, a speck of blue sky appeared through this canopy, illuminating a galaxy of flowers on its underside, blossoms of the Lamiaceae family — each like a purple pair of lips — as well as the bright yellow platypus-bill-shaped blooms on the *Platypodium elegans* trees, both native to Panama.

The men were more concerned with bongos, squat trees whose roots spread across the forest floor like tentacles, and pochotes, whose trunks were coated with thorns bigger and sharper than goats' horns. A pochote would shred any buccaneer who tried to climb it. Worse were the Chunga palms, whose long spines appeared designed to pierce human flesh and delivered doses of infectious bacteria when they did. The Chungas, in turn, were benign in comparison with the manchineel trees, known for their dangerous fruit, "in smell and colour like a lovely pleasant apple, small and fragrant, but of a poisonous nature," Wafer warned. The manchineel's bark was also to be avoided on account of its milky white toxic sap. While the buccaneer fleet had been stopped in the Bocas del Toro archipelago, en route to the San Blas Islands, rain had propelled some of the sap onto one of the men, and, as Wafer recounted, it "blistered him all over, as if he had been bestrewed with Catharides [blister beetles]. His life had been saved with much difficulty; and even when cured, there remained scars, like those after the small-pox."

As the company continued toward Santa Maria, a buccaneer who had either missed or ignored the warning ate a manchineel apple — *manzanilla de la muerte,* the Spanish called it, or "little apple of death." Not hyperbole, he would learn as he wasted away for six agonizing months. The budding naturalist William Dampier would consequently suggest a "general rule" that "when we find any fruits that we have not seen before, if we see them peck'd by birds, we may freely eat, but if we see no such sign, we let them alone; for of this fruit no birds will taste."

The steamy jungle air was troubling as well. Redolent of fresh rain, mud, and mushrooms, it seemed liable to stew the men or, worse, make them ill. Most of the buccaneers believed that toxic air rising from the ground was the principal cause of tropical afflictions such as dengue fever, malaria, and yellow fever, this last alternatively known as *vomito negro* (black vomit) for its signature symptom. Some of the men also believed that their profession made them especially susceptible to disease. As Wafer and most other surgeons of that era were taught: disease's primary cause was sin.

But for the time being, the buccaneers' greatest antagonist was the slope they had begun ascending at dawn. Three hours later, they were still climbing. It was one of several Darien mountains so tall that, as Wafer wrote, "I perceived a strange giddiness in my head; and enquiring both of my companions, and the Indians, they all assured me they were in the like condition." At the same time, they marveled at the view of clouds below them, a tropical phenomenon known as silvagenitus, created by water evaporating from the forest canopy. The problem was, they couldn't get any of the water for themselves. "On this hill wee could finde no water, so that the company weare almost famisht for the want theirof," wrote Povey. "The Indian pilotts gave us to understand that a little farther was water."

An hour later, however, the company reached the summit

without so much as seeing water. Two more sweltering hours, and the situation remained unchanged save for the increasing enormity of the buccaneers' thirst and their mounting suspicion that the Kuna were in league with the Spaniards. Like many of the buccaneers, Ringrose had heard the rumor of "a peace concluded between the Spaniards and the Indians." If there was truth to the rumors, and if word of the peace had reached Golden Island, Andreas might happily turn the buccaneers over to the Spaniards in exchange for his granddaughter.

Further, Dampier worried, if their Kuna guides had learned about the fate of John Gret, the buccaneers were almost certainly being led into an ambush. Gret was a Kuna boy who had been adopted by a crew of English privateers. Dampier had heard the story from one of the Miskito Indians who were among the company's three dozen non-Englishmen (the others were Frenchmen, Creoles, and escaped or liberated slaves). In 1665, Gret — whose original Kuna name is unknown — was paddling a canoe in the San Blas Islands when he crossed paths with a ship commanded by English privateer William Wright. Wright's crew took an instant liking to the boy and invited him to join them. He accepted and, while he was with them, learned their language, was clothed as an Englishman, was given an English name, and, at the end of the expedition, was invited to England. But the Miskito members of the crew prevailed upon Captain Wright instead to allow Gret to accompany them home to the Miskito Coast (parts of the eastern coasts of modern-day Honduras and Nicaragua). There, Gret learned the Miskito language, married, and lived until 1679, when Wright recruited him to broker a peace between the English and the Kuna. Returning to the San Blas Islands, Gret told his former tribesmen of his invariably positive experiences with the English, who were, he assured them, the antithesis of the murderous Spaniards. As a result, the Kuna not only welcomed English privateers into their territory but also guided them into the Darien to raid the Spanish settlement at Chepo.

The trouble started a few months later, when an English trading sloop sailed into the San Blas Islands. Gret and a small Kuna delegation went to greet the sloop and received a warm welcome. But the sentiment had nothing to do with the recent Kuna-English alliance. These Englishmen knew nothing about that. Instead, they had come to the San Blas Islands to capture Indians to sell as slaves. As soon as Gret and his cohorts learned this, they jumped overboard to escape, but while swimming away, they were all shot to death, unbeknownst to their friends and families on shore, who were left to imagine that the delegation had joined the noble Englishmen on another raid against the Spaniards. What if in the months since, Dampier wondered, John Gret's musket-ball-riddled body had washed ashore? What if the Kuna now knew of his murder at the hands of Englishmen?

At two in the afternoon, the company finally found water, a spring that flowed from the Santa Maria River (the modern Río Tuira) — the same river, according to Andreas, that ran past the settlement of Santa Maria and all the way to the South Sea. "Wee all dranck and refreshed ourselves bravely," Povey wrote. The march resumed at three with another hill that was even steeper than the first — "perpendicular," per Ringrose — and more rigorous, the "path so narrow that but one man at a time could pass."

They were still climbing when the sun set, at seven, and they didn't make camp until they had marched a total of eighteen miles. Not surprisingly, John Cox's reporting that night lacked its usual spark. "We took up our lodgings by a river-side," was all he wrote. The only detail Ringrose supplied: "Some rain fell." Povey added that along the way "one man more tier'd" and returned to Golden Island. Likely many more of them would have quit if they had had either the energy or any inkling of what lay ahead.

4

Golden-Cap

ON APRIL 7, the third day of the expedition, the buccaneers
marched on the relatively level and unobstructed banks of
the Santa Maria River, allowing them to avoid the steep inclines
and tangle of underbrush elsewhere in the jungle. But at a cost:
the river ran like an intestine, winding back on itself every half
mile. Making any sort of headway necessitated repeatedly fording the river, which was belly deep and as much as two hundred
feet across. Worse, the water was populated by caimans, the ferocious crocodilians known to reach thirteen feet in length in some
parts of the world. In the Darien, they are only six to eight feet
long, still more than large enough to kill a man. It did not help
that, like most Darien waterways, the river was as brown as coffee and no more transparent, entirely concealing the beasts. The
buccaneers' lone consolation may have been that caimans were
known to eat the anacondas that also inhabited the water. But for
many of the men, the water itself posed the greatest threat, given
that they had never learned to swim, especially those who grew
up away from the coasts of England and France. Even in places
where the river meandered, it remained capable of bowling over a

two-hundred-pound man and thrusting him into the sharp rocks and tree limbs on its bottom, trapping him underwater.

Still, the buccaneers emerged from the river without incident, and after a full day's trek through jungle and water they encountered a cluster of four houses on the banks of the river, each with cabbage-palm walls and a thatched roof, part of a Native village. From them appeared two Kuna laden with plantains, cassavas, corn, and drinks. Gifts for the Englishmen, they said, from the regional Kuna chieftain, Antonio, who eagerly awaited the company at his palace. The buccaneers happily accepted the refreshments and agreed to meet Antonio, Andreas's son and the father of the princess they had been engaged to rescue.

That evening, after a brief hike, they reached Antonio's village (near the modern town of Meteti, in the Pinogana District). None of the chroniclers described the village, though Wafer would later provide a picture of the typical Kuna community as consisting of a plantation and a 125-foot-long "war-house," or fort, scattered around which were houses twenty-four or twenty-five feet square, "walled up with sticks, and daub'd over with Earth." Hammocks hung around a fire in each house, the smoke from which escaped through a gap in the thatched palm roof. Evenings typically brought vibrant blue, green, and red macaws gliding out of the woods and through the doorways — the family pets, returning home for the night. "They will exactly imitate the Indians' voices, and their way of singing," Wafer wrote, "and they will call the chicaly-chicaly in its own note, as exactly as the Indians themselves."

The chroniclers also failed to record a single detail of Antonio's palace, but per Spanish accounts, a comparable Kuna chieftain's *bohío* was 450 feet long and 240 feet wide (by comparison, a football field is 360 by 160 feet), formed of timber beams fastened together and fortified by stone walls. Possibly the buccaneers'

Kuna smoking tobacco

reporting lapses were attributable to the entirety of their focus being drawn to the owner of the palace, which would be understandable. In addition to a white ankle-length royal robe, Antonio had a half-moon-shaped plate of gold dangling from his nose and, from his ears, thick golden rings nearly four inches in diameter, each ring in turn suspending a golden disk of a similar size. And that was nothing compared to his crown, woven from white reeds, lined with red silk, and ringed by an entire wreath of gold from which spouted three ostrich feathers and more golden beads. Bonete de Oro, the Spaniards called Antonio. The buccaneers took to calling him King Golden-Cap.

His queen was among those receiving them. She wore one red blanket around her waist and a second draped loosely over her head and shoulders. In addition to the young child in her arms, she was accompanied by three of Golden-Cap's sons, all clad in white robes like their father's, and two of his "very comely" daughters, who made the buccaneers forget all about Golden-Cap. *Marriageable* was the first word Ringrose used to describe them, echoing the sentiments of the other buccaneers. As Povey reported, during the lavish reception and entertainment that followed, "some of our peopple by signes would ask them if they should live with them and thay be their wives." Rescuing the older sister of these princesses from the Spanish garrison in Santa Maria now seemingly held a higher purpose.

The buccaneers were also smitten with the other women in Golden-Cap's kingdom. "The inhabitants for the most part are very handsome, especially the female sex," wrote Sharp, who would determine that the Kuna women were "so exceedingly loving and free to the embraces of strangers." His perception may have been colored by chicha co-pah, a sour beer with a high level of sweetness rivaled only by its alcohol content. He might have declined the beverage had he known it was mostly corn chewed into spittle by old women of the village, but probably not.

Two of the relatively sober buccaneers reported a much different story. While "very free, airy, and brisk," the Kuna women were also "very modest, and cautious in their husbands' presence, of whose jealousy they stand in fear," Ringrose wrote. Wafer, for his part, learned that the Kuna punishment for adultery was the death of both parties. "In addition," he wrote, "if a man debauches a virgin, they thrust a sort of bryer up the passage of his penis, and then turn it round ten or a dozen times: which is not only a great torment, but commonly mortifies the part; and the person dies of it; but he has the liberty to cure himself if he can."

Nevertheless, the evening likely exceeded the escapist fantasies any of the buccaneers had concocted once upon a time in gray London, and for a change, no one left the party to return to Golden Island.

The buccaneers resumed marching on April 9, their fifth day in the Darien, their numbers buoyed by the presence of Golden-Cap, three of his sons, and fifty additional warriors — according to Ringrose, that is. Sharp differed in his journal, reporting "an hundred and fifty indians in our company to go to the wars." (Sharp's reckoning is called into question, though, by his earlier estimation of Andreas's age at "no less than an hundred.") Whatever the actual number, it wasn't enough to extinguish the buccaneers' fear of being led into a trap. Two sublime days and nights of hospitality in Golden-Cap's kingdom had reduced their suspicion of the Kuna considerably. But a hint of doubt remained.

It is unknown whether that topic spurred the "words" that morning between the admiral, John Coxon, and Captain Peter Harris, but tempers flared to the point where Coxon was burning to draw his gun and blast Harris's head into the bongo trees. Of course, Coxon knew that discharging a weapon could compromise the expedition's secrecy; he had led as many clandestine raids as any buccaneer captain since Morgan, notably on Santa Marta in 1677, the Gulf of Honduras in 1679, and, most recently, Portobelo. And it was Coxon, after all, who had decreed that any man firing a gun in the Darien jungle would be killed (silently, one presumes). A mere cry could expose them to their enemies, and a cry was a likely response if Coxon were even to slap Harris.

Harris might also draw his own gun and shoot Coxon, but likely he would be more measured in response. A stout Kentish seaman who had seen his share of scrapes since accompanying Morgan to Panama in 1671, Harris had a reputation for discretion as well as valor. In December of 1679, shortly before hearing about the South Seas expedition from Sawkins, Harris found himself being pursued by a thirty-two-gun ("gun" meaning cannon in this context) Royal Navy frigate. His own 150-ton ship had twenty-five cannons in addition to muskets in the hands of 107 buccaneers — sharpshooters, in other words. But rather than engage the frigate, Harris let her trail him into shoal waters, where a sandbar destroyed her, allowing him to sail away.

The conditions couldn't have helped Coxon keep his cool. The Darien's average low temperature in April was seventy-five degrees, with a high in the low nineties, meaning a heat index in the low hundreds, since the humidity seldom dipped below 80 percent, even at night. In the daytime, trekking into the Darien jungle could feel like stepping into a hot bath fully clothed.

And then there were the bugs. The Darien's infamous clouds of mosquitoes are nothing compared to the chitras, nearly invisible flies that burrow into human pores and hair follicles and suck out blood, resulting in desperately itchy welts four times the size of mosquito bites. Worse still are the black botflies, which deposit eggs into human skin. The eggs hatch subdermally into larvae that each digs into its human host with dozens of black spines that make extracting it excruciating. The human host finds equal parts horror and relief three months later, when the baby botflies, having grown to the size of jelly beans, squeeze their way out.

A combination of such circumstances pushed Coxon to the edge of reason, where shooting Harris seemed like the only viable course of action. He drew his pistol, or possibly his musket, and loaded it — an intricate multistep process that afforded him plenty of time to come to his senses. Nevertheless he aimed at

Harris's head and pulled the trigger. The musket ball flew past Harris harmlessly — except for the sharp, ringing report that resounded through the jungle, audible for miles, possibly heard by the Spaniards and more likely by Indian tribes allied with them. Harris snapped up his own gun to return fire when, as Sharp would record in his diary, "I interposed, and brought him to be quiet."

As a buffer, Golden-Cap suggested that the company split into two, one party continuing ahead on foot and the other in canoes that his men could procure, presumably from a nearby village. Coxon consented, and shortly thereafter, he and sixty-nine other buccaneers — including Ringrose, Cox, Sharp, and Povey — followed Andreas to the riverbank. Waiting there were canoes, each of which was the trunk of a tall cedar or cotton tree that had been hewn flat on the side that would serve as the hull; the other side was either carved or burned to form a cockpit. "The wood is very red," Wafer noted of the cedars, "of a curious, fine grain, and very fragrant."

In addition to the buccaneers, each canoe carried two Kuna, one serving as guide, the other as pilot, propelling and steering the craft with a pole. The river, running "like an arrow out of a bow," led Povey to anticipate "a glide downstream." But in practice the swift current meant that "the least touch of a cannoe against a stump or rock oversets them if not staves them all to pieces." Also presenting a hazard were the floating tree trunks and limbs that blocked the way — so many, in fact, that the buccaneers considered the possibility that the Spaniards had felled the trees and placed them in the river for the purpose of impeding the expedition. Or, more likely, the Spaniards' Indian confederates, having heard Coxon's gunshot, were seeking to waylay the buccaneers until Spanish troops could arrive. Even without the obstacles, the river would be problematic, Ringrose reflected after navigating a number of waterfalls and hairpin turns. "For at the distance of almost every stone's cast, we were constrained to quit and get out of our boats, and haul them over either sands or rocks."

At the end of two such days, the river party made camp on a bank, beyond exhausted yet unable to sleep because of what they referred to as a "tiger" lying nearby, looking them over. Likely it was a jaguar, the largest cat native to the Americas and commonly mistaken for a tiger on account of its mustard-yellow coat and black rosettes. The threat easily could have been neutralized by a musket ball, but the buccaneers dared not fire — now more than ever, on account of a report of Spaniards nearby. That news, in combination with exhaustion and sleeplessness, reignited the buccaneers' suspicion of Kuna subterfuge.

When morning finally came, the party returned to the river, where, wrote Ringrose, "our pain and labour was rather doubled than diminished." The rowing was "intolerable," and the isolation was worse. They should have long since run into the 256 men who were on foot. To Cox this was proof positive that "the Indians had thus divided us, the better to execute some treachery, by the assistance of the Spaniard."

Sharp's journal entries during this period, by contrast, could be mistaken for those of someone on a leisurely canoe trip with friends. On the same day Ringrose called the way intolerable, Sharp experienced "a clear river and a pleasant day's passage of it." He even found gratification in hauling the canoes overland: "Our labor, I must say, was a pleasure to us, because of the great unity there was amongst us, all our hearts being fired with a general desire to proceed to the end of our land expedition." He made no mention of the tiger/jaguar; his journal entry that night consisted solely of a rave review of the supper Andreas's cook had prepared, "a very good sort of wild-beast called a warre, which is much like unto our English hog, and altogether as good." Finding no sign of the land party at the rendezvous point, however, Sharp turned "very suspicious."

The buccaneers' edginess was not lost on Andreas, who commanded a canoe to row up another branch of the river in search of the other party. Sharp, Ringrose, Cox, and their companions spent the rest of the day waiting around on a riverside beach, convincing themselves that Andreas had in fact sent the canoe to warn the Spanish contingent of the buccaneers' proximity and numbers. An hour before sunset, though, the canoe reappeared, carrying several profoundly relieved members of the land party, whose fears of Kuna chicanery had mirrored the river party's. The remainder of the land party arrived the next day, the expedition's ninth in the Darien. Between the joyful reunion and the affirmation of Kuna fidelity, something of a beach party ensued. Sharp wrote that Andreas, "in commanding his people to bring us several canoes laden with warre, and plantaines, did not a little contribute to exhilarate our spirits." The Kuna also procured another fifty-four canoes, so that the company might stay together going forward.

The remainder of the day was devoted to rest and cleaning weapons in preparation for the attack on Santa Maria, which, Golden-Cap told the buccaneers, they would reach the following night.

5

The Forlorn

AT DAWN ON April 14, their tenth day in the Darien, the 326 buccaneers joined the Kuna in sixty-eight canoes, everyone digging into the water with makeshift oars and paddles — in lieu of the poles they'd used previously — and every nerve straining; full speed was required if they were to reach Santa Maria in time to rest before attacking the garrison at dawn the following morning. The timing was critical. Waking up any later than six o'clock would cost them both the darkness they needed to conceal their advance to town and, at sunrise, the requisite light to see their target. Attacking at daybreak had the added benefit of catching the garrison in a state of disorganization. "Thus we rowed with all haste imaginable," wrote Ringrose.

The Kuna were already dressed for battle. Golden-Cap wore a "belt of tygers teeth" per the Kuna belief that animal body parts could supplement the wearer's own traits, in this case lethal prowess. Like his father, Golden-Cap was utterly bedecked with gold, including, according to Cox, "a hat of pure gold" and "a ring and a plate like a cockle shell" hanging from his nose. The gold jewelry, restricted to the Kuna elite, served as a statement of superior rank. Body paint also represented rank among the warriors; red, it was believed, imbued them with magic. Some of the warriors were wearing black paint as well, "a distinguishing mark of honour," as Wafer established, "to him who has killed a Spaniard, or other enemy."

Eighteen hours later, at midnight, when they should have been asleep, everyone was still rowing with all haste imaginable. Two more hours passed before the Kuna finally spotted the stretch of shoreline they'd had in mind for camp — a mere half mile from Santa Maria, a proximity that led to concerns over whether it was secure. It was, the buccaneers determined, thanks to the unlikelihood of Spaniards venturing into such an inhospitable area. "The country all about here is woody and low, and very unhealthy," Wafer explained, "the rivers being so lazy that the stinking mud infects the air."

On finally reaching shore, the men found forest so dense that they needed to carve their way into it to make space to sleep in the few remaining hours of darkness — if they could sleep, what with the stench, the fear of discovery, and the prefight nerves. As it turned out, twenty hours of rowing full-bore was a potent sleep aid.

The next thing Ringrose knew, he was awakened by a gunshot. The first flecks of dawn delineated the campsite from the darkness, revealing astonishingly tall trees all around and, more pertinently, no gun smoke. No Spanish attackers, either. Just Kuna and the buccaneers waking up and cocking their heads toward Santa Maria, from which the report seemed to have emanated. Their suspicion that it marked the garrison's changing of the guard was confirmed a moment later by the staccato beat of *à travailler,* a drummer's notification to soldiers that it's time to get out of bed and go to work.

The drumbeats also served as a go order for Captain Sawkins and his forty-eight-man "forlorn," or vanguard, the unit charged with leading an advance through the kill zone of a defended position. Some buccaneers volunteered for the forlorn; others were chosen on the basis of an unlucky throw of the dice. By seven o'clock, Sawkins's team, which included Sharp, had advanced to the edge of the woods and was staring out onto an open field. A few hundred yards across it stood the garrison, a fortress surrounded by a twelve-foot-high wall of palisades — stout wooden poles planted in the earth. To get into the garrison, the forlorn would either have to climb over the wall or find a way to breach it.

On Sawkins's command, the forlorn charged onto the field. The moment coincided with a paroxysm of gunfire from the garrison that transformed the air into a matrix of musket balls whining past at a thousand feet per second, thudding into tree trunks, and tearing into the ground. Eruptions of sod speckled the air with black mud. Clearly the Spaniards had known that the buccaneers were coming — perhaps since scouts had heard Coxon try to blow Harris's head off.

Without either cover by which to advance or an enemy weakness to exploit, Sawkins was left with two tactical options: first, he could order a retreat; a cardinal rule of buccaneer surprise attacks was to quit a fortification that had been alarmed. Second, he and his troops could drop to the ground, minimizing the targets they presented, and close in on the garrison in pairs, one man firing while his partner reloaded — the goal being to suppress enemy fire long enough for them to eventually breach the palisades. Sawkins dismissed both options. Instead he continued sprinting toward the garrison. He was, as one of the buccaneers remarked, "a man of undaunted courage." He was also observant. In that second or so following the forlorn's emergence from the woods, he had noticed that none of the men had become casualties of the paroxysm of gunfire, probably because they were outside the Spaniards' effective firing range of about two hundred yards.

Sawkins had also discerned that the Spaniards lacked training and experience. Otherwise they would have shot in small volleys, so as to maintain a constant fire, instead of firing all at once. Or they would have simply waited until the buccaneers were within range. As it stood, each of the defenders needed to reload his musket, which entailed pulling the hammer back into its safety — or "half-cocked" — position, withdrawing one of the paper cartridges from his cartouche box, biting the top off the cartridge, using a little of the black powder within the cartridge to prime the pan, closing the frizzen (which covers the powder in the pan and at the same time presents a surface for the flint to strike and create sparks), pouring the rest of the powder into the barrel followed by the paper cartridge itself and the musket ball, then withdrawing the ramrod from its base-of-the-barrel notch and plunging it into the barrel in order to ram the musket ball home as well as to properly seat it. Only then could the Spaniard fully cock the hammer (lest he "go off half-cocked," in which case the weapon wouldn't fire), find a target, aim, and, finally, fire. An experienced musketeer could accomplish all of the above in about twenty seconds — under good circumstances, as opposed to in the heat of battle, when his eyes and lungs were full of the acrid black gun smoke resulting from everyone in a garrison firing at the same time. And if, true to form, the Spaniards were using outmoded firearms like the arquebus (a larger, heavier, and more complex matchlock precursor of the flintlock musket), reloading would take them twice as long.

Sawkins and his men reached the fortress while the Spaniards were in all likelihood still fiddling with their ramrods. But the defenders would be reloaded momentarily, requiring the forlorn to climb the twelve-foot-high palisades while taking fire from above at point-blank range. Some of the buccaneers could fall back, providing cover fire for the others who were scaling the wall. Once a man reached the top, however, he would be assured of a sword or musket ball to the face.

Sawkins opted instead to go *through* the wall. The palisades stood embedded in the earth, the narrow gaps between them filled with moss and small sticks and, on the inside of the wall, sealed off with wooden battens. While under fire — arrows now, in addition to musket balls — Sawkins and two or three of his men wrestled with one of the palisades, trying to uproot it. Although they managed only to tilt it, the gap they created allowed them to get much better leverage on its neighbor. While trying to muscle the next palisade aside, Sawkins was struck in the head by an arrow, and one of the buccaneers alongside him was shot in the hand. Both were able to remain in the fight, though, dropping back and providing cover fire for another member of the forlorn who was attempting to squeeze through the since-expanded gap.

Unfortunately for this would-be breacher, the Spaniards within the fortress had clean shots at him. But by leaping in, he would at least present a moving target, which made the prospect less daunting, albeit not by much. Buccaneer articles of agreement took into account a man's natural disinclination to plunge into a hail of gunfire: Henry Morgan's, for example, promised fifty pieces of eight "to him that in any battle should signalize himself... by entering first any castle." Sawkins's man managed to squeeze into the garrison unscathed, perhaps having issued suppressive fire as he entered. A tide of the forlorn flowed in behind him, guns blazing, driving the Spaniards to seek cover.

The forty-eight members of the forlorn thus found themselves in a firefight with 260 Spanish soldiers inside the garrison.

In addition to being better marksmen, the buccaneers were able to fire two to three times as often, thanks to a technique that eliminated the ramrod: to seat the musket ball and the powder, each man simply banged the butt of his gun against the ground.

The firefight quickly tightened to close-quarters combat, whereupon the men drew their swords. The buccaneers were skilled swordsmen, and the cutlass was uniquely suited to their purposes: its short blade was thick and heavy enough to slash through canvas and ropes aboard a ship and, in a fight, to hack apart lighter swords, not to mention the men wielding them. Before the rest of the buccaneer force could reach the garrison, the forlorn had already killed twenty-six of the defenders and wounded fourteen more, prompting the Spaniards to surrender. Sawkins and the man shot in the hand comprised the totality of the buccaneer casualty list. The entire battle had lasted just half an hour.

Entering the garrison with the rest of the buccaneers, Ringrose thought it odd that there weren't more defenders. Not that he was complaining, but the buccaneers had expected to face closer to four hundred Spanish soldiers. The discrepancy signaled that something was amiss. Hurrying in after the buccaneers came Andreas, Golden-Cap, and the rest of the Kuna contingent. Their reaction to the outcome of the battle, as well as the details of the liberation of the princess, are, like her name, lost to history. Preoccupied with the spoils of victory, the buccaneers raced into the town of Santa Maria like children on Christmas morning.

The sole report on the princess's reunion with her father and grandfather came from Ringrose: "We found and redeemed the eldest daughter of [Golden-Cap]. She had, as it should seem, been forced away from her father's house by one of the garrison" — a Spanish soldier named José Gabriel. Ringrose also hinted at nascent doubt over the circumstances of her Santa Maria sojourn. Upon being rescued, she evidently did not, as expected, run into the arms of Andreas and Golden-Cap with tears of joy. Had she been traumatized? Or, perhaps, had she come to like Santa Maria? Seeing that she was pregnant, the Kuna leaders did not seek to investigate. Instead they dragged the nearest Spanish soldiers out to the woods and stabbed them to death.

Ringrose by then had joined the crowd of buccaneers rushing into town, anticipating Spanish settlement trappings such as magnificent colonial mansions full of the finest food and wine and even more magnificent cathedrals brimming with gold and jewel-encrusted iconography. Instead they found a handful of crude thatched houses assembled from wild cane and a lone forgettable church. The town of Santa Maria was not a town at all, they realized, but merely a rudimentary support system for the garrison. Inside the houses, Sharp wrote, were "neither riches to speak of, nor yet as much victuals as would satisfie our hunger for three or four days, of which our wearied carcasses at that time stood in no small need."

Sating their hunger for gold would be more than adequate compensation, however. The group eagerly proceeded to the gold-panning works, located on a stretch of the Santa Maria River that, according to Ringrose, was "twice as broad as the river Thames at London," or about two thousand feet across. To their consternation, they found only a small quantity of gold dust stored in jars made of hollowed-out pumpkins. A search of the rest of the settlement netted another twenty pounds of gold, worth nearly five thousand pieces of eight. That was enough, at fourteen pieces of eight per man, for each of them to buy a cow. Hardly what they'd braved caiman-infested rivers for. Where was the rest of the gold?

Reluctantly, their Spanish prisoners informed them that four chests full of gold dust and another three hundred pounds of gold ore from the mines had been shipped to Panama just three days earlier. The bad news didn't end there. Santa Maria's governor, the prisoners went on, had received advance notice of the buccaneers' approach and accompanied the gold to Panama, taking with him the priest and most of the town's higher-ups: everyone the buccaneers could have held for ransom. The gold mines themselves remained the buccaneers' lone opportunity for plunder — or would have, if not for the fact that in preparation for the raid, two hundred of the 460 soldiers stationed at the garrison had hurried up to the mountains to evacuate the mined ore. Ringrose took no solace in the vindication of his earlier analysis of the garrison's troop strength.

In addition to the scant gold, the buccaneers' haul included wine, brandy, bread, jerk pork, and likely clothing, too, for it was standard pirate practice to strip victims of coats, hats, and everything else down to their stockings. All in all, given their hopes, the take was paltry. As Ringrose reported, "Our great expectations of taking a huge booty of gold at this place being totally vanished, we were unwilling to have come so far for nothing, or to go back empty-handed, especially considering what vast riches were to be had at no great distance."

The gold mines were the closest. The troops from the garrison had evacuated the ore that had recently been mined, but, as Dampier noted, nearly infinite veins remained. He saw an opportunity to tap them, a plan he would call his Golden Dreams, in which the company stayed on in Santa Maria, fortifying the mouth of the river so that "if all the strength the Spaniards have in Peru had come against us, we could have kept them out." He envisioned the buccaneers panning and mining the gold themselves, then sending the ore upriver to the North Sea — as they called the Atlantic. And because thousands of members of the Brethren of the Coast — as Caribbean buccaneers referred to themselves — would no doubt flock to join them, they could seize control of gold mines as far away as Quito, Ecuador's capital, some five hundred miles south.

But most of the buccaneers were opposed to staying in Santa Maria. As Cox blithely explained, "Having no chymist to refine the ore, we thought it best to go look for it where it was to be had with the King of Spain's [coat of] arms on it." Panama was 120 miles distant, but most of that distance was traversable by an easy canoe ride, and, as Ringrose wrote, the city held "treasure enough to satisfy our hungry appetite for gold and riches." He was especially intrigued by the output from Potosí, a mountain said to be made entirely of silver. In fact the 15,827-foot-high Cerro Potosí (also known as Cerro Rico), located in modern-day Bolivia, is mostly shale. But in the century following its 1545 discovery, the mountain had done little to dispel the myth, yielding nearly half the world's silver. The ore was taken by llama and mule trains to the Pacific coast, then, like much of the 181 tons of gold and sixteen thousand tons of silver that had been extracted from Peru and Mexico since 1500, shipped to Panama. A successful raid of Panama could rank among the richest in the history of piracy — or, for that matter, in the history of raids.

6

The Second-Largest City in the
Western Hemisphere

P ANAMA PRESENTED A numbers problem. Five of the buccaneers had already returned to Golden Island during the trek
to Santa Maria, and now another dozen would have to haul the
Santa Maria loot back and notify the crews guarding the ships of
the change in plans, reducing the expedition to just 314 men. Captain Coxon had misgivings about attacking the second-largest city
in the Western Hemisphere (behind only Mexico City) with such
a small force — and that was before he learned that the governor of
Santa Maria was headed for Panama, meaning that the undersize
contingent would lose the vital element of surprise. When Henry
Morgan and his 1,200 men reached Panama in 1671, they had surprised the 3,600 Spanish troops and taken the city after just five
hours of fighting. But even caught off guard, Spaniards had managed in those five hours to load the bulk of the city's gold, silver,
and jewels onto a ship and sail away. Forewarned this time, the
Spaniards could evacuate the gold, silver, and jewels long before
Coxon and company were even within sight of Panama.

Accordingly, Coxon advocated that the company forget Panama

and instead return to the Caribbean Sea and rove there. The Caribbean was practically designed for pirating, with its countless islands, islets, reefs, cays, and coastal crannies all providing opportunities to resupply, wait in ambush for merchant ships, and careen — a critical maintenance procedure involving turning a ship on her side for cleaning, caulking, and repairs. Moreover, the water surrounding all those landmasses was too shallow for deep-drafted warships, allowing the smaller buccaneer vessels to evade them. As a Royal Navy admiral would remark, "Dispatching a large naval vessel after a pirate ship was like sending a cow after a hare." Lacking such natural advantages in the South Sea, even if the buccaneers were to take Panama and sail off with every last ounce of its gold, they would be an easy target for the potent Spanish warships sure to pursue them. For all the above reasons, it had been a century since English pirates had dared to sail into those waters, the last being Sir Francis Drake.

Coxon's argument failed to resonate with the crew, who maintained that pirates' historical aversion to the South Sea meant that the area was now virgin territory, where pieces of eight could be "gathered as easily as pears from a tree." They also suspected that Coxon's reticence was in fact rooted in sidestepping the dishonor of losing his admiralcy to Sawkins. The buccaneers had loved Sawkins before he shrugged off an arrow to the head and became the hero of Santa Maria; now they lionized him. If they did opt for an expedition to Panama, there would be no need for deliberation over their choice of admiral when they were drafting their articles of agreement for the expedition. The fear was that if they chose Sawkins, Coxon would return to Golden Island in a huff and his regular ninety-seven-man crew would follow, leaving the remaining buccaneers with too small a force even to think about taking Panama. Sure enough, when the company's pro-Panama majority promised that the new articles of agreement would stipulate that Coxon remain admiral, he came around to the plan.

The rest of their articles, like those for the Santa Maria expedition, are lost to history, but almost certainly they followed the Custom of the Coast, the de facto constitution of the Brethren of the Coast. Foremost among its statutes was compensation on a "no prey, no pay" basis: once buccaneers took a prize and their skilled crewmen—such as carpenters and surgeons—received salaries for their services, the balance was divided into shares, each seaman receiving a full share and captains and officers getting additional shares based on rank. The Custom of the Coast had myriad performance bonuses, too—for breaching a fort, for example—and even workmen's compensation: a member of the company who lost a left arm received either five hundred pieces of eight or five slaves; a man who lost a right arm received either six hundred pieces of eight or six slaves. Similarly, the loss of a left leg netted the beneficiary four hundred pieces of eight or four slaves; the loss of a right leg was worth five hundred pieces of eight or five slaves. Eyes and fingers were each worth a hundred pieces of eight or one slave.

To be eligible for a share of the bonuses, each man in the company had to swear his adherence to the articles, and many captains insisted that each man also apply his signature or mark. Signing the articles, however, gave pause to relatively judicious men such as Ringrose, Dampier, and Wafer. The moment they applied their signatures, the document became criminal evidence against them, making them accessories to all crimes perpetrated on the expedition. On this expedition, the company's legal justification would come to be more important than they could know.

For now they had Andreas, who was willing not only to commission the company to raid Panama but also, along with Golden-Cap, to lead the way, "out of the desire they had to see that place taken and sacked," as Ringrose recorded. But unlike Santa Maria, Panama was out of Andreas's dominion and lacked the justification that might allow a sympathetic jury in England to sidestep the 1677 antipiracy act that declared it a felony for an English subject "to serve under any foreign prince or state."

The company might still be able to justify the attack based on a "letter of reprisal" — a government-issued authorization for an individual to cross an international border and seize a ship or cargo in order to redress a grievance. Edmond Cooke, the captain who flew the colorful arm-and-cutlass flag, had been promised such a letter following a run-in with the Spaniards in May of 1673. He had been sailing from Jamaica to London when his 130-ton merchant ship, the *Virgin,* was stopped and boarded by Philip Fitzgerald, an Irish-born pirate operating on behalf of the *guardacosta,* the Spanish coast guard. Fitzgerald confiscated the *Virgin*'s forty-two tons of logwood as contraband. Cooke protested; he had a legitimate license for the logwood. In response, the Irishman confiscated the *Virgin* as well, with no explanation, then set Cooke and his crew adrift in a boat with two weeks' provisions.

Finally reaching Jamaica two harrowing months later, Cooke wasted no time in petitioning the Lords of Trade and Plantations (the committee formed by King Charles II to supervise England's colonies) for reparation. A year later, on July 3, 1674, the committee found that he was among "severall English merchants, who trading into the West Indies have been barbarously and inhumanely treated, despoyled of their ships and goods, and tortured and murdered by the Spaniards." The committee then dispatched him to Madrid to collect damages of £12,863 (one British pound was worth about four pieces of eight). Should the satisfaction of damages be delayed by more than four months, the directive added, he would receive letters of reprisal. Five years later, the case remained mired in court, Cooke had yet to receive a single farthing, and the letters of reprisal had yet to be issued. So with bills to pay, he returned to trading in the West Indies. Once again, his ship was illegally confiscated by *guardacostas* — or, as he now thought of them, Spanish pirates. Would any English jury now begrudge him the use of his unwritten letter of reprisal in procuring his rightful recompense in Panama? That line of defense could work, perhaps, but would restrict the buccaneers' take to £12,863.

Yet Morgan had raided Panama with much less justification — a letter of marque against Spain issued to him by the governor of Jamaica. He took the city six months after 1670's Treaty of Madrid had officially settled all disputes between England and Spain in the New World, however, rendering such commissions to privateers obsolete. Accordingly, following his return from Panama, Morgan was charged with piracy and taken to England for incarceration in the Tower of London in advance of his trial. The charge was altogether unwarranted, he argued, because he had been acting on behalf of the Crown by retaliating against a slew of attacks on English merchant ships by Spanish privateers. News of the Treaty of Madrid had yet to reach him in Jamaica before he departed for Panama, he added. Both claims were dubious, but in England, juries and lawmen alike were liable to consider all Spaniards vile Catholics who, after declaring the New World theirs "by the authority of Almighty God," deserved whatever they got. Not only did Morgan avoid a trial, he also received a knighthood, folk-hero status, and a snuffbox with a likeness of King Charles II set in diamonds, a gift from the king himself. And shortly thereafter Morgan returned to Jamaica as its lieutenant governor.

Portrait of Henry Morgan

But by 1680, as Ringrose, Dampier, and Wafer considered signing the Panama articles, England and Spain were at peace. Moreover, to stimulate further trade between them, the nations were actively working to eradicate piracy, and none other than Morgan was spearheading the effort in the Caribbean. He had been commissioned as commandant of the regiment in Jamaica as well as judge of the Court of Vice-Admiralty (Admiralty courts heard maritime cases, and Vice-Admiralty courts were colonial, juryless versions thereof). Of his suitability for this new role, Morgan said, "Nothing but a diamond can cut a diamond."

But did he mean it? Did he really intend to prosecute his buccaneering brethren for pirating Spanish vessels and settlements? The answer perhaps lay in a rumored account of a sloop that darted into Jamaica's Montego Bay under the cover of darkness one night, dropping anchor far enough offshore to avoid detection. Yet to the horror of the seventeen buccaneers aboard, an English coast guard vessel made a beeline for them. Rather than arrest them, however, the guardsmen invited them to dinner with Sir Henry Morgan, Jamaica's acting governor at the time. Because only men with something to hide would turn down such an invitation, the buccaneers accepted. They could only hope that the rumors were true — that the fox had managed to get himself put in charge of the henhouse.

The group was escorted to the gubernatorial mansion, where Morgan, a Welsh commoner with a drinker's ruddy complexion and a perpetual air of whimsy, appeared stifled by the staid milieu, perhaps explaining his welcome of the ragtag, hirsute "fellow mariners" as though they were long-lost family. At dinner, a lavish feast with goblet upon goblet of the island's finest rum, he told them that their choice to anchor so far from Port Royal had caused him to suspect that they were buccaneers, and he hoped so, because he was starved for Brethren of the Coast gossip. Also, he was always on the lookout for new "business partners." The men felt comfortable enough to confess, to his delight, and soon they were regaling him with pirate yarns, which he repaid with his own. A delicious back-and-forth ensued, lasting so late into the night that he suggested they stay over, if they could tolerate opulent guest quarters in lieu of their hammocks.

When the men rose from their feather beds the following morning, they were shackled and dragged to the Vice-Admiralty courthouse by soldiers who scoffed at the notion that there had been a misunderstanding. Fortunately, the buccaneers' friend Morgan was sitting at the judge's bench. "There's no need for a trial," he declared, to their profound relief. But then he added,

"These men are guilty of the crime of high seas piracy — they've already confessed it to me." He sentenced them to be taken to Gallows Point, and by day's end, they were all dead.

The story may be apocryphal; there is no mention of it in England's *Calendar of State Papers Colonial, America and the West Indies,* the 400,000-word tenth volume of which comprises a comprehensive index of every single proceeding involving the English government in the region between 1677 and 1680. For the buccaneer company pondering Panama, however, the reality was just as daunting. At the time, Lord Carlisle, the governor of Jamaica whom Morgan had temporarily replaced, was complaining bitterly to the Lords of Trade and Plantations about pirates — "ravenous vermin," he called them. Morgan himself told English secretary of state Sir Leoline Jenkins, "Nothing can be more fatal to the prosperity of this colony than the temptingly alluring boldness and success of the privateers... I spare no care to put down this growing evil."

Their raid of Portobelo two months earlier had placed Coxon and Sharp atop Morgan's vermin list, resulting in warrants for their apprehension as well as a proclamation that "the utmost rigour of the law" would befall their crews and anyone else daring to "harbour, deale with, comfort, aide, assist, or give intelligence, or hold correspondence" with them. With news and paperwork confined to the speed of ships, the warrants would not be issued until July 5, 1680, three months after the buccaneers left Golden Island. But in the interim, thanks to intelligence-gathering efforts such as his fabled dinner party, Morgan knew where to find them.

7

A Natural Pirate

I N CONTINUING TO Panama, William Dampier would have
more at stake, arguably, than anyone else in the company. For
starters, there were the hopes and dreams of his parents, who
had been tenant farmers. Both died while he was still a boy — his
mother as a consequence of the Great Plague — but not before
plotting a course on which his raw intellect and perspicacity could
be harnessed to facilitate both commercial success and the life of
a gentleman. Their first step was securing a scholarship for him,
evidently at King's Bruton, the Somerset boarding school founded
in 1519 by three eminent townsmen including the Bishop of London. There William received a classical education and an open
door to the prestigious career of his choice. Prior to plunging into
professional life, though, he wanted to indulge his "inclination for
the sea."

In 1669, an apprenticeship with a Weymouth merchant captain enabled the then eighteen-year-old to sail to France and
Newfoundland. He was so taken with the experience that he
soon signed on as a foremast hand for a yearlong voyage to Java,
in 1671. That experience in turn whetted his appetite for "seeing the world," and anytime he returned home between voyages,

he quickly grew "weary of staying ashore" and seized any opportunity to distance himself from it, even enlisting to fight in the Franco-Dutch War (in which England had allied with France). Aboard HMS *Royal Prince,* he took part in the two Battles of Schooneveld (fought a week apart in June of 1673, off the coast of the Netherlands) before being hospitalized with an illness. What precisely ailed him is unknown, but it was serious enough for him to return home to recuperate.

Upon recovery, he found himself at a crossroads. From a fiscal standpoint, the sea had dried up for him. The only thing poorer than the wages was the food, sailors joked, adding that if they were to mutiny over their meals and fail, the weight of their bodies wouldn't be enough to hang them. Twenty-three now, Dampier needed a career that would facilitate a proper countryside estate, a family, and the realization of his parents' dream — his dream, too, he would no doubt have hastened to add. Accordingly, he accepted a plantation management apprenticeship in Jamaica. Unfortunately, he abhorred the work. "I was clearly out of my element there," he wrote of his first six months. But a career as a plantation manager all but guaranteed the life of a gentleman, and so he stuck with it.

In the meantime, he could find diversion in nearby Port Royal. The second-largest English-speaking settlement in the New World (behind Boston), Port Royal was a warren of two thousand multistory redbrick Spanish Colonial buildings mixed in around the odd church. All manner of vessels streamed into its deep, accommodating harbor, the largest tying up at the wharves, where crewmen raced to unload exotic cargo and merchants to sell it, shouting the names of their wares from the dock and attracting swarms of customers. The city itself was home to a hectic vitality supplied by a caste of sailor that was at once familiar to Dampier and different from anything he'd ever seen. The men's windblown, rough-hewn faces were unmistakably those of mariners, as were their wide, rolling gaits (accustomed to swaying decks, seamen had difficulty readjusting to land) and their leathery hands, swung half open as though poised to grasp a rope. But some of these men, unlike the scruffy seafarers Dampier knew, wore elegant silk waistcoats, colorful sashes, and gold and jewels to excess — for example, a "necklace of pearls of extraordinary size and inestimable price, with rubies of surpassing beauty." Others were adorned with a parrot or a monkey. Because Jamaica was situated directly along the shipping route from the New World to Spain, it had become a natural base for English buccaneers and a convenient postplunder stop for their French brethren, who traded *bon butin* (good booty) to merchants for sacks of pieces of eight, then went to town to spend them.

Port Royal

The women of Port Royal threw the first-time visitor, too, with their skirts raised to expose brightly colored petticoats and bodices lowered to the edge of propriety. Their allure was augmented by bustiers, corsets, and, as a travel writer from London described it, a "proud lazy stalking gait with them, swinging and dangling their arms about as they walk and much addicted to a swearing obscene masculine talk and behavior." The air was heavy with their flowery perfume, and the sound of rattling dice and clacking billiards emanated from within the myriad taverns and punch houses. Dampier may also have heard the peal of a duel in progress, the cheers and groans and curses of crowds watching bear baiting or a cockfight, and the hoarse calls of street vendors hawking a local rum called kill-devil, despite the abundance of rum houses.

There was also debauchery in the air: one in four of Port Royal's buildings was either a drinking house or a brothel. Buccaneers flush with pieces of eight made stars of strumpets such as Unconscionable Nan, Salt-Beef Peg, and Buttock-de-Clink Jenny. The onetime British actress Mary Carlton became known throughout the West Indies as the Barber's Chair, for "no sooner was one out than another man was in." As a result, Port Royal was condemned — or lauded, depending on one's point of view — as "the Sodom of the New World" and "the wickedest city on Earth." "Pirates are found who will spend two or three thousand pieces of eight in one night, not leaving themselves peradventure a good shirt to wear on their backs in the morning," Exquemelin wrote of Port Royal, relating the story of a onetime master of his who would launch an evening by buying a barrel of beer or a pipe of wine (126–40 gallons), plopping it down in the middle of a sandy street, and then inviting passersby to drink with him, sometimes threatening to shoot them if they didn't.

In sum, Port Royal was antithetical both to the dreams of Dampier's parents and to the religious teachings of King's Bruton. But neither Dampier's parents nor his schoolmasters need have worried: he simply wasn't drawn to rum houses or debauchery. Yet Port Royal called to him in other ways. Perhaps the freedom from societal constraints made the air seem easier to breathe, all the perfume notwithstanding. Certainly he saw the city as a gateway to adventure.

Quitting the plantation, Dampier found a job with a trader who sold goods and provisions around the Caribbean and Gulf of Mexico. The new job took him to a place he liked even better than Port Royal: the Bay of Campeche. A shallow six-thousand-square-mile concavity in the Mexican coastline between Veracruz and the Yucatán Peninsula, the bay was surrounded by marshes and mangrove swampland inhabited by 250 English lumbermen who harvested logwood. Due to the singularly vibrant red dye produced from scarlet crystals in its core, logwood (*haematoxylum campechianum*) fetched £100 per ton in Europe, whereas the same amount of wheat sold for just £8.

Taking in the abundance of logwood trees between thirty and fifty feet tall and as much as six feet in circumference, Dampier didn't need his advanced math to determine there was "a great prospect of getting money here." Since the Bay of Campeche was part of the Spanish Main, though, Englishmen taking its logwood risked apprehension by the *guardacosta*. Nevertheless, in early 1676, Dampier invested all his money in cutting tools, a gun, and other logwood-related supplies, then took up residence in a crude thatched-roof hut at the Bay of Campeche's Términos Lagoon.

Sawing the unyielding logwood trees was like a wrestling match, during which Dampier and the other logwood cutters were continually looking over their shoulders for *guardacostas*.

They also contended with the cloying cheap-perfume scent of the logwood flowers as well as heat and humidity that all but brought the air to a boil. Their only relief came in the form of sporadic torrential rains that left them laboring thigh deep in floodwater, at risk of attack by alligators, and under attack from squadrons of plague-bearing gnats and ravenous mosquitoes, not to mention spiders as big as a man's fist and guinea worms that bored into human ankles and nested there. Nevertheless, Dampier relished the work.

Even better was the downtime: while exploring the surrounding savannah and forested ridges, he compiled notes that one day would earn him credit in the *Oxford English Dictionary* for the introduction of more than a thousand words to the English language, including *avocado, barbecue,* and *cashew.* His budding naturalism and enthusiasm for discovery also led him to become the first Englishman to detail in print the effects of smoking marijuana: "Some it keeps sleepy, some merry, some putting them into a laughing fit, and others it makes mad." Probably the best part of his life in the Bay of Campeche was the camp itself, especially the freedom from the stricture and mores of civilized society. In the logwood cutters — an assortment of outsiders, nonconformists, and former buccaneers — Dampier found a fraternity of kindred spirits.

Five months into the sojourn, with a fortune's worth of logwood stacked on shore, Dampier was looking out to sea in anticipation of customers' ships when his attention was seized by a darkening sky. He watched as all the seabirds raced inland — the sort of apocalyptic flight that preceded a hurricane, he concluded in his chronicle of the storm, which meteorologists would one day consider a landmark. But in the moment, the hurricane was a horror story, flattening the camp, casting all the accumulated logwood out to sea, and leaving the logwood cutters with nothing.

The onetime buccaneers in the camp saw it differently, because they still had the sea, where Spanish ships were just waiting to be plundered. But Dampier, the Old Brutonian, was no criminal. Buccaneers didn't see their vocation as criminal, however. Their rationale was rooted in an old story of a pirate who was captured and brought before Alexander the Great. The ruler asked him "what he meant by keeping hostile possession of the sea." The pirate proudly replied, "What thou meanest by seizing the whole earth; but because I do it with a petty ship, I am called a robber, whilst thou who dost it with a great fleet art styled emperor." Two millennia later, King Charles II of Spain was a stand-in for Alexander the Great. The upshot, according to Dampier, was that he "was forced to range about to seek a subsistence in company of some privateers." *Former* privateers, technically. In the Bay of Campeche they lacked any sort of legal authority. But in those days before the antipiracy act, if their mark was Spanish, a British Vice-Admiralty court might well regard the crime as victimless.

Dampier roved around the Caribbean and Gulf of Mexico with a band of sixty such privateers over the course of the following year. The highlight came during their raid of Veracruz, on the Mexican coast, which served as a way station for the Manila galleons of the Spanish treasure fleet. As had been the case in Morgan's raid of Panama, the battle lasted long enough for the defenders to evacuate the riches. When Dampier and company finally captured the fort, at a cost of ten or eleven of their comrades, they found only caged parrots — hundreds of them. While not as good as gold, parrots were nevertheless a New World status symbol and very much in demand, fetching five pieces of eight apiece.

Dampier's share of the proceeds was enough for him to cash out of pirating and return to England, where, over the ensuing

Portrait of William Dampier

two years, he seemingly laid to rest any doubts as to whether he could become a gentleman. He married a woman named Judith, a relative of the Duchess of Grafton who lived with her at Arlington House (located on the same Westminster plot where Buckingham Palace now sits). Shortly thereafter, he purchased a small estate of his own in Dorsetshire. All he needed was the right vocation, and his dream would be realized.

While exploring opportunities, he seized on the idea of procuring logwood-cutting supplies in England and selling them for a huge profit in the Bay of Campeche. Accordingly, he purchased bulk quantities of saws, axes, and other logging instruments, booked himself a transatlantic passage, and, leaving Judith behind, set sail on a quick business trip — at least that was the plan. Once again, Port Royal upended his world. He stayed there for eight months until embarking on — if he is to be taken at his word — "a short trading voyage." No sooner did he and the traders depart Port Royal, his story went, than they ran into Captains Sharp, Sawkins, and Coxon and their crews, and the trading-ship crewmen "all left" to join the buccaneers. What choice did Dampier have but to go, too?

Now, in Santa Maria, he was faced with the choice of signing on to a pirate expedition he knew to be both illegal and among the riskiest of all time. But like Ringrose and Wafer and the rest of the company, he couldn't pass it up.

8

An Easy Canoe Ride

WITH THEIR KNOWLEDGE of Panama's defenses, the captured Spanish soldiers of the Santa Maria garrison became critical to the buccaneers' raid on the city. Returning from the town to the garrison to collect that intelligence, Coxon and his men discovered, to their horror, that the Kuna had already executed as many as twenty-six of the Spaniards.

The company straightaway put an end to the Indians' "barbarous cruelty," as Ringrose put it. As far as the Spanish soldiers knew, though, the slaughter had merely been paused. Given the choice between answering questions about Panama or being sent out to the woods with the Kuna, the Spaniards proved fonts of actionable intelligence. A key piece was the news that the governor of Santa Maria had left not three days earlier in a ship, as the buccaneers had previously believed, but only two days earlier, and in a canoe. Accompanying him were just two men and two women. With elite rowers, the buccaneers might overtake them on the way to Panama and thereby maintain the element of surprise for their attack on the city. At once, Sawkins gathered ten good oarsmen into a canoe and raced downriver.

One Spaniard especially eager to please the remaining buc-

single-handedly fulfilled their prisoner criteria. Additional prisoners might net the buccaneers more intelligence and, as hostages, a measure of leverage, but those benefits were outweighed by the risks associated with shepherding as many as a hundred soldiers who, just the other day, were trying to kill them. Yet in an astonishing display of mercy, or foolishness, Coxon and company consented.

A flotilla of some thirty-five canoes and the one periagua — bearing a group of buccaneers, Kuna, and Spaniards and totaling 450-odd men — started down the Santa Maria River toward the Gulf of San Miguel, the confluence of the river and the South Sea. In hindsight, Ringrose would have been wise to trade his own canoe for one of the newly available craft. Put in charge of three buccaneers and José Gabriel, the most important Spanish prisoner, he had been given a canoe that, like the others, was about twenty feet long and a foot and a half wide. If anything, it appeared more durable, with a hull some six inches thick. But that solidity made it slower, he realized belatedly. He and his crew fell behind right away, and soon the rest of the flotilla was out of sight.

The Gulf of San Miguel sat thirty miles due west as the crow flies, but for a canoe subjected to all the river's bends and undulations, the distance was closer to fifty miles. Still, reaching the gulf was a simple matter of following the current, in theory. But not in practice, Ringrose discovered, because of the Santa Maria River's innumerable tributaries, channels, and other offshoots, many of which were indistinguishable from the river itself. Although there were no maps, the Kuna knew the way. The trouble was since Ringrose had been entrusted with Gabriel, his canoe could not carry a Kuna guide — for the Spaniard's safety. After losing sight of the flotilla, the Ringrose party rowed for two miles before realizing they had inadvertently turned down a dead-end channel. At the same time, they had to contend with a receding tide. "We were forced to lay by until highwater came," Ringrose wrote in his journal, "for to row in such heavy boats against the tide is totally impossible."

The setback presented an opportunity. Ringrose had begun learning Spanish on the expedition and was making so much progress that the assignment to chaperone Gabriel was probably no coincidence. Likely he was expected to deepen the company's knowledge of Panama through conversations with the Spaniard. Pirates made it their business to thoroughly question all prisoners about their hometowns, cities, and countries. Consequently pirate ships were floating census bureaus, with information on each area's manufacturing, wealth, fortifications, military strengths, and susceptibilities that would have rivaled the dossier compiled by any intelligence agency. Between Latin, gesticulation, and his smattering of Spanish, Ringrose was able not only to make conversation with Gabriel but also to establish a rapport. Thus began an unlikely friendship during which the Englishman would learn that the Spaniard had been born in Chile and that he was innocent of the charge of kidnapping Golden-Cap's daughter — in fact, he professed, he and the princess had married. But for now, if the Spaniard had actionable information on Panama — the correct route, for example — he was keeping it to himself.

Eventually the tide turned, allowing Ringrose and company to resume their voyage, which they did in double time to catch up to the flotilla. "But all our endeavours were in vain," Ringrose recorded. He and his men found no trace of their companions, who evidently viewed Gabriel as less of a commodity now that they had a hundred other Spanish prisoners in tow. At about ten that night, "the tide being low, we stuck up an oar in the river, and slept by turns in our canoe, several showers of rain falling all the night long, which pierced us to the skin."

At first light, they wasted no time in starting downriver — or at least in the direction they thought was downriver. The Santa Maria, Ringrose was sure, ran down from the mountains into the South Sea, which, of course, was to the south. Yet the sun was rising over the wall of trees on the right side of the river, meaning that the canoe was heading north. This vertiginous dynamic persisted for two full leagues, as though the laws of nature simply did not apply in the Darien, until the river twisted once more, bringing into view an Indian embarcadero, or landing place. Banked there was a periagua and a throng of canoes whose 450-odd passengers were on shore, in the process of breaking camp. Ringrose and his companions would have been no happier to find 450 bars of gold.

They were greeted by the others with instructions to hurry inland to the pond, the last opportunity to collect enough drinking water to sustain them through the next few days of travel on the brackish river and salty sea. As soon as they had filled their calabashes — hollowed-out melons also known as bottle gourds — they hastened back to the embarcadero. On return, they found just one canoe. Their own. Once again, the rest of the flotilla was nowhere in sight. Ringrose was at once furious, crestfallen, and, mostly, flabbergasted: "Such is the procedure of these wild men that they care not in the least whom they lose of their company, or leave behind," he wrote. It was like a recurring nightmare. He and his men jumped into their canoe, the one they'd been dying to get rid of, and "rowed after them, as fast as we possibly could, but all in vain."

At the start of the journey from Santa Maria the day before, as Ringrose and his canoe party were being left behind, Richard Sawkins and his own canoe party had been doing everything in their power to prevent the governor of Santa Maria from reaching Panama, a task that turned out to be challenging for reasons beyond the Spaniard's head start. One of the problems was the great width of the river, in some stretches three miles, the outer limit of human eyesight. Yet even if the governor's canoe came within visual range, Sawkins's view of it could be obstructed by glare or haze or a low-hanging banyan tree bough. And if the governor and his party had gone ashore and banked their canoe behind the mangroves, there would be no way of descrying them.

Sawkins's Kuna guide, however, had an idea: about six leagues downriver from Santa Maria was an embarcadero that was all but a mandatory stopover en route to the gulf, because the pond there was the last chance to collect fresh water. It was a good bet, therefore, that the governor and his party would make camp there for the second night of their journey. To catch them, Sawkins and his ten elite rowers simply needed to double the pace of the governor and reach the embarcadero by their first night.

Indeed, the Sawkins party made it to the embarcadero by nightfall — while Ringrose and his companions were still miles upriver, sleeping in the rain — but they found no canoes. There was a chance that the governor had dragged his vessel onto the bank and concealed it, but a concerted search revealed that the whole of the embarcadero was deserted. The pond, too. Sawkins's best hope now was that he had unwittingly passed the governor's canoe between Santa Maria and the embarcadero. If so, it would be arriving at the embarcadero soon. Indeed, at midnight, a canoe landed on the bank. But, damnably, it was a buccaneer canoe, the first of the flotilla's three dozen. The odds that all of them had breezed past the governor's canoe were minuscule. More likely the governor had long since passed the embarcadero and was now beyond their reach.

But the next day, shortly after Ringrose and his fellow stragglers finally turned up and the flotilla got under way, the buccaneers came upon the two women from the governor's party, now stranded on one of the river's many small islands. The governor had put them ashore that very morning "to lighten his canoe," they said. Sawkins and his elite rowers again raced ahead in pursuit, soon reaching the end of the Santa Maria River and entering the South Sea at the Gulf of San Miguel. Here, unfortunately, the governor's canoe would be a mere speck on the horizon, even on a clear day. And now, the gulf was stormy, with tides and winds so fierce that Sawkins rethought his pursuit.

Back upriver, Sharp was watching in alarm as the turbulent waters overset a canoe carrying seven Frenchmen, who would have "certainly perished" if not for divine providence on top of an extensive buccaneer rescue effort. All the buccaneers, Sharp thought, were now "in exceedingly great danger to lose both our lives and all of our substance in one dash." The indomitable Cox may have been the only member of the crew to remain calm — "it being a certain truth that those who are born to be hang'd shall never be drown'd," as he explained.

9

Castaways

ON APRIL 18, the same day that the rest of the flotilla tried to access the Gulf of San Miguel only to be repulsed by the storm, Ringrose and his canoemates still lagged far behind, trapped in a virtual hall of mirrors. The cluster of verdant islands in the lower part of the Santa Maria River reflected so perfectly on the water's glassy surface that the men could hardly tell where one island ended and the next began. In addition, veritable walls of trees blocked their view past the islands. Soon they were lost. Once again.

"Much trouble and toil" was Ringrose's summation of their effort to extricate themselves. But it paid off. At last the Boca Chica — the Spanish name for the mouth of the Santa Maria River — appeared, along with, on its far side, the Gulf of San Miguel, a vast, glittering mosaic of blues, grays, and greens. Now reaching the fleet's rendezvous point near Panama would be a simple matter of rowing along the Pacific coastline for a couple of days. Or so Ringrose and company thought. But with a mere hundred feet to go before entering the gulf, a strange thing happened: the seawater began to rise, spilling into the river. Unlike the comparatively tideless Caribbean, the South Sea rose and fell daily, by as much as twenty feet, creating a tidal stream known as a "young flood." It came at the canoe like a dam bursting — "violently," wrote Ringrose, "so that though we were not above a stone's cast from the said mouth, and this was within a league broad, yet we could not by any means come near it." He and his companions were forced to put ashore — in the same cluster of islands that had so vexed them all day long — and wait for the Boca Chica to level off.

The delay at least afforded another opportunity for him to get better acquainted with his prisoner. Gabriel had certainly had better weeks. He had narrowly escaped a brutal death at the hands of the Kuna, and his extraordinary life in Santa Maria — a tropical paradise where he had a steady income, bountiful food and wine, and a bed he shared with a princess — had been reduced to ashes by murderous English thieves who, despite being pirates, had turned out to be inept navigators. Ringrose's kindness was perhaps the lone ray of light, and the Spaniard appreciated it.

Some two hours later, the tide turned, giving the party another chance to extricate itself from the Santa Maria River. At long last, they succeeded in entering the Gulf of San Miguel. Given what he had heard of the gulf, Ringrose was expecting "a mere mill-pond" — water as flat and calm as that of a pool formed by damming a stream in order to turn a mill wheel, or the perfect antidote to the serpentine Santa Maria River. Instead it was a conflagration of high waves, each one amounting to a crisis: the canoe was about twenty feet long but not quite a foot and a half wide, leaving the men barely enough room to sit down. Even a modest wave could swamp them. There was no choice but to put ashore once again.

The party retreated to a small island they had passed while entering the gulf, and they made camp — or tried to. As Ringrose would write, "It was, from the loss of our company, and the great dangers we were in, the sorrowfullest night that until then, I had ever experienced in my whole life." Rain lashed the men throughout the night, leaving them wet from head to foot and without "one dry thread" among them. By starting a fire, they could warm and dry themselves, but each time they managed much more than a spark, the storm swiftly annihilated it — along with their efforts to rest. Notwithstanding their exhaustion, no one managed a single minute of sleep, leaving them to chew over their predicament, which Ringrose summed up as being "totally destitute of all human comfort; for a vast sea surrounded us on one side, and the mighty power of our enemies, the Spaniards, on the other." More troubling was the seeming permanence of the situation, because "all that we could see being the wide sea, high mountains and rocks; while we ourselves were confined to an egg-shell, instead of a boat."

That day would be easy and uneventful, however, compared to the next one, April 19, which began, as ever, with Ringrose and his team hauling their leaden canoe into the water. They were still wet and cold, but fortunately the gulf had calmed. Still, at all times, at least one of the men had to bail the water pouring over the side of the canoe. After they rowed for about two miles, as they entered a range of small, richly forested islands, a large wave surged their way, picked up their canoe, and flipped it over. Cast into the gulf, the five men had little choice but to watch helplessly as the subsequent wave whisked the canoe away. To swim after it through the turbulence — to do anything but get themselves ashore — meant death.

No sooner had they dragged themselves onto the nearest island (likely the eighty-nine-acre Isla Conejo) than the gulf spat out their canoe, sending it tumbling onto the beach after them. It was their first bit of good luck since Santa Maria. And more followed: they recovered their weapons and ammunition, which had been secured to the inside of the canoe and remained fully operational on account of having been thoroughly waxed down. Their supplies of bread and fresh water, however, had washed away.

The three other buccaneers had now had it with the expedition. Anything, they told Ringrose, was preferable to proceeding. Instead they wanted to return to Golden Island, and, failing that, to live with the Kuna. Ringrose argued for continuing to Panama, the rewards of which greatly outweighed the risks, and eventually he "prevailed with them to go forward, at least one day longer, and in case we found not our people the next day...then I would be willing to do anything which they should think fit."

But before he could devise a plan to go forward, the party faced yet another difficulty — a canoe full of Spanish soldiers who had seemingly materialized from the sea spray and were now headed for the island. As the canoe approached, though, the Spaniards received the same one-two punch the sea had landed on the buccaneers: one wave violently upended their canoe, and a second threw them into the froth. Their slender canoe was slammed against the rocks surrounding the island, shattering the craft and giving Ringrose a newfound appreciation for his own six-inch-thick clunker.

Dragging themselves onto the beach and looking up through burning eyes into the barrels of English muskets, the six Spanish castaways must have wondered why they had bothered swimming for their lives. And they must have been astounded, subsequently, when Ringrose invited them to supper. To his way of thinking, the two factions were now neither Englishmen nor Spaniards so much as fellow citizens of this desolate, uninhabited rock at the end of the earth; their chances of survival would benefit from an alliance.

The Spaniards accepted the invitation, and, while they built a fire, the buccaneers hunted, procuring meat. Next, with one man assigned to stand watch "for fear of any surprisal by the Indians, or other enemies," the other ten sat amicably around the fire, broiling and then eating the meat — boar, perhaps — all the while trying to communicate. Ringrose gathered that the Spaniards, who knew Gabriel, had been among the combatants in Santa Maria taken captive by the Kuna after the battle but had escaped in an old canoe. There was no misinterpreting the dinner conversation's main topic: the castaways' desperate need for fresh water. The island, it appeared, had none whatsoever. Save for inadvertent mouthfuls of salt water, no one had had anything to drink since capsizing.

Their watchman interrupted with news of an Indian intruder, a problem that was at the same time a potential solution. But the Indian, alerted to the large party, turned and bolted into the woods. Ringrose sent two of the buccaneers after him. What might have been a dramatic chase through a dark and unfamiliar jungle was defused by recognition: the intruder, the two buccaneers happily realized, was "one of our friendly Indians" — one of Andreas's men, in other words. The Indian in turn recognized them and, gesturing for them to follow, led them to a beach where seven more Kuna from Andreas's contingent were waiting by a large canoe. Andreas had sent a rescue party, the buccaneers hoped.

The two buccaneers returned with the eight Kuna to the bonfire. Ringrose asked the Indians — "by signs," as he related it — if they knew the whereabouts of the rest of his company. They replied that if he and his men would accompany them, they would catch up to Andreas and the buccaneers no later than the following morning. The news, Ringrose wrote, "not a little rejoiced our hearts."

The rejoicing came to an abrupt end, though, when the Kuna realized that the six newcomers seated alongside Ringrose were Spaniards and declared that they ought to be put to death. Ringrose protested, but the Kuna insisted. Gabriel, they admitted, had value as a prisoner, but not the other six *wankers* — the Kuna word for Spaniards. These six could die with no ill effect on the mission. Ringrose, though, "would not consent to have it done." The Kuna eventually backed down, or so he thought.

A short while later, though, when his back was turned, "a sad shriek and outcry" in Spanish drew his attention to a plot by his own men. Having isolated two of the Spaniards, the buccaneers were beckoning the Kuna. Rushing to the Spaniards' defense, Ringrose now found himself at odds with his fellow buccaneers, who maintained the need to "oblige the Indians." Otherwise there would be no fresh water, much less an escape from this godforsaken island. Were Ringrose to stand in their way, he would likely draw their ire himself. Nevertheless he demanded that the Spaniards' lives be spared, and ultimately he succeeded, albeit with one weighty concession to the Kuna: "I was forced to give way and consent that they should have one of them for to make their slave."

As the other buccaneers followed the Kuna to the canoe, Ringrose — along with Gabriel, presumably to help translate — lingered at the bonfire to give the five remaining Spanish castaways the canoe his party had arrived with. He advised the soldiers to use it to leave the island as soon as possible, "lest those cruel Indians should not keep their word."

He and Gabriel then rejoined their party, their time as castaways concluding as they climbed into the substantial Kuna canoe, which had space for twenty men. The Indians had fitted a sail to it, allowing a strong gale to hurtle the party away from the island, "to the infinite joy and comfort of our hearts," according to Ringrose, who was "so happily rid of the miseries we but lately had endured." His sanguineness seemingly provoked the Fates. Almost at once, rain fell — "vehemently" — resulting in the sort of darkness that, at sea, can be like complete immersion in India ink. As the party neared the mainland promontory known as Point San Lorenzo, where the rest of the company was supposed to have made camp, the current intensified, creating "a very great rippling of the sea" that "often almost filled our boat with its dashes."

Finally, two far-off flames pierced the darkness off the starboard bow, elating the Kuna, who believed them to be campfires. They aimed for the promontory, and as the canoe cut through the breakers near the shore, they called out to Andreas and Golden-Cap. In response, sixty Spaniards emerged from the woods and, brandishing clubs, charged into the surf.

Ringrose drew his gun, thinking he might mount some sort of defense or at least keep the attackers at bay until the canoe could reverse course. But four or five of them swarmed him before he could get off a shot. Others grabbed hold of the canoe by the gunwales and began hauling it toward shore. Turning to his own company for help, Ringrose found the three other buccaneers sitting and watching, stupefied. Gabriel, who now stood to be liberated, certainly wasn't going to put up a fight. The only action taken was by the Kuna, who leaped overboard and ran off through the surf, disappearing into the woods.

While the canoe was being dragged onto the beach, Ringrose tried to make sense of this band of club-wielding Spaniards on an otherwise deserted promontory. He asked whether any of them could speak either French or English, receiving only "no" in response. Next he tried Latin and thus learned, by degrees, that most of the men were the soldiers from the Santa Maria garrison who had persuaded the buccaneers to take them to Panama as prisoners. Along the way, Admiral Coxon and company had become increasingly concerned about the possibility of one of the Spaniards escaping and warning his countrymen in Panama of the attack. The buccaneers' solution was to turn the Spaniards ashore on Point San Lorenzo — a marooning, effectively, because the promontory was surrounded by turbulent sea on one side and impassable jungle on the other.

Upon reaching shore and removing Ringrose and his companions from the canoe, the Spaniards "made great shouts for joy, because they had taken us." It became clear to Ringrose that the Spaniards intended "to use us very severely for coming into those parts, and especially for taking and plundering their town of Santa Maria." Separating Ringrose from the other buccaneers, the soldiers prodded him toward a small bough-covered hut they had constructed, where he was to be "examined" — a euphemism, it stood to reason, much like the word *inquisition* in "Spanish Inquisition." Volunteering his knowledge of Latin, it seemed, had been a fatal misstep. The Spaniards would now attempt to extract from him every detail of the buccaneers' Panama attack plan.

As a conversation starter, Ringrose might expect thumbscrews, pincers, or the strappado, wherein his hands would be bound behind his back with one end of a rope while the other end was spooled through a pulley, allowing the Spaniards to raise him off the floor an inch at a time — rapid elevation wasn't as excruciating. Or he might experience the *tormenta de toca,* the torment of the cloth, in which the subject was bound in place on a trestle, his head lower than his feet, with a prong holding his mouth open so that a *toca* — strip of linen — could be lowered into his throat,

An "examination"

after which water would be poured in, causing the toca to swell and giving him the sensation of drowning. This Spanish interrogation mainstay is best known today as waterboarding.

Ringrose stood before the Spanish captain and faced his fate stoically. He would report nothing of the ensuing examination save José Gabriel's sudden entry to the hut. Gabriel related to the captain how kind Ringrose had been not only to him but also to the Spanish castaways, "saving their lives from the cruelty of the Indians." Having heard Gabriel out, the captain rose from his seat, advanced on Ringrose, and then, astonishingly, embraced him. Next he invited Ringrose to eat dinner with him. During the meal the captain said that for the kindness Ringrose had shown to his countrymen, he and the other Englishmen could have their lives and liberty, which otherwise he would have taken. Pardoning the Kuna as well, the captain allowed that the entire party could "go in God's name" the following morning.

Although it was then late at night and the weather was foul, Ringrose thought it best to leave before the captain changed his mind. First, though, Ringrose wanted to search the adjacent woods for the Kuna. The other buccaneers, champing at the bit to get away, could not have been overjoyed by his concern for the Indians. He persisted, though, eventually finding them and relaying to them the news of their reprieve. As he returned to the canoe with them in tow, however, the Spanish captain and his men caught up to them. Had the Spaniards reconsidered? Ringrose wondered. On the contrary, he wrote: "As they at first hauled us ashore, so now again they pushed us off to sea, by a sudden and strange vicissitude of fortune."

Stranger still, José Gabriel opted to continue on with the buccaneers. Ringrose provided no explanation of the Spaniard's motivation or the extent to which it had factored into the captain's decision to release them. Possibly the buccaneers had added a financial interest to Gabriel's leading them to the "bedchamber door of the governor of Panama," which previously he had agreed to do solely in exchange for his life. Or perhaps he saw facilitating a buccaneer success in Panama as a means of redemption in the eyes of the Kuna, allowing him to reunite with his wife in Golden-Cap's village and to meet their newborn child.

Once safely away from the Spaniards, the canoe party sailed west, a hard rain notwithstanding, rather than put ashore anywhere in the vicinity of Point San Lorenzo. They continued throughout the night, whittling away at the seventy-five miles between them and the fleet's planned rendezvous point near Panama. In the morning they alternated between sailing, rowing, and paddling, making it a record four hours without any major reversals of fortune before they caught sight of a craft coming toward them "with all speed imaginable." If it was a Spanish vessel of any consequence, there was little Ringrose and his companions could do but wait to be taken prisoner again.

As it sailed closer, Ringrose could tell that it was a canoe of some sort. When it came into firing range, he recognized the sailors. The buccaneer flotilla had been hiding in a nearby bay, it turned out, and, having mistaken the Kuna canoe for a Spanish periagua, opted to attack. "We were all mutually rejoiced to see one another again," Ringrose wrote, "they having given both me and my companions up for lost."

Thus his canoe ordeal finally ended — just in time for him to fight in one of the bloodiest naval battles in South Sea history.

10

Surprizal

O N THAT SAME afternoon, April 20, while continuing across the Gulf of San Miguel, the newly reunited party of buccaneers spotted a bump on the horizon. As they rowed closer, it took on blues and grays and the shape of a whale; closer still, and the hue deadened to a leafy green, with gaps and protrusions appearing upon its surface. They hoped it was Plantan Key, a small island at the entrance to the Gulf of Panama. If so, they were on the right course. The greenery soon revealed itself to be primarily trees resembling palms but with disproportionately large canoe-shaped fronds, each nearly the size of the trunk itself. They were plantain trees, realized Dampier, who had developed a fascination with them during his time in the West Indies. "The King of all Fruit," he called the plantain.

Likely the botanical identification, suggesting to the buccaneers that they had indeed come upon Plantan Key, would have spurred cries of *huzza* (pronounced *huzzay*), the seventeenth-century mariners' exultation of choice, believed to have been derived from an older mariner's cry, *heeze,* meaning "hoist." But what the men saw on Plantan Key next would have changed the *huzzas* to curses (commonly *damn,* as opposed to *argh,* which, in reality, pirates never said prior to the 1950 film version of *Treasure Island*). Perched atop the island's highest hill was a hut, undoubtedly a lookout post installed to capitalize on the location's singular vantage of the entrance to the Gulf of Panama. Almost certainly watchmen would now climb its roof and light its beacon, a stack of wood sitting at the ready for just such a bonfire, and Spanish soldiers on the mainland would be alerted to the pirate threat.

Coxon and company knew they needed to stop the watchmen — or at least douse the fire — before the soldiers could get the message. Accordingly, they banked their canoes and periagua on the island's northern coast and quickly began climbing the steep hill, all the while braced for an ambush or gunfire from above. There was no sign of the enemy, however, until they burst into the hut and met its lone occupant, an elderly watchman who lived there by himself and hadn't noticed the flotilla. For Dampier, the pathetic lookout post was right in line with the Spanish letters intercepted at Portobelo bemoaning the South Sea colonies' vulnerability to pirates. But although the watchman had been of no use to the Spaniards, he might prove invaluable to the buccaneers by sharing the specifics of Panama's preparations for their attack.

To loosen tongues, the buccaneers, like the Spaniards, had many draconian methods, among them placing captives' thumbs or genitals in vises or holding just about any of their body parts to a fire. Such tactics were unnecessary in the case of the old watchman, who quickly established his credibility with his claim that he had become aware of pirates in the South Sea only moments earlier, when he looked out his window and saw a horde of scruffy men arriving with guns and cutlasses. He went on to tell them that the Spaniards were also unaware of the threat — otherwise the governor of Santa Maria, whose party had stopped at the island the day before, surely would have said something about pirates. The buccaneers could easily catch the governor in the twenty leagues remaining between here and Panama, the watchman added, spurring Sawkins and his team of elite rowers back to their canoe.

The visit yielded another valuable piece of intelligence via the lookout post's view of the Gulf of Panama. Sailing on a direct course for Plantan Key at that moment was a thirty-ton barque — or bark, as the chroniclers recorded it — a broad term for a small ship. Fortune again seemed to be smiling upon the buccaneers, who desperately needed such a vessel to prevent the Spaniards from evacuating Panama's gold and silver. As the sun dissolved into an especially dark night, the barque anchored off Plantan Key's southern coast, where her sailors could not see the periagua and thirty-six canoes — more good luck for the buccaneers.

Ringrose was among the small team — perhaps ten men — deployed to seize the barque. To all appearances, he was unafraid, perhaps because he was preoccupied with the planning of the operation, known as a "surprizal at anchor." To begin with, the unit needed information, including the target ship's strengths, weaknesses, and likely response to being boarded. Unfortunately, the combination of darkness and the barque's distance from shore afforded the team no opportunity for reconnaissance without jeopardizing the most important part of their surprizal — namely, the surprise.

They advanced in two canoes, rowing around the island in the barque's direction, sticking to the shoreline to lower their profiles. The darkness was good for veiling their approach, and nighttime in general was best for surprizals, because most men would be asleep belowdecks. Further, on this night, given that they had anchored off an all but uninhabited island absent any discernible threats, it was reasonable to assume they would have the fewest possible men on watch. The buccaneers kept the noise to an absolute minimum as they approached the barque, paddling "as softly as if they had been seeking manatee," as Dampier described it. They aimed to board the barque amidships — typically a vessel's lowest and thus most accessible point from the water — and on her leeward (downwind) side, which blocked the wind and waves, affording the men the steadiest possible purchase when they sank their boat hooks and grapnels into the hull and scaled it.

In the best-case scenario, they would take the sailors standing watch by complete surprise. Even so, they would still need to contend with the sailors belowdecks, who might use their familiarity with the ship to gain the upper hand over the attackers. To keep the majority of the crewmen out of the fight, the buccaneers would secure the doors, ports, and hatches as soon as possible, trapping the defenders belowdecks. Next they would try to neutralize the captain — doing so affected a crew the way decapitation does a body, especially on a merchant vessel such as this one.

Neither Ringrose nor the other members of the sortie provided details of the weapons they carried, but typically for a surprizal at anchor, pirates packed light in favor of maneuverability, each man with a pistol or two in lieu of a musket. Boarding axes came in especially handy — a quick, quiet solution to the problem of a sailor standing watch. Once aboard, cutlasses became their primary weapon. Fists also came into play in close combat. As did elbows, knees, skulls — for headbutting — and however many teeth a man had. With life in the balance, any tactic was justified. A sharp kick to the enemy's groin was wise, backstabbing nothing but pragmatic. To keep from inadvertently being stabbed or shot by one another, meanwhile, pirates wore distinctive bands or scarves around their arms.

As soon as they reached the barque, Ringrose and his companions began climbing aboard. The crewmen on watch were indeed surprised but still managed to gather themselves up and fire at the attackers. The bullets struck only water, however, and within seconds, the overwhelmed crew surrendered. The ensuing interrogations brought more evidence that the buccaneers were on a lucky streak: in addition to its crew, the barque was usually packed with Spanish soldiers, but as it happened, the soldiers had all disembarked earlier that week "to fight and curb certain Indians and negroes, who had done much hurt in the country thereabouts." Panama, the buccaneers excitedly concluded, had absolutely no idea they were coming.

The newly acquired barque allowed 137 of the 314 buccaneers to sail rather than row the remaining thirty leagues to Panama. Priority was given to those who had the slower of the thirty-five canoes, reported Ringrose, who, for a change, was not in that category. Of his third canoe in three days, he wrote, "It was something lesser than the former, yet was furnished with better company." Although his journal never mentions Wafer and Dampier by name, their own accounts relate their burgeoning friendship with Ringrose — Baz, they called him — and on that day, April 21, it is likely they were among the passengers in his canoe who spotted another Spanish barque and "instantly gave her chase."

It is easy to imagine Dampier during the pursuit, redoubling his strokes without interrupting his discourse on Plantan Key's plantains. In his memoir, *A New Voyage Round the World,* he would devote just twenty-nine words to the buccaneers' march across the Darien and the raid of Santa Maria: "In about nine days march we arrived at Santa Maria, and took it, and after a stay there of about three days, we went on to the South-Sea Coast." To the plantain, however, he devoted well over a thousand words, including this description:

> The shell, rind or cod, is soft, and of a yellow colour when ripe. It resembles in shape a hogs-gut pudding. The inclosed fruit is no harder than butter in winter, and is much of the colour of the purest yellow butter. It is of a delicate taste, and melts in one's mouth like [marmalade].

To be fair, Dampier, whose account was published after Ringrose's, felt Baz's chronicle of the Santa Maria raid made his own redundant. Also, understandably, he avoided self-incriminating details. Still, piracy was becoming the day job that facilitated his true avocation, naturalism.

Ringrose and Wafer would have been more focused on the demands of capturing a barque on the open sea, an operation fraught with all the risks of a surprizal at anchor and compounded by both an enemy cognizant of the threat and, of course, the sea itself. Unless the enemy surrendered, the buccaneers needed to clear her decks of defenders, requiring them to fire muskets with extreme precision at a moving target from their flimsy, wave-tossed canoe, all the while under fire themselves. Before they could even get close enough to take aim, though, the canoe captained by Peter Harris swooped in, pulling up alongside the barque and engaging her twenty-man crew in what Ringrose characterized as "a sharp dispute." Fifteen minutes later, Harris and his men were aboard the ship and in control.

* * *

Ringrose and his friends would get another chance at a Spanish barque the very next day, April 22, when they were but ten leagues from Panama. Once again, another canoe — Coxon's this time — beat them to her. Having capitalized on a light wind to overtake her and pull alongside, Coxon and his men launched a resounding volley of musket fire from their canoe. It made hardly a dent among the men on deck. This was no feeble merchantman or ferry they had picked a fight with but a hardened "man-of-war's tender," a vessel used to carry intelligence and orders between warships as well as to refill their supplies of gunpowder and provisions. Probably the enemy crew had muskets and *pedreros* — rail-mounted swivel guns between four and seven feet long designed to repel boarders. *Pedreros* issued blasts of grapeshot, pellets, or langrage, a mix of bolts, nails, metal scrap, and whatever other sharp objects happened to be handy. When a boarder took a volley of langrage and survived the initial wounds, the resulting infections almost always caught up with him. The English translation for *pedrero* at the time was *murderer.*

The first volley from the tender wounded five of Coxon's men, one fatally; Ringrose identified him as Mr. Bull — probably one and the same as Bullman, the old buccaneer whose tattoo Wafer had tried in vain to remove. Before Coxon's men could get off a second volley or Ringrose's crew could add fire to the fight, the wind freshened and the ship flew off, which was perhaps fortunate, inasmuch as she could easily have turned both canoes into splinters. She headed toward Panama, though, imperiling the entire company.

That night at their rendezvous point — the tiny, uninhabited Isla Chepillo, near the mouth of the Río Chepo, six leagues from Panama — the buccaneers grieved the loss both of Mr. Bull and their element of surprise. If, for whatever reason, the man-of-war's tender had not raised the alarm in Panama, surely Santa Maria's governor had — Sawkins and his team had arrived at Chepillo with the news that they had once again failed to catch the governor's canoe. As the buccaneers tried to figure out their next move, only Dampier seemed to have escaped the prevailing black mood. "Chepelio is the pleasantest island in the Bay of Panama," he wrote before detailing the landscape, soil, and vegetation that included "extraordinary sweet" plantains.

Invading Panama, which maintained a garrison of 1,500 troops, would be a fool's errand now that the city was apprised of the buccaneers' imminent arrival. Even Sawkins, for whom no plan was too crazy, agreed with that. The buccaneers wondered, though: What if they left Chepillo immediately, allowing them to reach Panama by first light? Might they still surprise the warships defending the city? If they could take the warships, the thinking went, they could blockade the harbor and lay siege to Panama. The Spaniards certainly wouldn't expect them to take on Spanish men-of-war with only a couple of barques and a handful of canoes. That was crazy—which Sawkins liked. Consequently, a majority of the buccaneers sparked to the idea.

There were two problems with it, though. The first was manpower. The company was now down by 137 men, because Captain Sharp had sailed away with them on the barque from Plantan Key in search of water. What if they didn't return in time for the battle? Sawkins liked the company's chances even without the 137 men, and his sentiments prevailed. With that settled, the buccaneers were left with the issue of prisoners, because that very day they had taken captive fourteen Spaniards who'd had the misfortune of landing their periagua at Chepillo. If the Englishmen left those prisoners to their own devices, they might go and forewarn Panama of the buccaneers' revised plan, altogether compromising it.

Ringrose could think of several more appealing solutions than the gladiatorial display the company settled on. The Kuna were asked to fight the prisoners — "or rather to murder and slay [them]," as Ringrose put it, "in view of the whole fleet." The Kuna happily complied, but although the prisoners had no weapons with which to defend themselves, all but one of them managed to escape into the woods. The Kuna killed the straggler and then went on the hunt. While remaining on the island to await Sharp, they would track down and kill several if not all of the fugitives.

The exigency of reaching Panama, however, forced the buccaneers to miss the spectacle. To his journal, Ringrose added only, "We rowed all night long, though many showers of rain ceased not to fall."

11

The Dragon

NATURE, IT SEEMED, was trying to deter the buccaneers from their mad undertaking, hitting them head-on with a north-westerly wind that transformed the driving rain into a fusillade. They rowed through it all night long, hopeful that the conditions would both forestall the arrival of the man-of-war's tender and force the governor of Santa Maria to put ashore. In the morning, as though Mother Nature had been moved by their resolve, the skies suddenly cleared and the darkness lifted, revealing a collection of resplendent white stone buildings, pert brick houses with red tile roofs, and churches in various states of construction, all laid out in a grid with balconies overhanging the narrow streets to protect pedestrians from rain. Dampier called the city "one of the finest objects that I did ever see, in America especially."

Known locally as New Panama, the settlement was situated on a small peninsula five miles west of Old Panama, where the former incarnations of these resplendent churches, municipal buildings, and thousands of homes had once existed. As a result of the fire set during Henry Morgan's 1671 raid, all that remained of Old Panama was the famous Cathedral of St. Anastasius and, as Wafer described it, "rubbish, and a few houses of poor people."

New Panama, with a population of eight thousand, appeared to Ringrose to be better built than its predecessor, and larger, spanning a mile and a half of coastline. But as he scanned the city now — along with Sawkins and thirty-four other buccaneers whose five canoes had reached Panama Bay ahead of the rest of the flotilla — Ringrose was more interested in the Spaniards' preparations for the pending attack.

Of primary concern were the city's imposing fortifications. Rumor had it that they had been so expensive that auditors in Spain wrote to inquire whether the wall surrounding the city was made of silver and gold. In fact the wall was stone, twenty to forty feet tall and ten feet thick, fronted by a deep moat on land and by a mass of coral reefs seaward, and crowned by watch-towers every two or three hundred feet with "a great many guns." All the guns were pointed landward, at the gentle savannah, where herds of cows and oxen now grazed. Morgan's force had come by land, as, the Spaniards presumed, would any attacker. But just in case attackers did come by sea, Panama had the Barcos de la Armadilla, a trio of stout and hardened hundred-ton barques, each more than three times the size of either of the buccaneers' barques.

Ringrose spotted the three Spanish barques among a half dozen merchant ships moored at Perico, one of a cluster of three small islands two leagues south of Panama that served as the city's commercial port as well as the locus of the Spaniards' treasure storehouses. As Ringrose was inspecting the islands, the Barcos de la Armadilla weighed anchor and, in a flash, were under sail with the wind behind them, heading straight at the canoes and leading to his stomach-knotting conclusion that, "according to the intelligence they had received of our coming," they had decided to fight.

Retreat was the buccaneers' lone avenue of escape, but the armadilla, sailing before the wind, could quickly run them down. They looked over their shoulders in hope of assistance. Both of the fleet's periaguas (the first, from Santa Maria, and the second, captured at Chepillo) were too far behind to mount any sort of rescue. The thirty-ton barque acquired at Plantan Key, with Sharp and 137 men aboard, had yet to return from her mission to find drinking water. Meanwhile, the other barque, which had been seized by Harris en route to Isla Chepillo, was nowhere to be seen. Before the advance on Panama had been moved up, Harris had instructed thirty of his men to take the vessel and procure provisions, and because those men decided to do some extracurricular pirating along the way, they would not arrive in Panama Bay for several days. The company's ninety-two other buccaneers, in canoes, were currently at various points between Chepillo and Panama, their progress having been slowed by the northwesterly wind and rains. Thus Ringrose, Sawkins, and their thirty-four companions realized they would have to fend for themselves against three Spanish warships, which were now hoisting blood-red flags, signifying that no quarter would be given.

In this impending calamity, one of the buccaneers — Sawkins, perhaps — saw opportunity. All anyone recorded was the idea itself: row the canoes straight at the oncoming armadilla, as though to joust. On approach, there would be no risk of taking cannon fire because the great guns were stationed only on the sides of each ship, not on the bows or sterns, according to the naval convention of the era, which was to engage the enemy by sailing alongside and issuing a broadside, a simultaneous discharge of all the artillery on one side of a vessel. At the last possible moment before impact, the buccaneer canoes would swerve out of the barques' way and then continue ahead, parallel to the ships, as close as possible to their hulls. Were the Spaniards to fire their cannons from their relatively towering decks, the balls would fly harmlessly over the buccaneers' heads. In seconds, the canoes would be behind the barques. At that point, if any of the Spaniards tried to turn around and come after the buccaneers, the oncoming wind would deprive the barques of steerage and leave them "in irons" — dead in the water. To continue pursuing the buccaneers, therefore, the Spaniards would need to repeatedly tack, or proceed into the wind in a zigzag pattern. To this day, the same maneuver challenges even state-of-the-art racing yachts. In the seventeenth century, for even the nimblest wooden square-rigged ships, it was a nonstarter. Therefore, Sawkins and company assumed, the Spaniards would not tack, meaning that the barques' cannon-free sterns and helmsmen would be exposed, likely relegating their defenses to assorted outmoded firearms and the odd swivel gun. Given the buccaneers' superior marksmanship, they would at least stand a chance of clearing a deck and boarding.

This stratagem, founded on transforming a seeming advantage — powerful cannons — into a liability, would warm the heart of any iconoclast and, one would imagine, draw *huzzas* from every buccaneer in the five canoes. But some of the buccaneers had problems with the plan, not least of which was that with a mere tap at the whipstaff — the bar that, prior to the advent of the steering wheel, controlled the ship's tiller — a Spaniard could alter a barque's course enough for her to flatten any canoe trying to swerve past. The other issue was that even if the buccaneers gained the vaunted "weather gage" position, windward of the enemy, to capitalize they would need still to be close enough to fire at the enemy, meaning that the enemy would also be close enough to fire at them — from a higher, more stable platform. And although in normal circumstances the buccaneers believed themselves to be the better shots, in their current state they were, as Ringrose put it, "in very unfit condition to fight, being tired with so much rowing, and so few in number" against as many as 250 rested and ready Spaniards aboard the three ships.

Ultimately the calendar played a decisive role in the deliberation. It was April 23, or, as Ringrose noted at the beginning of his journal entry, the "day being dedicated to St. George, our Patron of England." Every English buccaneer — and every Englishman — identified with George, the chivalrous, dragon-slaying knight-errant. St. George's Cross was a fixture on both the flag of the Kingdom of Great Britain and the banners under which English soldiers went into battle. Although buccaneers opted to live outside of English law, they remained English patriots, and on April 23, 1680, in Panama Bay, Spain was their dragon.

Wrote Cox, "We made a resolution rather than drown in the sea, or beg quarter of the Spaniard, whom we used to conquer, to run the extreamest hazard of fire and sword." For banners they had only Sawkins's flag — red with yellow stripes — and probably it was still folded up or stuffed into his satchel. But effectively, as the buccaneers dug their oars into the waves and launched themselves toward the armadilla, they flew standards emblazoned with St. George's Cross, all aglow in the early morning light and snapping in the steady northwesterly wind.

12

The Extreamest Hazard of Fire
and Sword

A s THE SUN rises in April, the temperature in modern-day
Panama City typically warms from seventy-five to seventy-
nine degrees, and Panama Bay transforms from indigo to a classic ocean blue. During that span of time on April 23, 1680, three
dozen buccaneers rowed the hollowed-out trunks of five cedar
trees into the maw of more than two hundred soldiers in three
warships, each built from a thousand full-grown oaks. As Ringrose
soon realized, the buccaneers had underestimated the Spanish
vessels' sheer velocity. The barque leading the charge was already
all but upon his and Sawkins's canoes, leaving them no time to get
out of the way. Depending on the whim of the ship's commander,
one canoe or the other would momentarily be crushed.

But that commander, Don Diego de Carabaxal, steered
directly between the two canoes, placing Ringrose's canoe to his
left side and Sawkins's to his right — precisely where the Spanish captain wanted them. Waiting for the buccaneers on either
side of the barque's deck, weapons at the ready, was his crew of
sixty-five soldiers. As the canoes passed below the soldiers, the

buccaneers raised their own muskets and fired a volley of small shot — multiple pellets per shot, as in a buckshot cartridge. Birding, they called it. The soldiers, meanwhile, unleashed broadsides.

Ringrose, the only one of the expedition's seven chroniclers in the fight, did not itemize the Spaniards' weapons. Probably they had muskets, pistols, and swivel guns. Given cannons' limited range of motion and the height differential between the barques and the canoes, their tactical value was primarily psychological, though the sum total of the broadside did plunge the buccaneers into an earsplitting thunderhead, leaving them dazed, their ears ringing with warbling, high-pitched whines that could continue in their heads for hours and, sometimes, days. Some of the buccaneers were struck by musket balls, pellets, and knifelike splinters emanating at high speed from their own canoes. (In naval battles at that time, combatants were more likely to be injured or killed by shrapnel than by the projectiles themselves.)

As the two canoes emerged from the maelstrom and reunited by the stern of Carabaxal's barque, Ringrose saw that only one of his boatmates had been wounded. The Spaniards on the other side of the barque had proved better shots, however, hitting four of Sawkins's men and turning his canoe into a sieve. But both buccaneer canoes were windward of Carabaxal; they had succeeded in attaining the weather gage position. It would be exceedingly difficult now for the Spaniards to turn around and come after them. In addition, the buccaneers' birding had been incredibly effective. Through the dissipating gun smoke, Ringrose saw several of Carabaxal's men lying dead on their deck. And the resulting deficit in manpower was slowing the Spaniards' adjustments of their sails as they tried to turn the ship around, rendering them easy targets.

The buccaneers quickly reloaded, but before any of them could pull a trigger, the armadilla's flagship — and most formidable fighter — was upon them. Commanded by Spain's high admiral of the Pacific, Don Jacinto de Barahona, her crew consisted of eighty-six Biscayers — Basques from the western Pyrenees region of Spain, along the coast of the Bay of Biscay — who, according to Ringrose, had "the repute of being the best mariners, and also the best soldiers amongst the Spaniards." Massed along the flagship's starboard rail, the Biscayers let loose a broadside more than twice as powerful as the barrage delivered by Carabaxal's crew, and, again for the buccaneers, the world ceased to exist beyond a deafening, gun-smoke-gray abyss.

Ringrose fired back in the general direction of the barque, then dropped as far beneath the gunwale as he could to reload his four-and-a-half-foot musket. As he felt around his cartouche box for a fresh cartridge and then bit it open, the thwacks and thunks of musket balls against the flimsy cedar hull must have unnerved him, yet each served as a reminder that the canoe had been hit, not him. Once he'd managed to seat his own musket ball, he snapped his hammer back to full cock, and, raising the musket to a shoulder, he peered over the canoe's gunwale, took aim, and squeezed the trigger. As the flint slammed into the frizzen, it created a spark that transformed the powder into flame, generating a cloud of hot gas that swelled until it propelled the ball out the far end of the barrel through the murk and, ideally, into a Spanish head or upper torso. Soon the smoke began to thin, revealing to Ringrose that, amazingly, no one in either his canoe or Sawkins's had been hit by the Spanish volley. Sawkins's canoe, though, was sinking.

The flagship, meanwhile, was attempting to turn counterclockwise, into the wind, apparently to face the buccaneers again. But she was taking the wind from the wrong side. Her sails inverted until they pressed against the masts, abruptly stopping her. It was puzzling: How could her helmsman allow this to happen? The answer, Ringrose realized, was that the helmsman was dead, the result of a shot that stood to be the stuff of gunslinging lore, given the angle, distance, and the ship's fortifications.

Other Biscayers scrambled to the quarterdeck (the raised platform behind the mainmast) to take the slain helmsman's place. One after another, they were cut down by the buccaneers, whose canoes were now perfectly positioned beneath the stern. At the same time, in a phenomenal display of marksmanship, the buccaneers blasted apart the flagship's mainsheet and brace, the ropes used to control the mainsail. Now even if one of Barahona's men succeeded in regaining the whipstaff, it would make no difference.

Fortunately for Barahona, the third of the armadilla's three barques was speeding to his rescue. She was under the command of Don Francisco de Peralta, "an old and stout Spaniard, a native of Andalusia," per Ringrose, with a reputation for bravery and resourcefulness dating back to 1671, when it was he who sailed out of Panama under the noses of Morgan's raiders with the bulk of the city's gold and jewels. Against this new group of would-be invaders, Peralta commanded seventy-seven men, all of whom, according to Ringrose, were Black.

By this time, the smaller of the two buccaneer periaguas had reached Sawkins's swamped canoe in time to rescue him and his men. Once aboard the periagua, Sawkins took command and, rather than fall back, advanced to meet Peralta's barque, pulling parallel to her starboard side and staying as close as he could. From Ringrose's vantage point, "The dispute, or fight, was very hot, [the crews] lying board on board together, and both giving and receiving death unto each other as fast as they could."

Trading deaths was not a viable long-term strategy for Sawkins and his team, who had about sixty fewer combatants than Peralta's barque did, but they had at least created a diversion, allowing Ringrose and the others to complete their capture of the flagship. Parked behind Barahona's stern and firing at will, they decimated the flagship's rigging as well as her elite Biscayer crew.

In response, Barahona rushed onto his quarterdeck and waved a handkerchief. But not to surrender, as the buccaneers might have hoped. Instead he was instructing Carabaxal, in the first barque, to tack about and rejoin the fight. While the maneuver was exceedingly difficult, it was not impossible, and now, with even a minimal advance upwind, Carabaxal could regain the weather gage position from the buccaneers as well as place their four canoes between his barque and Admiral Barahona's, exposing the invaders to the full firepower of the two ships and their 150 men.

Ringrose anticipated the maneuver and sought a way to thwart it. The only question was how. He huddled with his cohorts. If they stood off and intercepted Carabaxal, Barahona could escape with the flagship. If, on the other hand, two of the canoes stayed in place to keep Barahona in check, the other teams might be able to take on Carabaxal. But to what end? Best case, the two teams would duck a Carabaxal broadside, get off a volley of their own, and take out a few Spaniards, only to watch helplessly as Carabaxal breezed past them and obliterated the first two canoes. It would be better, they decided, to divert Carabaxal.

Although lacking a clear idea of how exactly they would do it, the buccaneers nevertheless chose two canoes, one of which was Ringrose's, to try to divert the tacking ship. As they rowed to meet Carabaxal, one thought likely lingered in their minds: it was high time for Bartholomew Sharp and his 137 men to show up.

And just where was Sharp? The previous morning, April 22, one of the prisoners on Isla Chepillo, perhaps in an effort to curry favor, had told the captain about a newly launched brigantine sitting in the nearby Pearl Islands, ripe for the plucking. A brigantine was typically a two-masted merchant ship with a square-rigged fore-mast and a fore-and-aft-rigged mainmast. This one, the prisoner suggested, would be perfect for use against the Barcos de la Arma-dilla in Panama Bay.

Sharp was intrigued. Probably he was even more intrigued by the Pearl Islands, well known for their copious oyster beds since the early days of the conquistadors. In 1513, after ousting the islands' twenty Indigenous chiefs in brutal fashion, even by conquistador standards — they set their dogs to tearing apart and eating the local leaders — the Spaniards took over and established pearl fisheries, forcing the remaining Natives to dive to the ocean bottom and fill baskets with oysters. In 1680, the oyster beds remained bounteous.

The same morning Sharp learned about the brigantine, he also heard some of the buccaneers "complain grievously for want of water." It was just the pretext he needed — although in his jour-nal, he would claim that he was "forced" to go in search of water. Taking 137 men, he sailed the ten leagues in the barque the com-pany had seized at Plantan Key, arriving before noon. Quickly the crew spotted the brigantine — presumably anchored at the largest of the 250 islands, the ninety-square-mile Isla del Rey. "Happily finding [the prisoner's] words to be true," Sharp wrote, "I presently, with seven men along with me, went on shoar and took the vessel."

As his crew set about fitting out their new brigantine, Sharp wandered to a nearby house in the hope of obtaining provisions. No one was home, or so it seemed until he caught a glimpse of a woman and two children in the adjacent woods. They were hid-ing, cowering in fear of the pirates. The woman happened to be "very young and handsome," prompting Sharp to suspend his quest for provisions. Instead he took her into the house, found "a case or two of wines," of which he drank a bottle or two. Soon he was "presenting [his] services to the woman" — evidently his deadpan rendition of such seventeenth-century euphemisms as "dancing the cushion dance," "making the beast with two backs," and "joining giblets." Of course, while those other phrases imply mutual consent, in refusing Sharp's "services," the woman would have been placing her own life and those of her children at risk. And without his protection, she would have faced the prospect of his entire crew "presenting their services" as well.

Afterward, Sharp said, "she returned me thanks, in her lingua, which I understood very well," and, as the afternoon progressed, "I was yet a more pleasing guest to her, when she understood what country-man I was." The captain decided to stay on the island for supper. Unbeknownst to Ringrose, Sawkins, Wafer, and the other buccaneers under fire in Panama Bay, Sharp and his 137 men would not come to their aid until well after the conclusion of the battle.

Two of the canoe teams, including Ringrose's, rowed as though they meant to strike Carabaxal's barque head-on. But by now Carabaxal was wise to that game. The mystery for the buccaneers was how he would counter. If he had his men fire their small arms forward, their shots would be obstructed by their bowsprit (the large pole projecting from the bow that provides the anchor point for the foremast stays) and its forest of canvas, ropes, lifts, blocks, braces, and deadeyes. Not all their shots, though. If just a fifth of them reached the canoes, the fight would be even, at least numerically, because Carabaxal's men outnumbered the buccaneers in the two canoes five to one. And probably many more than one in five shots would reach the canoes. In addition, the Spaniards' elevated forecastle — the raised deck on the bow — gave them a significant height advantage. In sum, attacking Carabaxal was a terrible idea. It was the buccaneers' only recourse, though — if they failed and Carabaxal reached Barahona's barque and repelled the other canoes, none of the buccaneers would leave Panama Bay alive.

They fired a volley as soon as they were within range of the barque, and the Spaniards returned in kind, letting fly a swarm of projectiles. The exchange left several Spaniards dead, while, remarkably, the buccaneers sustained no casualties. In spite of the Englishmen's stunning marksmanship, Carabaxal ordered his men to fire again, evidently content to fight a battle of attrition as he continued toward Barahona's ship. But before firing their second volley, his men had to reload. While they did, the buccaneers reloaded and fired as many as three times. Carabaxal's men fell dead to the deck all around him. Still he stayed the course. After a few more such exchanges, however, he had no choice but to retreat — and even that was problematic. "We killed so many of them," Ringrose explained, "that the vessel had scarce men enough left alive, or unwounded, to carry her off."

The buccaneers may have been too successful for their own good, though. By knocking Carabaxal out of the fight, rather than merely diverting him, they sent him toward the city, where as many as 1,500 garrisoned soldiers stood ready to serve as reinforcements. Revising their objective to the seizure of Carabaxal's barque, Ringrose and company set after him. But the wind picked up, carried the Spaniards off, and, as Ringrose put it, "saved their lives."

The two canoes hurried back to the flagship, where the fight continued to rage between the Spaniards and the buccaneers in the other two canoes and the periagua that had rescued Sawkins and his men. Presumably. A fog of gun smoke made it impossible for Ringrose and company to see who exactly was fighting. The men in Ringrose's canoe "gave a loud halloo" through the smoke. In response they received distant shouts from Captain Harris and Golden-Cap and a dozen others who had joined the fray — in the larger of the two periaguas — and, at that moment, were attempting to board Barahona's barque. Reckoning that the Spaniards would be preoccupied by repelling the boarders, Ringrose and his companions rowed close to Barahona's stern, hoping to get within reach of the rudder. If they could wedge an oar or even a thick piece of flotsam between the sternpost and the rudder, they would prevent the rudder from moving, effectively paralyzing the vessel.

Wise to their ploy, Barahona and his chief pilot fired down at them. Ringrose and company returned fire, killing both men. The problem was the seemingly endless reserves of elite Biscayers ready to take their places. But as Ringrose related, at last the Biscayers "were almost quite disabled and disheartened likewise, seeing what a bloody massacre we had made among them with our shot. Hereupon, two-thirds of their men being killed, and many others wounded, they cried for quarter."

The timing of the surrender was fortuitous for Captain Harris, who had been shot through both legs while attempting to scale the side of the flagship. He was helped aboard by Coxon, who a week earlier had tried to shoot him, an irony that was lost on none of the buccaneers, now sixty-eight strong. They also noted that Coxon had been conspicuously absent from the fighting. He was still their commander, though — pirates never switched commanders midbattle — so they did not hesitate to follow his orders to go attack Peralta, whose barque stood between them and an escape from Panama Bay.

13

Blood Ran Down the Decks in Whole Streams

I T WAS CLEAR to the surgeons that one of Captain Harris's legs would not survive. Nor would he himself unless the leg was amputated straightaway, right there on the deck of the captured flagship. No record exists of Harris's response, but if he was like most patients prescribed amputation, he pleaded for an alternative treatment — until given the choice between life with one leg or death with two. His acquiescence would have been rewarded by a belt or two of whiskey, which also constituted the only anesthesia for the procedure.

As the whiskey took hold, the surgeon — Wafer, it is assumed — opened his instrument case, which was, pragmatically, dyed red. Beside the sailcloth-draped platform that would serve as the operating table, he laid out his instruments, including an "amputation knife" that resembled a curved dagger, along with a scissors-handled "crow's beak" clamp used to constrict blood flow and, for the same purpose, several metal cauteries that he would heat in his firepot. (The streaks of dried blood on these tools were not a poor reflection on his sanitary practices; surgeons never washed instruments at sea, lest the metal rust.) Last but not least of Wafer's implements was the wooden rod or stick given to Harris to bite down on during the operation; with any luck it would divert the captain's focus from the dismemberment taking place before his eyes, in turn curtailing screams that might interfere with the surgeon's focus. And if ever a surgeon needed focus, it was during a shipboard above-the-knee amputation, which was analogous to carving a large rib roast while it was still attached to a living cow.

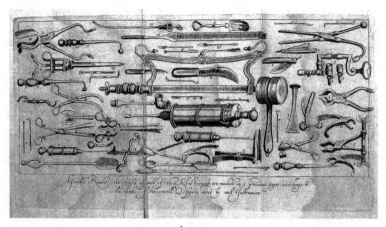

Surgeon's instruments

The operation was performed as quickly as possible to minimize the patient's agony. Five minutes would be on the long end; two or three was optimal. In such a scramble, Wafer would hardly have been the first surgeon to inadvertently slice off the fingers of either the flailing patient or the assistants attempting to restrain him. The young surgeon began by drawing a line around Harris's thigh, indicating where he would cut. Next he tied a tourniquet just above the line, the idea being to reduce both the flow of blood and — albeit not by much — the pain. Then came the moment of truth: he took up the amputation knife and sliced, as quickly as he could, through the skin and muscles, circling the femur. Once the tissue was removed, he used the crow's beak to clamp shut the freshly severed femoral artery, the main source of blood to the leg. This mitigated the significant bleeding from what remained of the limb. If the femoral artery were left agape, Harris would bleed to death in as few as four minutes. When time permitted, Wafer would stem additional blood flow with the now-glowing cauteries, or with styptics such as vitriol and turpentine. Eventually he would also ligate — sew shut — the vessels. For now, he attacked the femur with a specialized amputation saw that could be mistaken for an ordinary hacksaw. He tried to cut the femur slightly shorter than the remainder of the limb around it, allowing him to pull the surrounding muscle tissue and skin over the end of the bone, forming a stump. If Harris were lucky, at this point he had passed out either from the pain or from shock.

While Wafer stitched Harris's stump closed, Sawkins was being repulsed from Peralta's deck for a third time. "To give our enemies their due, no men in the world did ever act more bravely," Ringrose said of the defensive effort by Captain Peralta's crew. Pulling their canoes alongside Peralta's barque, Ringrose and his companions delivered a full volley of shot before dropping below the gunwales to reload and brace for the cumulative thunderclap of return fire — that sensation of the planet being knocked off its axis accompanied by a squadron of hot projectiles.

Those expectations were met, but not as the result of any action undertaken by the enemy. Instead, behind the barque's mainmast, a small earthenware jar of gunpowder — likely about the size of a quart of milk — exploded. Paradoxically, there was nothing more perilous to bring to a gunfight than gunpowder, particularly on a deck crowded with discharging guns and the resulting spray of sparks. Accidental explosions of gunpowder accounted for a quarter of all injuries and deaths during sea battles.

When the gunpowder on Captain Peralta's deck detonated, it compressed the air particles around it before discharging them as a supersonic blast that turned Peralta's men into bowling pins, knocking several overboard. In the same fraction of a second, the flash swelled into a massive orange-yellow fireball, engulfing the nearby men and roasting them. As quickly as the fire had materialized, it dissipated, leaving only a blackened deck — actually a good sign for the Spaniards. The real danger would have been for the explosion to ignite more powder or the powder room itself.

Peralta looked over his gunwales at the men who had just been thrown into the bay by the blast. Many were now either unconscious or unable to swim. Although seriously burned himself and at risk of taking fire from the buccaneers, the captain leaped in after his men and managed to return several safely to the ship. "But as one misfortune seldom comes alone," Ringrose wrote, "whilst [the captain] was recovering these men to reinforce his ship withal, and renew the fight, another jar of powder took fire forward, and blew up several others upon the forecastle." The barque and her surroundings were shrouded by black smoke heavy with the stench of burning flesh and permeated only by muzzle flashes. Regarding the smoke as cover to board, Sawkins led the way, and he and his men gave Peralta little choice but to surrender.

Now two of the three Barcos de la Armadilla — Peralta's and Barahona's — were under buccaneer control. As was Panama Bay, since the third barque — Carabaxal's — had fled. Carabaxal might yet return with reinforcements. But for the time being, the

Surrender

buccaneers enjoyed a respite. Their adrenaline-charged world could slow to its normal pace. It was noon. They had been fighting for a full five hours. Ringrose was euphoric: "These three captains against whom we fought, were esteemed by the Spaniards to be the valiantest in all the South Seas." Now the buccaneers owned that distinction. But it had come at a steep cost: eighteen of them had been killed during the course of the battle, and another twenty-two lay seriously injured.

For whatever it was worth, the Spaniards had it far worse. Of Peralta's ship, Ringrose wrote, "Such a miserable sight I never saw in my life, for not one man there was found, but was either killed, desperately wounded, or horribly burnt with powder, insomuch, that their black skins were turned white in several places, the powder having torn it from their flesh and bones."

It didn't take long for him to see an even more miserable sight, aboard the late Admiral Barahona's flagship. Of her original complement of eighty-six Biscayers, just twenty-five were still alive, and of those twenty-five, only eight remained able to bear arms, "all the rest being desperately wounded, and by their wounds totally disabled to make any resistance, or defend themselves. Their blood ran down the decks in whole streams, and scarce one place in the ship was found that was free from blood."

All the while, Ringrose kept an eye, in the distance, on the progress of the third barque, whose commander, Carabaxal, had flagged down two ships departing the port at Perico. Watching the three vessels rise and fall with the waves, Ringrose could imagine their three captains conversing and formulating a plan of attack. The buccaneers lacked the manpower to use the cannons on the captured ships, Carabaxal had no doubt observed; a loader, a rammer, a gunner, and at least two more men were required to maneuver and fire just one of the big guns. Accordingly, the Spaniards could simply glide downwind and, while keeping out of range of the buccaneers' small arms, destroy them with artillery. In reality, though, as Ringrose was about to learn, Carabaxal's discussion with the two other captains was going much differently: Carabaxal "gave them so little encouragement that they returned back, and dared not engage us." The new threat was altogether eliminated.

Sawkins asked Peralta's men — now the buccaneers' prisoners — about Spanish troop strength on Perico Island, the location of the treasure storehouses. Overhearing the question, Peralta warned Sawkins against moving on the port. He pointed to the largest ship at anchor there, a four-hundred-ton galleon named *La Santísima Trinidad* (Blessed Trinity), the very same galleon, as it happened, that he had used to evacuate Panama's riches in 1671, thwarting Morgan. Aboard the *Santísima Trinidad* alone, Peralta said, were 350 men.

With the canoes that had lagged on the way from Isla Chepillo — only now trickling into Panama Bay — the buccaneers had 136 able fighters. Given what Sawkins had seen of the Spaniards, he had to like the buccaneers' chances. Again, Peralta attempted to discourage the buccaneers. Even as he flattered them, referring to Englishmen as "the valiantest men in the whole world," he said the ships at Perico were too well provided for them to defeat. He advised Sawkins and company to flee Panama Bay while there was still a chance. They could still go and plunder the lightly defended Spanish settlements on the Pacific coast, he suggested; at least they would come away with their lives.

Peralta was immediately contradicted by one of his crewmen, who "lay a-dying upon the deck," as Ringrose put it. Either a victim of the fighting or the gunpowder explosions, the dying man told Sawkins that the ships in view were empty — every able sailor had been sent aboard the three barques of the armadilla. The Englishmen were not sure whether to believe the crewman or Peralta. There was some possibility that Peralta was telling the truth with an eye on his own interest rather than those of his countrymen. But a man at death's door — would he dare utter false last words, placing him at risk of being turned away by Saint Peter from the gates of heaven? A fundamental principle of testimony in English law at the time was *Nemo moriturus praesumitur mentire* — a dying person is not presumed to lie. All of a sudden, Peralta's silver-tongued spiel appeared as the first step in a long con.

Sawkins set the captured barque on a course for Perico Island.

14

Mutiny

I T WAS ODD. Waves patted the Perico Island pier. The usual creaks and groans rose from the moored ships. But there were none of the creaks and groans of deck boards beneath Spanish soldiers shifting their weight as they readied their weapons and tensed their knees to leap out in ambush. Similarly, the air did not carry the sour prefight scent of fear. Seabirds aside, the only sign of life in the port was the smoke billowing from the largest of the ships, *La Santísima Trinidad,* which was also sinking. Before evacuating the island, the Englishmen reasoned, the Spaniards had scuttled the big galleon to keep her out of buccaneer hands. "We quenched the fire with all speed, and stopped the leak," Ringrose wrote. Thus the buccaneers gained control of "the greatest sea port of all the South Sea" and clinched one of the most improbable victories in the history of naval warfare.

They gave no thought to their place in history, though. Their full focus was on the spoils: Perico's merchant ships and, of course, the storehouses. In them they found a sizable haul of wine, sugar, flour, sweetmeats, skins, soap, and iron bars. But no gold, no jewels, no silver, not so much as a stray piece of eight. Suddenly the day ranked instead as a colossal Pyrrhic victory.

Crestfallen, the buccaneers deliberated the matter of how they might extract gold and silver from the city instead. The first order of business was tending to their wounded. To do so effectively, they decided to take up quarters aboard the salvaged *Santísima Trinidad*. On Spanish ships, officers' cabins typically included mattresses, bed linens, and chamber pots — luxuries that were antithetical to the pirate esprit de corps that espoused hammocks in a communal berth. Moreover, cabins added to a ship's weight, hindering speed. But the buccaneers would not be sailing the *Santísima Trinidad,* and after three weeks of sleeping on the ground or in hollowed-out tree trunks followed by a draining battle, the indulgence could be seen as necessarily restorative. The ship also offered a convenient place to keep prisoners, including Peralta and Gabriel, who could be of immense value in the coming days, both as intelligence sources and trade chips.

While settling in, the buccaneers saw how, with some retrofitting for speed, the *Santísima Trinidad* might become the ultimate pirate ship, and they drooled over the prospect of using her to plunder more cities in the South Seas, after first ransoming Panama. Coxon, however, advocated taking their Perico haul and returning overland to Golden Island right away, before Panama could rally its considerable military force against them. But an examination of their prisoners was leading his men to a downward revision of their previous estimates of Spanish troop strength. Ringrose's ever-improving Spanish yielded the critical piece of intelligence that the three hundred elite king's soldiers were currently out of town. He also discovered that, true to the testimony of Peralta's dying crewman, upon receiving word of "pirates in these seas" the night before, all the city's remaining troops had been herded onto the three Barcos de la Armadilla. "Had we gone ashore, instead of fighting their ships," he concluded, "we had certainly rendered ourselves masters of the place."

Still, Coxon wanted to leave. It dawned on the men that their touchy admiral was, once again, motivated by saving face. Following the battle, he had been "much dissatisfied with some reflections which had been made upon him by our company," according to Ringrose, on top of which Sawkins would almost certainly be the company's choice for admiral if the expedition continued. "We ought justly to attribute to him the greatest honour we gained in our engagement before Panama," Ringrose wrote of Sawkins, mirroring the sentiments of most of the company.

The anti-Coxon ardor was further inflamed by news that two of the wounded, including Peter Harris, had expired. Of Harris's leg, Povey wrote, "itt fester'd so that itt pleased god he died." Again speaking for the company, Ringrose eulogized Harris as "a brave and stout souldier, and a valiant Englishman...whose death we very much lamented." Coxon, who had tried to murder Harris in the Darien jungle, was suddenly, according to Cox, "in disgrace amongst our men." Yet — especially among the surviving members of his original ninety-seven-man crew — Coxon still retained a good deal of support.

The resulting tension, in combination with fatigue and disappointment with the Perico haul, turned the *Santísima Trinidad* into a four-hundred-ton powder keg. And the local marine life didn't help. Ringrose described Panama Bay as "full of worms" — likely *Teredo furcifera* Martens, commonly known as deep-cleft shipworms: "We found worms of three quarters of an inch in length, both in our bedclothes and other apparel." That night, most of the men slept poorly, if at all, and in the morning they mutinied.

The story comes from seaman William Dick, the seventh of the expedition's seven chroniclers. All that is known of him before he fell in with Bartholomew Sharp is that he was born in England, in approximately 1644, and sometimes used the alias William Williams — or, possibly, he was born William Williams and Dick was the alias. Either way, in 1684, he wrote an account of his South Sea experiences that was published as part of the second English edition of *The History of the Bucaniers of America.* To avoid self-incrimination, he used the nom de plume W. D., and to shield his shipmates, he sidestepped or altogether omitted incriminating details, naming no names save those of the men who by then had already become famous for their roles in the expedition. The lone exception was John Coxon. On the topic of the admiral, Dick's account reads like a tell-all.

About the deliberation aboard the *Santísima Trinidad* following the Battle of Panama Bay, Dick wrote that the men were furious with Coxon and that they "reproached him for his ill-behavior in the engagement we had with the Armadilla of Panama; for in that dangerous action, to speak it in a word, he shewed himself more like a coward than one of our profession, that is to say a true bucanier." The company, Dick contended, ought to remain in the South Seas until they had loaded "our vessels with gold, or at least as much silver as they could carry." As will come as no surprise, Dick was also part of the faction that organized a mutiny against Coxon.

For buccaneers, a mutiny was not the classic maritime blade-held-to-the-captain's-throat affair but rather a parliamentary procedure — in essence, a vote of no confidence. On the *Santísima Trinidad*, they met in council, a vote was held, and as a result, Coxon was out: Sawkins was elevated to admiral and Sharp to vice admiral, as soon as he returned from the Pearl Islands.

The company also voted to facilitate Coxon's departure by allotting him one of the periaguas as well as a fifty-ton merchantman taken at Perico. It was addition by subtraction, they thought, until seventy members of his crew opted to depart along with him. That would leave the company with just 223 men, limiting potential actions against Panama as well as severely restricting future opportunities in the South Sea. Worse, another twenty of Coxon's original crewmen had wanted to return to Golden Island with him, but he turned them down; their battle injuries would make them too great an encumbrance on the march up the Darien. The exigencies of caring for those twenty men — on top of another twenty injured — would hobble the remaining bucca-neers, especially since the company's top surgeon had also elected to join Coxon, taking with him the bulk of the medication needed for treating the forty wounded.

Moreover, the Kuna had also decided to pack it in, though not without parting gifts for the buccaneers. Andreas granted them a "full commission" in their South Sea venture, Dick's appraisal of which was characteristically blunt: "Thus we disengaged from the pretended service we had proffered unto that Emperor — I call it pretended, forasmuch as anyone would easily guess that the real intent thereof was only to serve ourselves with gold and silver." Golden-Cap's gift was more practical. As Ringrose reported, "The King desired we would not be less vigorous in annoying their enemy and ours, the Spaniards, than if he were personally present with us." As an affirmation of his hope for the future of the Kuna-buccaneer alliance, he left both his son and nephew in the charge of Admiral Sawkins.

Still, the drastic reduction of their ranks raised the question of how the rest of the buccaneers should proceed — or indeed if they should proceed at all. Ringrose, Dampier, and Wafer shared an outlook reflected by the company as a whole. On the one hand, they'd had their share of adventure and had come away with a cut of the Santa Maria and Panama haul, which, despite its gold deficiency, was more than any of them could have earned in a year in their legitimate occupations. In the process, though, they had learned just how easily and arbitrarily pirating could cost them their lives. But at the same time, they had seen that the worst fears of the Spanish merchants expressed in the letters intercepted at Portobelo were spot-on: the Darien had indeed served as an open door to the South Seas for buccaneers. Now the South Seas presented them with a direct path to anything they might ever want for the rest of their lives.

Part II

The South Seas

15

The Muzzles of Our Guns

RICHARD SAWKINS'S ADMIRALCY commenced with an effort to ransom the port of Panama: until the Spaniards met his price, his men would prey on incoming merchant vessels, which might be even more lucrative than sacking the city. At the same time, Sawkins undertook measures to make the Spaniards willing to pay simply to be rid of the company. First he sailed the *Santísima Trinidad* the six miles from Perico Island to the city of Panama, anchoring her close enough to be within plain view of its inhabitants yet out of the range of their cannons. As Povey reported, "Thay fierd their gunns off from Pennamau to us butt did us no damage."

Next Sawkins urged his men to go and celebrate their capture of the port. They complied with bacchanalian enthusiasm. In one case, on the small island of Taboga, six leagues south of Panama, they accidentally started a house fire that spread to twelve houses before they could extinguish it. Wafer earned his surgeon's salary — between 200 and 250 pieces of eight — as a result of such carousing, not by salving burns or stitching lacerations but by contending with the outbreaks of sexually transmitted diseases that invariably followed.

To treat syphilis, then known as the Spanish disease (or, to the Spaniards, as the French pox), he had to use a urethral syringe to inject each patient with mercury, often more than once. Sometimes the treatments continued for months, hence the old refrain "Two minutes of Venus, two years with Mercury." Because mercury induced urination and salivation, seventeenth-century medical wisdom went, it expelled the invisible properties responsible for syphilis. In fact, the only way the treatment could bring the condition to an end was by killing patients via mercury poisoning.

The partying on Taboga benefited the company overall, however, by drawing Spanish merchants from Panama. The merchants came by stealth on account of their governor's strict prohibition of all commerce with the invaders. Their objective was not to sell their own wares but instead to purchase the goods the buccaneers had plundered from Perico Island. Taboga's secluded beachside village — inadvertently reduced from a hundred houses to eighty-eight — thus became an animated commodities exchange, with polished Spanish capitalists haggling over prices with sellers who were their sartorial opposites. The Panamanian merchants drove hard bargains — just not too hard, in deference to the murderous tendencies of the sellers. Any awkwardness for the merchants attendant to buying their own goods back from the men who had stolen them was outweighed by the opportunity to replenish their inventories at bargain prices.

The Spaniards were also in the market for slaves, paying two hundred pieces of eight for each Black prisoner with whom the buccaneers were willing to part. Neither Ringrose nor the other chroniclers touched on the ethics of the practice, probably because enslaved people were commonly regarded as plunder. Typically pirates either sold such prisoners or kept them as servants. On occasion, however, they liberated them or welcomed them into a crew as full and equal partners. Trafficking slaves, however, was not what these buccaneers had had in mind for their blockade of Panama, and after two weeks of it, they began to question the plan, which to that point had netted them just two merchant ships of any consequence, each laden with nothing but fowl and poultry.

On the night of May 10, eighteen days into the blockade, Sharp found himself in the unenviable position of sailing from Perico to Taboga to fetch some men who had been enjoying themselves too much, neglecting their shipboard duties. It was no easy task to wrangle pirates back aboard a ship when they still had money to spend. Sometimes a captain had to resort to a false claim of a ripe Spanish merchant ship in the vicinity. As it happened, on the way to Taboga, Sharp spotted just such a vessel. He gave chase, easily caught up, and hailed her. Gathering that she was the *San Pedro* on her way from Lima, he bid her captain to strike — to lower topsails or colors in acknowledgment of the other vessel's superiority.

When the captain complied, Sharp sailed alongside the *San Pedro,* and his men boarded her. He himself couldn't be bothered to join them, because the *San Pedro*'s sailors were armed only with rapiers, and he had no reason to think that the plunder would be anything other than more fowl. Yet his men found, as he recorded in his journal, "1400 jars of wine and brandy on board, besides several more of vinegar, a considerable quantity of powder, and some shot which came very luckily, for we had almost spent all our ammunition." The plunder included one other item of note. Sitting at his desk that night, writing about the brandy while likely enjoying a jar of it, Sharp added, almost as an afterthought: "I am not to forget that there were also in the vessel fifty thousand pieces of eight."

The money had been sent from Lima to pay the soldiers in the Panama garrison, according to Ringrose, who recorded the total as 51,000 pieces of eight. John Cox had it at 60,000 pieces of eight, adding that when the company divided it the next day, each man received 247 pieces of eight. Even if Sharp's low figure is correct, each buccaneer's share would have exceeded the two hundred pieces of eight Morgan's men netted for their entire 1671 expedition. In 1680, 247 pieces of eight equated to two and a half years' worth of wages as a farm laborer, or enough to start a farm of one's own and furnish it with a dozen cows.

But any of the buccaneers who contemplated cashing out were given pause by the intelligence they gathered from the *San Pedro*'s crew: a second ship was due from Lima in ten or twelve days, this one carrying twice as much money. Sawkins and company corroborated the intelligence two days later, when Sharp seized another ship, this one laden with flour that he sold to the Panamanian merchants. The more significant prize was her crew's affirmation that, yes, the ship with 100,000 pieces of eight had already sailed from Lima. She was due in Panama in eight to ten days.

While waiting for her, the buccaneers shifted their residence from the *Santísima Trinidad* to Taboga, providing themselves not only with an excellent view of vessels arriving in Panama but also with recreational opportunities unavailable at an anchorage in the middle of a bay. Sharp wrote of their new base of operations as "an exceedingly pleasant island abounding in all manner of fruits, including pine-apples, oranges, lemmons, albecatos, pears, mammes, saportas, cocao-nuts." The meanings of "mammes" and "saportas" are casualties of time or, perhaps, brandy, but if by "albecatos" Sharp meant avocados, he likely deserves the credit William Dampier would be awarded by the *Oxford English Dictionary* for introducing *avocado* to the English language.

A few days later, Spanish merchants landed at Taboga as usual, with goods the buccaneers had ordered. This time they also brought a message from the governor of Panama, asking what the Englishmen "came for in these parts." Invoking Andreas's commission, Sawkins composed a response, which he gave the merchants to take back to the governor: "We came to assist the King of Darien, who [is] the true Lord of Panama and all the country thereabouts," he said, adding that since the buccaneers had come so far, there was no reason they shouldn't have some satisfaction. Accordingly, he demanded that the governor "send us five hundred pieces of eight for each man, and one thousand for each commander, and not any farther to annoy the Indians, but suffer them to use their own power and liberty, as became the true and natural lords of the country." If the buccaneers were paid, Sawkins went on, they would "desist from all further hostilities, and go away peaceably." Otherwise they would remain in Panama and take whatever they could, meanwhile causing as much damage as possible.

While awaiting the governor's reply, Sawkins played another angle — the Catholic Church, whose influence in colonial affairs could not be overstated. As it happened, he knew the Bishop of Panama, Lucas Fernandez y Piedrahita. The two had met during the buccaneers' sack of Santa Marta in 1677, when Fernandez was the city's bishop and Sawkins held him for ransom. The difficult circumstances notwithstanding, they had developed a rapport, which Sawkins believed was strong enough to leverage now.

By way of greeting, he sent Fernandez a gift of two loaves of sugar. The bishop responded the next day with a gift of a gold ring for Sawkins along with a new message from the governor. It did not contain the acquiescence Sawkins had hoped for, however. Instead the governor called into question the validity of the buccaneers' commission. They were Englishmen, and their country and Spain were at peace, he said. To whom should he complain about the damage they had done to his city?

Sawkins replied that the entirety of his company had yet to land in Panama, but when they did, they would go to visit the governor and "bring our commissions on the muzzles of our guns, at which time he should read them as plain as the flame of gunpowder could make them." In time, the threat would become the lead item in Sawkins's legacy, but the truth was that he had no additional company, and now, with the return to Panama of the three hundred king's soldiers, should the buccaneers attempt to land in the city — or even sail within range of its guns — they would face obliteration. Moreover, if the governor had known just how many of the buccaneers had left Panama following the battle, he would likely have answered Sawkins's message on the muzzles of his own guns.

The governor received an accurate assessment of the buccaneers' troop strength shortly thereafter, however. It was given to him by one of their own — "a certain Frenchman," according to Ringrose, "who ran from us at the island of Taboga unto the Spaniards." Consequently, in his next message, the governor challenged Sawkins — according to Povey — to "meete him on shoare with a hundred men to try their manhoods" against a hundred Spaniards. Sawkins replied that he would gladly meet, but only if the governor brought 100,000 pieces of eight for the two sides to fight over. In fact, Sawkins would not have met under any circumstance, because it was far too likely that the governor would bring a thousand soldiers instead of a hundred. But the challenge itself amounted to good news. It told Sawkins that as long as he and his men remained on the island of Taboga, they were out of the governor's reach, at least until the Spaniards built new ships.

The company only needed to hold its position for another five to seven days, until the merchantman with 100,000 pieces of eight arrived from Lima.

But to Sawkins's dismay, his men were unwilling to wait that long, in part because they lacked confidence in the intelligence they had about the Lima ship. Even if the crew of the flour-laden ship Sharp had taken was correct about her departure, if she ran into contrary winds, an unfavorable current, or a storm, her arrival in Panama would be delayed for weeks. Also, as they would soon discover firsthand, sometimes vessels simply vanished. Sawkins's case for waiting was predicated on the weather: at that time of year, a ship bound from Lima to Panama benefited from ideal conditions. Indeed, the crews of the last two barques from Lima (both captured by the buccaneers) had reported smooth sailing. Ultimately, just as Sawkins's weather argument appeared to prevail, a bigger issue came to the fore: after weeks of subsisting on fowl, the men were hankering for red meat. As an incredulous Ringrose reported, "Our men were so importunate for fresh victuals, that no reason could rule them."

Sawkins was well aware that his crew would be far from the first to mutiny over provisions. "Among privateers," Dampier noted, "nothing emboldens them sooner to mutiny than want." So the new admiral presented his men with an alternative to waiting for the Lima ship: a raid of Pueblo Nuevo (also known as La Ciudad de Nuestra Señora de los Remedios), a town 250 miles up the coast, where they would have access to plenty of meat. Even better, Pueblo Nuevo was utterly swollen with money from its pearl fisheries. Sawkins proposed sailing there as soon as possible so as to outpace the messenger the Spaniards in Panama would send up the coast the moment the buccaneers sailed that way. As soon as the messenger delivered word of the raid to the citizens of the Spanish coastal settlements, they would begin hardening their defenses and, worse, evacuating their money. The company voted in favor of the plan, but with one stipulation, which Povey reported: "Our peopple, being headstronge, would have meate to eate first."

16

Swallowed by the Sea

O N MAY 15, 1680, the company set sail for Pueblo Nuevo with a planned stop at Otoque, an island near Panama known to be rich in victuals. The fleet consisted of the *Santísima Trinidad* — now renamed the *Trinity* — along with two small barques captured while the buccaneers were in Panama and, under the command of Edmond Cooke, a 180-ton merchantman that had been moored at Perico Island. The rest of the prize ships the buccaneers had burned, lest the governor of Panama have a means of pursuing them.

After six weeks of being penned in by land, the buccaneers could now breathe deeply of hot, salty air and exult in the feeling of bounding over whitecaps toward another adventure. For Sawkins, though, the thrill was blunted by the exigencies of stealth. To keep out of sight of anyone on land, he needed the fleet to stay just over the horizon, with only low sails set. If any of his vessels was spotted, either by a Spanish craft or a well-positioned coastal lookout, the buccaneers would be in a race to Pueblo Nuevo, one they would almost certainly lose. The issue was the doldrums, the often windless waters near the equator that were now constraining them to a speed of one knot (one nautical mile, or 1.15 standard miles, per hour). In spite of the jungle terrain, a messenger carrying word of the pirate threat from Panama to Pueblo Nuevo could travel over land more than twice as fast, which meant, in Sawkins's opinion, that the fleet simply could not afford a stop at Otoque for meat. But he would sooner be able to persuade his men to forgo oxygen.

No record exists of the duration of their time at Otoque. Ringrose was the lone chronicler to mention the visit at all, writing only, "Being arrived there, we lay by it while our boat went ashore and fetcht off fowls and hogs and other things necessary for sustenance." That the men "fetcht" — a euphemism in this case for "stole" — created yet another headache for Sawkins. The victims' report of the theft would reveal the fleet's whereabouts to the Spaniards, allowing the governor of Panama to surmise that the buccaneers were bound for Pueblo Nuevo. Although the stop at Otoque left the crew sated, Sawkins had to wonder whether they had just had the costliest pork dinner in history.

As it transpired, the stop at Otoque had no ill effect on the Pueblo Nuevo effort; word of the incident would not leave the island. The buccaneers would continue sailing undetected up the coast of Panama. The snag was the Frenchman who had betrayed them in the city of Panama. Unbeknownst to the company, when they dissolved the Taboga blockade and began sailing up the coast, the Frenchman had predicted that they would move on Pueblo Nuevo, and the Spaniards immediately sent word there.

The doldrums continued to hold the fleet to a speed of one knot, the same rate at which an iceberg floats. It was frustrating for the men, given the exigency of reaching Pueblo Nuevo, a frustration that was exacerbated by their confinement. Even the most spacious of their four vessels, the *Trinity,* was cramped, with some 150 men packed into less habitable space than is found in a four-bedroom house. A man could scarcely move during the day without brushing against another, and at night, when there was less topside activity, the crowding was even more pronounced: the men slept primarily belowdecks in hammocks fourteen inches wide, crammed side by side and above and below one another, stewing in unventilated air, heavy with snoring and the odors to be expected of seamen who often went months between baths. The stench was nearly strong enough to mask the odors of rotting wood and canvas, moldering urine, stale vomit, chickens and pigs and other live animals (serving as either pets or future meals), and the putrefying detritus sloshing around the bilge, within the base of the hull, where water naturally settled. Later in the expedition, some combination of air and gas in the bilge would be potent enough to blind Ringrose and several shipmates for the better part of a day.

Fortunately, the crew was divided in half by four-hour "watches," during which one group worked while the other slept. The ship's bell was struck every thirty minutes, the interval measured by a half-hour sandglass. Eight bells signaled the end of a four-hour watch — time for the men on the next watch to get out of their hammocks. If Baz Ringrose happened to sleep through the bells, he would be roused by the "mate" who shared the hammock and was now dying to drop into it. If Ringrose lingered between the sleeping quarters and the deck, he stood to be punished by John Hilliard, the ship's master, who, in addition to navigation, oversaw the watches.

Once Ringrose was on deck, a good wind could sweep away any of life's frustrations. The deck required no end of scrubbing and scraping, but that chore was a pleasure compared to others he might have been assigned, such as cleaning the pissdales — the basins that served as urinals. Still, even the best chores had their limitations. Tending to the sails, for example. On a tall ship such as the *Trinity*, the sails could be magnificent, especially when aglow in a propitious sunset and filled by favorable wind. But very quickly into a four-hour watch, they could become cumbersome masses of canvas — some as large as a high school basketball court and weighing hundreds of pounds — in constant need of maintenance and repositioning. All the while the scenery rarely changed, causing a man to be driven to distraction by something as picayune as the way a shipmate breathed.

Fortunately, there were antidotes for shipboard tensions and tedium. Music was to sailors' morale as wind was to the sails. The right jig or chantey could inspire Ringrose to leap out of his hammock and scrape a deck. Fiddlers, drummers, pipers, and trumpeters were prized at sea. For a sailor on a vessel captured by pirates, the ability to play even a penny whistle could mean the difference between life and death. The crew also had meals, of course, and alcohol, which provided a measure of escapism. But drinking also inflamed tempers that were already prone to run hot, especially when the men were in close quarters. This dynamic gave rise to the rule in some crews that anyone wanting to drink when it was dark had to do so on the open deck. As a result, sunset could transform the deck into something of a nightclub, where a buccaneer like Ringrose might find friends like Dampier and Wafer on the moonlit deck firing guns at waves or toasting to a successful raid of Pueblo Nuevo. Other men might be seen gathered around the binnacle (the illuminated compass housing) playing card games, and others still rattling dice, stomping their feet to accompany the fiddler, or belting out chanteys.

And all that revelry was ephemeral in comparison to the camaraderie. Indeed, as Ringrose was beginning to appreciate, it was more than camaraderie, which could be found in any old seafaring crew. Those who shed blood together and were willing to die for one another formed a much stronger bond. It was love — not that any hardened warriors would have called it that. Still, the sentiment was there among men who referred to themselves as brothers. And the sentiment was stronger among buccaneers than it was in any old band of warriors, because they only had one another — it was them against a world that declared them *hostis humani generis,* enemies of mankind. More than firepower or ammunition or their preternatural toughness, that love was what kept them alive. Together, they could face down any challenge.

Except storms. As Ringrose and company sailed past Punta Mala, about halfway to Pueblo Nuevo, they were troubled by the dark clouds ahead. "We met with very bad weather, much rain and hard gales, cloudy and dark," Sharp wrote. Aboard the 180-ton merchantman, men raced either to take down or to furl the sails, all but the few that were essential to controlling the ship. As they headed into the brewing storm, every instinct told them to turn and flee. But sailing in the opposite direction was often even more dangerous, placing a ship at risk of being hit from behind by enormous waves. Dropping onto her stern deck, a wave that was thirty-three by sixty-six feet — nothing extraordinary for a South Sea storm — could deliver nearly a million pounds of pressure, enough to crush her.

But the buccaneers were better off risking that than they were heading for shore, where, in the darkness, with the wind and waves in command of their ship, the hull would inevitably be torn apart by rocks, the sea bottom, or the shore itself. By sailing ahead at an angle to the waves, they avoided the repeated impact of the hull slamming into the troughs between the waves. In doing so, though, they put themselves at risk of a wave broadsiding them and rolling their ship onto her side until her topsails dipped into the water. From that point, it would be just a matter of time before she lay on the sea bottom. Pirate ships were particularly vulnerable to capsizing because of their combination of empty cargo holds and tall masts flying tons, literally, of canvas, which made them dangerously top-heavy. Pirate ships on the Spanish Main were more vulnerable than those anywhere else because of the region's unique susceptibility to low-pressure systems. As a result of air mass and temperature differences between the upper atmosphere and the surface of the earth, pressure systems created vertical columns of swirling winds that acted as giant vacuums. Sometimes, the temperature difference between the warm water and overriding cold air could create waterspouts — several-hundred-foot-tall columns of mist, as big as a hundred yards in diameter, rotating at fifty miles per hour — meteorological phenomena that could have the effect of a blender on a ship's mast and rigging. Dampier had heard of only one way a crew could try to counter a waterspout: "Fire shot out of their great guns into it, to give it air or vent, that so it may break." He'd never heard of the tactic working, however.

The wind and rain began their assault on the fleet just as night fell, reducing visibility and heightening the dangers of falling spars and other heavy chunks of loosened rigging that could crush a man's skull, waves that permanently swept men overboard, and gobs of gelatinous seafoam that had the same effect by greasing the already slippery decks. All the while the men needed to work the pumps furiously to bail the ever-increasing amount of excess water in the notoriously putrid bilge.

Despite these hazards, the *Trinity* emerged from the storm intact as the sun began to rise. Cooke's ship, too, had escaped damage other than to her mainsail, which the wind had "split all to pieces," as Sharp reported. That was far better than he could say for the two small barques, though. They were gone altogether, as if they had been swallowed by the sea. Ringrose's entire report on the missing vessels amounted to a sentence: "We lost two of our barks, the one whereof had fifteen men in her, and the other seven."

Sharp's record was similarly terse: "One of the barks after this night we saw no more." And the second barque? "Lost," he wrote. Neither Povey, Cox, Dampier, nor Wafer said a word about either barque. As for Dick, two days later, when the barques still remained unaccounted for, he wrote in summation of the voyage, "Nothing remarkable happened." While at sea, sailors believed it was bad luck to raise a number of topics, including drowning, church, pigs, and good luck. But lost ships was not among them. The chroniclers' indifference was instead a result of the fact that, as Dick said, nothing remarkable had happened. Ships disappeared as often as house keys, mostly because they became separated from one another, especially during storms. Accordingly, fleets prearranged rendezvous points — in this case, the buccaneers had agreed to meet near Pueblo Nuevo at Isla de Coiba, which at nearly two hundred square miles was Central America's largest island and therefore one of its easiest to find.

The next night was merely gusty, but still it scattered the fleet. As dawn distinguished sky from sea on May 21, Sharp, Cooke, and the rest of the merchantman crew saw only wave tops where the *Trinity* ought to have been. Scanning the Panama coast to the north and the horizon in the other directions, they saw not so much as a sail. Climbing the hundred-foot mainmast and standing on the crosstrees expanded a lookout's view to 350 square miles (roughly the size of Dallas, Texas), but again, no sign of the *Trinity*.

Might the Spaniards have had something to do with her dis-appearance — and those of the two barques? Possibly, though had there been any sort of battle within ten miles, Cooke's crew would have heard it — and probably seen the muzzle flashes. The buccaneers did not rule out a sea monster as a possibility. Sail-ors heard plenty of tales of cephalopodic krakens, colossal squids, and leviathans that were part whale and part sea dragon, and they took their existence for granted.

Reaching Isla de Coiba on May 22, however, Cooke's crew found the *Trinity* anchored off the island's northern shore. "We had the good luck to join them again the next day," said Sharp, the only chronicler to mention the incident at all. The fate of the two small barques, however, remained a mystery.

17

As Valiant and Courageous as
Any Could Be

A T Isla DE Coiba on May 22, the company—down to
two hundred men in the absence of the crews of the two
barques—formulated a plan for the attack of Pueblo Nuevo.
The town was sixty miles away, fifty across the Gulf of Panama
to the Gulf of Chiriquí and then ten up the Pueblo Nuevo River
(now called the Chiriquí Nuevo). Sawkins chose sixty men to go,
including Ringrose, Sharp, Cooke, Cox, and Povey.

They set out the next morning, May 23, aboard Cooke's ship,
and by late afternoon had entered the Gulf of Chiriquí, which
at that time of day could be a fairy-tale setting, the waning sun
turning the placid water gold and projecting rainbows onto the
rising mist. That afternoon, the surreal atmosphere was augmented by the sounds of violins and a pipe organ emanating
from an uninhabited island ahead—seemingly an instance of
the supernatural, in which the buccaneers firmly believed. As the
ship sailed closer to the island, however, Ringrose realized and
explained that the music was produced by air whistling through
the trees—on the map he drew of the area, he labeled the island

Silva, from the Spanish verb *silbar,* to whistle. Probably not all his shipmates were entirely comforted by the explanation, because whistling was also on sailors' list of prohibitions at sea; it provoked the wind, many of them thought, resulting in storms.

They also passed the unsettling Isla Muerto, or Dead Man Island, a two-and-a-half-mile-long strip of land with elevations at either end that gave it a haunting resemblance to a man lying beneath a burial shroud. Rounding Isla Muerto brought the buccaneers to the mouth of the Pueblo Nuevo River, where Ringrose and seven others stayed to guard the ship while Sawkins and the rest switched to canoes for the ten-mile trip upriver.

Their first nine miles proved uneventful. But on the tenth, they came upon one freshly cut tree after another laid across the river. The clear attempt to impede them did not bode well for their element of surprise, nor for a chance to rest prior to the attack. Indeed they spent the remainder of the night getting in and out of the canoes to haul trees out of their way.

Reaching Pueblo Nuevo at daybreak, they found the town fronted by a stockade, a brand-new defensive structure perfectly tailored to repel an incursion force such as theirs. The design was no doubt the work of the Frenchman who had betrayed them in Panama. But although impressive as hastily constructed fortifications go, it was nothing compared to the garrison that Sawkins and his forty-eight-man vanguard had made short work of in Santa Maria.

After landing his canoe ahead of the others, Sawkins strode into the savannah adjacent to the town. He was, Cox remarked, "a man whom nothing on earth could terrify." In the undeveloped savannah, the admiral was expecting to find the path of least resistance into the town for his raiders. Instead he discovered a trio of strong breastworks — temporary fortifications made of earth, wood, and rock piled breast high to protect defenders while they fired at onrushing attackers. Behind the breastworks now stood dozens of Spaniards. Sawkins was undeterred. The town would have some defenders — he had known that — but fewer than in Santa Maria, and farmers and fishermen rather than soldiers.

A moment later, the defenders spotted Sawkins, and one of them leaped over the breastwork, charging him. Unruffled, the admiral leveled his gun and fired, knocking the man off his feet. Unfortunately, the report drew more defenders from within the town, dozens of them. Sanguine about the buccaneers' prospects nevertheless, Sawkins started back to the river to rally his troops. Partway there he ran into Povey, Cox, and about nine others. Once they had assured him — incorrectly, it would turn out — that the rest of the canoe party had landed, Sawkins said, "Follow me and do not lie behind, for if I do amiss, you will all fare the worse for it." He then turned and launched himself toward the breastworks.

Along with the five swiftest of the men, he was met by as many as a hundred Spaniards—and at least that many were still streaming down from the town. These men were not soldiers, though, just farmers and ranchers, as expected; they had no guns whatsoever, just the odd lance. Yet they climbed over the breastworks and advanced on the six buccaneers — confidently, as though entirely ignorant of the consequences of a run-in with a musket ball. Sawkins offered a demonstration, raising his pistol, plucking at the trigger, and effectively transforming a minuscule soft lead ball into a bolt of lightning, felling one of the defenders. Before the man's comrades had time to react, they, too, were targets. Following some combination of five more percussive reports, the stomach-turning whine of incoming projectiles, and the howling of their recipients, the rest of the Pueblo Nuevans were given pause, or they simply froze in terror.

Intent on cutting down six more Pueblo Nuevans and sending the survivors scurrying back to the breastworks, Sawkins and his men reloaded — cartridge, powder, pan, frizzen, ramrod, and hammer, all in rapid succession. But it was not rapid enough for them to fire before the defenders resumed their advance. Bolstered by a staggering number of reinforcements — as many as a thousand, estimated Cox, who was just then running up to the breastworks along with Povey — the Pueblo Nuevans fell like a tidal wave onto the buccaneers, of whom there were just a dozen now. As a result of a miscommunication, only a quarter of their canoes had landed. Which was probably for the best. If all the buccaneers had been there to fight, they all would likely have died. As it stood, the rain of Pueblo Nuevan lances killed three of them, including Sawkins.

All of a sudden, Cox, Povey, and the remaining buccaneers were out of options save turning back to the river and running for their lives. As they ran, one of their comrades was snatched from behind them by the trailing throng. Because any attempt to stop and help him would mean certain death, they continued across the savannah, forced along the way to endure his bloodcurdling screams. Finding their canoes unmolested, they bounded in, and with the Spaniards "comeing downe so fast uppon us," as Povey put it, they shoved off, joining the balance of the raiding party in retreating downriver with all haste imaginable.

The Pueblo Nuevans kept up the pursuit, piling into their own boats. With periaguas and other sailing vessels, they could easily catch the buccaneers and again overwhelm them. There was a chance the buccaneers would be rescued by Cooke and his skeleton crew, which included Ringrose, now sailing upriver.

However, Cooke and company's unfamiliarity with the river proved their undoing: not only did they run the ship aground, they also landed on a rock. In a flowing river, rocks can act as saw blades on the wooden hull of a ship that is rocking and pitching in the current, turning her into a shipwreck long before either the tide or her crew can dislodge her. Cooke's crew would eventually manage to free her, but not in time to be of any help to their comrades trying to flee Pueblo Nuevo.

With the Pueblo Nuevans bearing down on them, meanwhile, those men were overdue for good luck, and they got some when Sharp spotted a sleek barque that could facilitate the buccaneers' escape — if they could take her. Planning to do so or die trying, Sharp and his canoemates advanced, finding her at anchor with, amazingly, no one aboard. They quickly installed themselves, helped the rest of the men in the canoes onto her deck, and weighed anchor. Not only was the barque swift — she whisked them out of harm's way — she was also packed with valuable booty, including indigo, oil, butter, and pitch (a glutinous tar-based composition used in waterproofing hulls).

But it was small consolation for the loss of Sawkins. Back at Isla de Coiba, echoing the buccaneers' collective sentiments, a gutted Ringrose wrote that the admiral had been "as valiant and courageous as any could be" and "the best beloved of all our company." Sawkins had been more than their leader; he had been the expedition's glue. The men concluded that their fortunes had died with him. Unwilling to serve under his prearranged successor, Sharp, they mutinied again and prepared to go their separate ways.

Sharp tried to change their minds, gathering everyone aboard the *Trinity* and making a case for them to stay together. Under his command, he said, they would "prosecute the design Captain

Sawkins had undertaken," which was to remain in the South Sea and plunder Spanish ships and settlements. He maintained that once they were farther onto the Spanish Main, where the citizens weren't expecting them, they would regain the element of surprise, and in no time they would each be worth £1,000 (four thousand pieces of eight) and on their way home.

The entreaty won him support from the diehards, including William Dick, who were "determined to be buried in those seas rather than to return home without the gold they had fought for so long and through so many dangers." Sharp's promise of £1,000 also resonated with the substantial number of men who had already gambled away their shares of the expedition's plunder. But for the rest of the crew, the issue remained Sharp himself. He was a brilliant sailor and tactician, they acknowledged, but also a rash hothead barely capable of managing himself, much less an entire fleet.

That, too, was a sentiment shared by Ringrose, who was now "totally desirous in my mind to quit those hazardous adventures and return homewards." The trouble was that his route home would entail a trek up the Darien Isthmus, and he was "much afraid and averse to trust myself among wild Indians any farther." And, regardless, with the rainy season now under way, the crossing would be nearly impossible. Ringrose's friends Dampier and Wafer both enthusiastically advocated for continuing the adventure, which may also have influenced his decision.

On May 30, he was not among the breakaway party of sixty-three buccaneers who sailed for the Darien along with the remaining Kuna, who would serve as their guides. About 140 buccaneers remained on Isla de Coiba. Ringrose was given reason to regret his decision almost at once: first, as he was standing beneath a manzanilla tree, a shower of rain happened to fall, dumping the tree's toxin onto him and causing his entire body to break out with red spots that wouldn't abate for a week. Next, while hunting for supper, he and several shipmates found themselves face-to-face with several twenty-foot-long alligators. The men managed to shoot and kill the alligators, at the same time solving the problem of supper.

Buccaneer infighting and politicking proved trickier. Sharp chose to keep the swift barque he'd taken during the flight from Pueblo Nuevo, which he christened the *Mayflower*. In her he saw the ideal consort for the *Trinity*, enhancing both the buccaneers' tactical options and reconnaissance capability. He gave Edmond Cooke command of the new ship, a reasonable choice given Cooke's seniority and track record. But the radically democratic crew bristled at being denied a say in the matter, and after just a few days under Cooke, his men simply refused to follow his orders, as Ringrose reported. "Determining to rule over such unruly company no longer," Cooke quit the *Mayflower* and rowed over to the *Trinity*. Sharp appointed John Cox to be Cooke's replacement on the *Mayflower*, a move that amounted to throwing gunpowder on a fire. Again the men resented Sharp's unilateral approach. In their opinion, the glib New Englander's lone qualification was being one of Sharp's cronies. As a result, mutiny was again brewing before the reconfigured fleet had sailed even an inch.

Those mutineers put their plan on hold, however, to weigh an offer from one of their prisoners, Captain Juan Moreno, who had commanded the *San Pedro*, the merchant ship that yielded some fifty thousand pieces of eight in Panama Bay two weeks earlier. As Ringrose related, Moreno "promised to do great things for us, by piloting and conducting us to several places of great riches." Foremost was Guayaquil, a burgeoning Spanish port city (in modern Ecuador) where the buccaneers "might lay down our silver, and lade our vessels with gold."

Another incentive to raid Guayaquil was chocolate, which had only recently been introduced to England and — despite its exorbitant price — become an immediate sensation because of its taste as well as the prevailing belief that it was an aphrodisiac. The buccaneers enjoyed chocolate, to say the least; the chroniclers' oft-repeated exaltations of it lead to the conclusion that pirates placed its value somewhere between rum and the company of women. And, as Ringrose reported, Guayaquil's "cacao-nut, whereof chocolate is made...is supposed here to be the best in the whole universe." Dampier differed, writing that it was only because of the limited travels of his "worthy consort" that he could hold such an opinion. Had Ringrose benefited from Dampier's breadth of experience, his friend maintained, he "would prefer the Caraccos nuts before any other."

Chocolate and riches aside, Ringrose, Dampier, and company feared that Moreno was either leading the company into a trap or trying to facilitate his own escape — or both. They took their concerns to their other prisoners, including José Gabriel and Francisco Peralta, the old and stout Andalusian captain who had tried to deceive them in the aftermath of the Battle of Panama Bay when he warned them away from Perico Island. Hearing that Moreno had told the buccaneers about Guayaquil, Peralta became enraged. A good sign, the buccaneers thought — that is, unless they were watching a piece of theater the Spaniards had scripted during their time together in confinement.

Again, Ringrose's nascent Spanish proved a boon. Since the Battle of Panama Bay, he had managed to strike up a friendship with Peralta — just as he had done before with Gabriel — and found the Andalusian to be an eager raconteur as well as a font of information about the South Sea. In that time, notably, Peralta had said nothing about Guayaquil, suggesting that his ire now was legitimate. Accordingly, the buccaneers decided it would be best to keep him and Moreno apart. They transferred Peralta to the *Mayflower*, to the dismay of Ringrose, who would be sailing aboard the *Trinity* — if the fleet ever weighed anchor.

Several of the buccaneers were unsure that, with a force of fewer than 150 men, they could manage a city of Guayaquil's size and might. Those who gave weight to omens were given further pause by the weather's sudden turn. "That night we had such thunder and lightning as I never had heard before in all my life," Ringrose wrote. If nothing else, it was a sign that the rainy season was well under way. In late spring and early summer in the vicinity of the equator, weather systems from the Northern and Southern Hemispheres butt heads, forming sixty-thousand-foot thunderclouds that produce rain whose intensity defied the chroniclers' description. Wafer would later write that it felt as if "Heaven and Earth would meet." The clouds would also throw off sparks in the form of five-mile-long bolts of lightning, which carried a charge of a hundred million volts and gravitated toward ships' masts — the sea's highest points — and could detonate stores of gunpowder.

As it happened, at the same time the buccaneers were ratifying the plan to attack Guayaquil, lightning ripped into the waves around the *Trinity* and the *Mayflower*, clipping the former's mainmast. Thankfully, it did no harm save electrocuting fish in the vicinity. Their crews were fortunate to be protected by Isla de Coiba, a landmass with an elevation of more than two hundred feet. But they would have no such luck on the 650 miles of open sea between the island and Guayaquil.

18

Snake-Haired Sisters

THE *TRINITY* AND the *Mayflower* departed Isla de Coiba for Guayaquil at five o'clock in the evening on June 6 and proceeded to sail in the wrong direction. It wasn't a navigational error, or anything Sharp or anyone else had drunk, but rather the result of so little wind that the current drove the ships northwest — in reverse, essentially. Over the following two days, there was enough wind to get the ships back on course but not enough for them to outpace an average middle-aged swimmer. The morning of the third day brought what Ringrose called "an easy gale." It was just a tease, though. By suppertime the ships had advanced just five leagues, a speed of 1.5 miles per hour, or one-quarter the speed of horsemen carrying news of the attack on Pueblo Nuevo and warnings to settlements throughout the Spanish Main. At the rate the buccaneers were going, the voyage would take five weeks — assuming they remained on course.

In the hope of determining their position, Ringrose turned to an astrolabe, a stack of adjustable brass disks that allowed him to first sight a familiar star at sunrise, then calculate the sun's position at its apex relative to the horizon, and finally translate the relative position of the two into the distance north or south of the equator, or latitude. He thereby determined that the ships were thirty-two miles south of Isla de Coiba. But he couldn't tell whether they were east of the island, as they should have been, or west. It would be another seventy-nine years before the invention of the marine chronometer allowed sailors to determine their positions east or west of the meridian, or longitude. In Ringrose's time, "discovering the longitude" was a popular way of saying "attempting the impossible."

Steady rain the next day ruled out an astronomical observation, but Ringrose didn't need it to determine that the company was again drifting the wrong way. The rain was falling straight down, rather than at an angle, as it would have been had there been any wind. That left the current to push the ships back toward Isla de Coiba. In desperation, the buccaneers turned to their Spanish prisoners, who were veterans of those waters. But some were more reliable than others. According to Ringrose, José Gabriel had been consistently honest, going so far as to share the plots and conspiracies of other prisoners to escape or kill the buccaneers. By interviewing the prisoners individually and comparing notes, Ringrose and company hoped to isolate the truth. They thus learned that there was no consistent wind until the third parallel, or a latitude of three degrees, which was nearly three hundred miles south.

The prisoners also told them about two other, bigger problems. First, when trying to sail down the coast of South America, as the company was now, vessels ran smack into the southeast trade wind, which originated in the southeast and blew in the opposite direction — northerly, parallel to the Pacific coast of South America. Second, ships also had to fight against the strong northward-flowing Peru Current. The best way to counter the two forces, the Spaniards said, was to take a long enough tack to circumvent them. In this case, that would entail sailing some eight hundred miles southwest to the Galápagos Islands, just below the equator. There, the *Trinity* and the *Mayflower* would attain the wind and be able to dart 750 miles due east to Guayaquil. The roundabout route would add nearly a thousand miles to their voyage but potentially save weeks. It sounded legitimate to Sharp, who revised his course accordingly.

Over the following week, though, there was hardly any wind. The men engaged in little more than fishing as they "lay tumbling in the calm," as Ringrose put it. At five o'clock on the morning of June 17, the twelfth day of a journey that under decent circumstances would have taken a week, land was sighted on the eastern horizon. Had the fleet reached the Galápagos? Unsure, Sharp sailed in for a closer look, revealing a vast, low-slung coast notched with countless creeks and bays. Much too vast to be one of the Galápagos, Sharp thought. No one else aboard the rain-drenched *Trinity* was sure where they were. Sharp summoned Cox from the *Mayflower* and had him bring Peralta, who had restored his credibility with his recent navigational advice. The veteran South Sea captain would be able to identify the landmass better than anyone else, Sharp expected. Probably he could name the individual creeks and bays.

Peralta indeed knew it: Barbacoas, he said, a wild country on the South American continent (in modern-day Colombia). The buccaneers were now a hundred miles farther from the Galápagos than they were when they'd started. Groans spread throughout the crew, followed by rumblings that it was time to cash out. Buccaneers relied on the element of surprise even more than wind; these misadventures, Ringrose complained to his journal, had given the Spaniards time "to send advice of our coming to every port all along the coast."

Sharp argued that, in fact, the delays would work to the company's advantage. Concluding that the pirates must have left the South Sea by now, the Spaniards would relax their guard. The matter was put to the men in council. Should they continue the expedition or not? The result, according to Ringrose, was that the members of the company "who had got money by the former prizes of this voyage" were outvoted by "the others who had lost all their booty at gaming." The men also voted on a new piece of advice from Peralta and agreed to sail to Gorgona, an island just ten leagues away, for a badly needed careening. Gorgona was ideal for it, Peralta said, since the Spaniards never went there because of the seemingly incessant rain, "scarce one day in the year being dry at that place."

Ringrose saw a detour to Gorgona for careening as a further boon to Spanish preparedness. When the company voted in favor of it, he wrote, "I seriously repented my staying in the South Seas."

Rain, it turned out, was the least of Gorgona's problems. Conquistador Francisco Pizarro, who was stranded on the island with his crew for seven months in 1527, called the island an "inferno" in spite of the showers, which served to mitigate the heat. The reference to hell was instead founded upon the rank soil, which seemed to exhale venomous insects by the swarm, and a superabundance of snakes, including fer-de-lances and even more lethal coral snakes. Snakes killed several of Pizarro's men, leading him to name the island after the Gorgons of Greek myth, a trio of snake-haired sisters with the power to turn anyone who looked at them to stone.

But the buccaneers were more concerned about a Spanish ambush than they were about rain, bugs, or snakes. On approach, the ten-square-mile island was inviting, swathed in lush rain

forest and topped by striking mountains. The Colombian mainland, seventeen miles east, provided a backdrop of the Andes
Mountains, their enormous snowy peaks ablaze in the sharp
equatorial sun. Anchoring the *Trinity* and the *Mayflower* at the
mouth of a tranquil river on the island's southern side was like
arriving at a maritime Eden — uninhabited and unspoiled, everything glistening in mist rising from the waterfalls. The whales
and dolphins cavorting by the shore seemed like a fantasy. How
could Pizarro have been so wrong?

Sharp decided to rename Gorgona after himself; Ringrose
would dutifully label it "Isla de la Gorgona or Captain Sharpes
Isle" on the map he drew, which included the tiny adjacent
island of Gorgonilla. Meanwhile his shipmates tried to shoot
the whales and dolphins, but as Ringrose wrote, "Our bullets
rebounded from their bodies." The men searched for victuals on
shore instead, finding an abundance of conch, turtle, and oysters. They also caught all the fish they could want as well as a
sloth, which Ringrose described as "a beast well deserving that
name." "It takes [sloths] eight or nine minutes to move three
inches forward," Dampier reported after conducting a number
of experiments. Unfortunately for Povey and the contingent who
couldn't do without meat, the sloths were "nothing but skin and
bones." But the island's monkeys and Indian coneys — guinea
pig-like rodents the size of rabbits — were more than adequate
compensation.

The Gorgona honeymoon ended all at once, with rain that
returned as though making up for lost time, "there falling a
shower of rain almost every hour of the day and night," according to Ringrose. The weather increased the difficulty of careening the ships, at best a grueling two-week process of repairing

damage to the hulls caused by dry rot or cannon fire, then scraping, burning away, or otherwise excising organisms such as barnacles, shipworms, and, primarily, weeds. Veritable jungles of weeds formed on hulls, especially in the tropics, slowing down a ship like the *Trinity* by as much as three knots, or up to half her average speed, which would be more than enough to prevent the buccaneers from escaping the men-of-war almost certain to pursue them after their raid on Guayaquil.

Careening the *Trinity* began with unrigging her, which the downpour immediately put on hold — canvas sails could not be taken down in the rain because of their tendency to rot when stored wet. The ship was not completely unrigged for four or five days, at which point the men connected a series of blocks and tackles between her fore and mainmast and the trees on shore. As they heeled the ship onto her side, the mainmast cracked, necessitating another delay for repairs.

Meanwhile, snakes — including one eleven feet long and fourteen inches around, the approximate circumference of a man's neck — settled any doubt the men had over Pizarro's choice of the island's name. More troublesome, from the buccaneers' standpoint, was the state of their stores, "nothing considerable of any sort but flour and water," Ringrose lamented. As opposed to meat and wine or brandy.

Amid this deprivation, the crew was stricken, for the first time on the expedition, by an outbreak of disease. José Gabriel came down with calenture, a delirium-intensive fever believed to be brought on by tropical heat. To treat it, doctors like Wafer used the seventeenth-century cure-all, evacuation of "superfluous humors from the whole body" by way of bloodletting, transpiration, enema, or vomiting. In Gabriel's case, the evacuation came by means of transpiration — essentially, sweating — a procedure that typically involved placing the patient in a warm bed, covering him heavily, and administering a medicine like London treacle (a concoction of wine, herbs, spices, honey, and opium) that induced perspiration.

It didn't help. For two days, Gabriel lay senseless, as far as his friend Baz could tell, though perhaps the Spaniard was dreaming of the company's successful raid of Guayaquil, of his own triumphant return — laden with gold and silver gifts — to Golden-Cap's village, and of the happy life he would lead with his beautiful princess and their newborn, the first of their many children. On the third day of his battle with calenture, however, Gabriel succumbed. "He had all along been very true and faithful to us," Ringrose wrote in memoriam.

The company would continue to endure such miseries on Gorgona for a total of thirty-eight days, until July 25, when, at long last, the ships were ready. Looking over the *Trinity*, Ringrose marveled at the difference: with the addition of topgallant masts, staysails, and lengthened topsails, and with the subtraction of her roundhouse coach and the elaborate carvings on her stern, the only thing slowing her down would be the weight of all the gold from Guayaquil. But Sharp no longer wanted to go to Guayaquil — not for any love of "Captain Sharpes Isle" but because the buccaneers had spent so much time there that they had almost certainly been descried either by passersby or the Spaniards who lived on the neighboring island, Gorgonilla — a total of three families, the buccaneers had established. Since Guayaquil would have its guard up, Sharp thought, "it would be in vain to go thither."

Like most of his shipmates, Ringrose was taken aback. Sharp ought to have considered that risk before subjecting them to more than five weeks in this snake-infested stew pot. Yet it was clear that he was right about Guayaquil, and so the buccaneers waited to hear his new plan. He didn't have one, unfortunately. Nor did anyone else in the company, at least anything able to gain traction. Tempers rose as the indecision wore on. Finally, one of their prisoners spoke up — "the old Moor," as everyone called him. (Likely he was one of the Muslims from the vicinity of the Iberian Peninsula who were occasionally found in Spanish crews at the time; it is recorded only that he had long sailed with the Spaniards.) He offered to lead the buccaneers to "a place called Arica," to which "all the plate" — or *plata,* the Spanish word for silver — "was brought down from Potosi, Chiquisaca, and several other places...where it was dug out of the mountains and mines." The plate simply lay in storage in Arica, the old Moor went on, "until such time as the ships did fetch it away." He had no doubt that the buccaneers would get "at least two thousand pounds every man."

Crewmen waiting to hear the captain's plan

The buccaneers knew of Arica; the port city (in what today is northern Chile) was the stuff of legend. In 1579, Francis Drake had seized a ship from Arica carrying 240 tons of silver, more than his ship could accommodate; he was forced to dump much of it overboard in order to continue sailing. A century later, the city remained the repository for all the silver mined in the region, which is to say, most of the silver mined in the world. Arica's mint also transformed a good deal of that silver into pieces of eight that, according to the buccaneers' new intelligence, now sat in the port, largely undefended, waiting for treasure ships to transport it to Spain.

The problem was the distance. Arica was nearly two thousand miles down the South American coast. To get there, as the buccaneers now knew, they would have to sail three thousand miles — nearly a thousand miles west out to sea in order to circumvent the trade wind and the Peru Current, then two thousand more miles southeast. It dawned on them, though, that the great distance might be a positive: it could restore the element of surprise, because they were likely to get to Arica before the Ariqueños received any warning of the threat.

Arica was additionally appealing because of its weather. Rain could kill a land raid, particularly one reliant on surprise. But it almost never rained in Arica, located in Chile's Atacama Desert. In fact, the city ranks as the world's driest inhabited place, with an average annual precipitation of 3/100ths of an inch — sixteen times less than even towns in the Sahara receive. After thirty-eight sopping days on Gorgona, the buccaneers would have been captivated by Arica even if it had no riches.

Early on the morning of July 28, three days after the fleet had departed Gorgona, the *Mayflower*'s commander, John Cox — who had survived his crew's initial objections and remained at the helm — awoke to discover that the *Trinity* was gone. It was a cloudy day, limiting visibility. It seemed likely that she was simply veiled by the fog. When the sky had cleared, however, Cox and his crew still couldn't locate her. This was no ordinary separation, Cox suspected, given the disagreement that he and Sharp, the *Trinity's* commander, had had the night before.

Since weighing anchor at Gorgona, the *Trinity* and the *Mayflower* had been sailing south along the South American coast — in advance of their planned tack out to sea — and suffering, unsurprisingly, from too little wind. Cox figured out, though, that the closer he sailed to the coast, the stronger the wind blew. Accordingly, when the cover of darkness permitted, he plied the shore. The practice brought Ringrose rowing over from the *Trinity* as a messenger. "An ingenious man," Cox thought of Ringrose, but that ingeniousness was neither here nor there when the Englishman was serving as Sharp's mouthpiece. Sure enough, Ringrose said, Sharp had ordered him to convey to Cox that he should stand off from the shore lest the *Mayflower* run aground.

Cox was no fool. He'd been taking fastidious notes on the *Mayflower's* position relative to the shore as well as on her speed and direction. He was certain, he told Ringrose, that he could maintain a course along the coast from sunset until at least two in the morning without the slightest risk of running aground. Ringrose thought Cox was being obstinate, and before returning to the *Trinity*, he advised the New Englander to "come about" — to sail away from the coast. Cox complied, but not until 2:00 a.m., without ill effect — except, perhaps, the hotheaded Sharp's reaction.

It was easy now, in the clear light of day, with no sign of the *Trinity*, to imagine Sharp ordering his crew to drop back, to leave

Cox to regret his insubordination, if only because of the uproar it would provoke among the *Mayflower* crewmen when they realized their captain was responsible. According to Povey, more than anything else except storms, the men feared being left alone "in an enimies cuntry and unknowne seas." And indeed, as a result of losing the *Trinity*, panic reigned on the *Mayflower*.

Judging himself windward of the *Trinity*, Cox had his men lower the *Mayflower*'s topsails and haul up the lower sails in order to slow her and enable the *larger ship* to catch up. But the day ended without any sign of her. As did the following day. And the day after that. After a week, the crew became convinced that the *Trinity* had succumbed either to the Spaniards or to the vagaries of the sea. As William Dick wrote, "This loss occasioned sundry distractions in our minds, not knowing what would become of us after so many misfortunes."

Nevertheless, Cox proceeded to the appointed rendezvous point, Isla de la Plata, three hundred miles southeast of Gorgona. If the *Trinity* were still afloat, he reasoned, Sharp would wait there for the *Mayflower* crew before proceeding to Arica. And if the *Trinity* were indeed lost, Isla de la Plata — which translates to "Silver Island" — offered Cox an intriguing alternative means of obtaining silver from Arica: it was there, in 1579, that Francis Drake had unloaded much of the excess Ariqueño silver weighing down his ship.

Cox continued to direct the *Mayflower* down the coast, battling the wind and current much of the way. Over the course of the first week in August, he passed the highland of Santiago, the white cliffs of Cape San Francisco, Cape Pasado, Manta, and Cape Lorenzo. Finally, on August 10, one of his men sighted Isla de la Plata. The two-square-mile uninhabited island was steep all around but flat on top, like a pillbox. There were no trees; the vegetation consisted

Francis Drake's crew seizing the silver that may still lie on Isla de la Plata

solely of low shrubs, evidently sustaining the many wild goats the men observed. The sheer rocky coastline afforded just one viable landing spot, on the northeastern side. There were no other ships there, meaning both that the *Trinity* crew was not on the island and that a reunification was not in the cards.

Nor was there silver, at least that Cox's men could find. Deciding to instead search for a prize at sea, Cox set about reprovisioning the *Mayflower*. While some of his men dug for fresh water, others rowed a canoe around to fetch goats, and they captured several. It would have been prudent to slaughter the animals before bringing them aboard their canoe. As it stood, their opposition to going to sea led to the craft sinking, in turn significantly delaying the goat hunters' return. As a result, the *Mayflower* was prevented from departing Isla de la Plata that day, as Cox had planned. This turn of events proved to be for the best. Otherwise the men would have missed out on the feeling of "infinite joy," as Dick described it, when the *Trinity* sailed up shortly thereafter.

The men on the *Trinity*, too, were euphoric. Two weeks earlier, Ringrose related, they had arrived at the conclusion that "we had lost [Cox] in the obscurity of the night, through his obstinacy in standing in too long, and not coming about when we spoke unto him." The joy of the reunion flowed into the following week: there were celebratory feasts and men bounding around the island like little boys, hunting treasure and spearing anything that moved, including dozens of tortoises. "These creatures here are so little fearful," observed Ringrose, "that they offer not to sink from the fishermen, but lye still until such time as they are struck." Even Admiral Sharp cut loose. "Our commander showed himself very ingenious in striking [tortoises]," Ringrose added. During that week, the company also figured out how to hunt the island's goats, killing more than a hundred, then salting them away along with massive tortoises, some of which weighed three hundred pounds. Dampier's review included, "Their fat is yellow, and the lean white, and their flesh extraordinary sweet."

For the most part, the buccaneers' spirits were so high that their failure to turn up even one of Drake's pieces of eight engendered no more than a shrug. A notable exception was the contingent that lost money on Isla de la Plata gambling with Sharp. His skill at dice — and more so, perhaps, his bombastic style of play — created a resentment that would fester over the course of the expedition.

On August 17, the well-rested and fully provisioned buccaneers set sail, as Cox wrote, "fit for new adventures." They would not have to wait long.

19

The Merry Blades

THE *TRINITY'S* SPEED stunned everyone, even old Captain Peralta, who had seen it all — and had once commanded her as part of the Spanish navy. Thanks to the buccaneers' structural modifications and the careening, she was slashing through the waves, sending salty foam sizzling past her waist, all but flying to Arica and no doubt able to outrun any Spanish warship — or any ship in the South Seas, for that matter. The *Mayflower* was a problem, though. As Ringrose explained from aboard the *Trinity,* "We were forced to lye by several times, besides raising our topsails, to keep our other ship company, lest we should lose her again." Waiting for the *Mayflower* was burning two or three hours every day.

On August 24, a week after departing Isla de la Plata, Sharp had had enough and decided to take the *Mayflower* in tow, sacrificing the *Trinity's* singular speed in the interest of reaching Arica sooner. His timing had been awful, he realized that night in the Gulf of Guayaquil, when, through the darkness, one of the men spied sails on the horizon. Spaniards from Guayaquil, Sharp suspected. At best, this was a blow to the element of surprise. At worst, men-of-war. Only the time of night was fortuitous: Sharp had several hours of darkness remaining to elude them. As the sails drew closer, however, he saw that they belonged to neither a fleet nor a man-of-war but instead to a single undersize galleon. At once his point of view shifted from that of prey to that of predator — a predator who had yet to deliver his men a prize in three months as admiral. He also sorely needed to redeem himself for his lone attempt at seizing one — just a day earlier, off Point St. Helena, on the northern coast of Guayaquil. Spying sails that looked to belong to a barque, he sent canoers in pursuit. But the "barque" turned out to be a worthless pair of abandoned rafts rigged with sails, and, worse, in pursuing them, the fleet had drawn the notice of a man at one of Guayaquil's lookout posts.

Sharp understood, now, that attacking the galleon carried great risks. If the previous day's blunder had not already sounded the alarm in Guayaquil, then failing to take this galleon certainly would: her crew was bound to put an armada on his tail. Also, should the galleon mount a solid defense — even a well-placed cannonball or two could splinter the *Trinity*'s masts — she might altogether compromise Arica.

Despite these concerns, he didn't hesitate, commanding the *Trinity* crew to cut the *Mayflower* loose and chase the galleon. In a flash, the languid pace of the night watch exploded into preparations for battle. Every man and weapon were needed topside, with everyone racing to clear the deck of sea chests and anything else that might impede them during the engagement. Ringrose may have been among those assigned to help the carpenter ready shot-plugs — pieces of plank and sheets of lead used to seal any breaches in the hull below the waterline. This job included clearing the sides of the holds so that when there were breaches from incoming fire, the carpenter could find them without having to trace the flooding to its source.

Dampier was likely among the crew sent aloft by the boatswain — the officer in charge of the boats as well as the sails, rigging, anchors, and cables — for a litany of tasks that included furling sails, which allowed the ship to be sailed by fewer men than were ordinarily necessary, and securing yards (the spars from which sails are set) with chains or ropes to prevent them from falling onto his shipmates during combat.

Wafer's job at this point was to secure space belowdecks for treating casualties. Typically during battle, surgeons stationed themselves in the cockpit, which earned its name from its onetime use by the cockswain, who was responsible for managing and steering a vessel.

Cannons usually required the most complex and elaborate preparations. But although the *Trinity* had swivel guns, she had no cannons, which was atypical for a merchant ship of her size and value. The buccaneers may now have regretted their failure to add some; alternatively, they may have belonged to the tactical school of thought that muskets were the more effective means of suppressing fire from a vessel while trying to board her.

As the two vessels came within plain view of each other and the battle drew nigh, Sharp's men would have expected him to deliver a speech. No record exists of what he said. Perhaps he invoked the memory of Sawkins or channeled the crew's rage. Given his laconic tendencies, it's more likely that his exhortation bore a closer resemblance to Blackbeard's famous rally cry, "Let's jump on board, and cut them to pieces." It's a near certainty that Sharp supplemented the crew's courage with wine or brandy.

Abruptly, the galleon turned to flee, giving Sharp and company the impression that her sailors had just noticed them for the first time. She caught a wind that transformed her into a gazelle. But the *Trinity*, by comparison, was a cheetah, and as she devoured the gap between her and her prey, the buccaneers' boatswain blew his whistle, signaling "all hands to quarters" and spurring Ringrose, Dampier, Wafer, and their shipmates to their appointed stations. On some pirate ships, to prevent crewmen from deserting their posts and slinking belowdecks when the hot metal started flying, the carpenter bolted or lashed shut all the hatches except those leading to cabins essential to the job at hand, such as the surgeons' station and the powder room.

Quickly the *Trinity* closed to within hailing distance of the galleon. Sharp ordered one of his Spanish-speaking prisoners to command the enemies to strike their topsails. From the darkness came defiance: a claim that they would make the pirates lower theirs. In response the buccaneers opened fire, which their enemies returned with equal ferocity. Ringrose and his shipmates found themselves ducking a squall of langrage — nails, bolts, and other scrap metal traveling a hundred feet per second, capable of turning a wooden rail into splinters and an exposed man into stew. Enemy fire battered the *Trinity* and sent debris raining onto the deck. The Spaniards also used their weapons to devastating effect on her rigging, shredding it.

Several buccaneers were hit. Those with only slight wounds were encouraged to remain in action. Three, though, had to be carried down to the cockpit, where Wafer and his fellow surgeons had readied beds — platforms covered with stretched sailcloth — as well as tourniquets, needles of all sizes, thread, splints, bandages, tape, and lint mixed with flour to absorb drainage from the gunshot wounds. The surgeons endeavored to maintain a professional detachment, to act as though they were entirely unaffected by the piercing cries of the wounded men.

As Wafer labored to save lives, Dampier and others would likely have needed to climb the rigging to make repairs. While aloft, he could observe the enemy, and, if it could be done judiciously, take shots. Top-fighting, as it was called, carried the risk that sparks from one's own pistol would set fire to the sails, not to mention that it made one an irresistible target. The good news, gleaned by the top-fighters, was the absence of cannon fire. If the galleon had any cannons, she wasn't using them, meaning that unless Spaniards were massed belowdecks, perhaps preparing a surprise gambit, the thirty or so sailors topside comprised the entire enemy force. This virtually guaranteed that, unless the *Mayflower* were damaged so badly that she could not sail away, the buccaneers would eventually prevail.

If the fight lasted too long, however, neither vessel would be capable of sailing away; the buccaneers would then be sitting ducks for the men-of-war inevitably arriving from Guayaquil. Therefore, as soon as possible, Sharp and company needed to board the galleon, a fraught procedure on the open sea in the dark. Between the waves, the limited visibility, and the two heaving decks, men might easily fall short and be crushed between the two hulls. For now, the darkness neutralized the buccaneers' two advantages, numbers and marksmanship. Although each enemy shot created a muzzle flash, the glow dissipated before a buccaneer could acquire a target and pull a trigger.

The firefight continued to rage in that fashion for another half hour, until one of the *Trinity*'s sharpshooters managed to zero in on the Spaniards' helmsman, killing him. "None of the rest dared to be so hardy as to take his place," Ringrose would write. At the same time, another buccaneer shot split apart the galleon's maintop halyards, the ropes used to raise and lower the main topsail, at once causing the sail to fall, eliminating the Spaniards' hope of getting away and prompting them to cry out for quarter. Sharp granted it and prepared to board his new galleon.

* * *

The galleon was odd, thought Ringrose as he wandered her deck. She was neither a warship nor any sort of *guardacosta* nor, to his dismay, a merchantman — at least the boarding party had yet to discover any cargo. The mystery deepened when Sharp examined the survivors, among whom was a band of twenty-four young men claiming to be in charge — as a group. They professed themselves to be civilians who had recently relocated from Spain to Guayaquil, where they had hired a crew of ten experienced seamen and soldiers along with a friar to serve as their chaplain. The only way for Ringrose and Sharp to make sense of this crew configuration was to regard the twenty-four young Spaniards as aspiring pirates.

Their actual story was stranger. As they proceeded to explain, they had met one another the night before in a Guayaquil tavern, where the news of the English pirates was on every lip. To a man, they were galled by the notion of such English blackguards violating their waters. When one of them proposed they all go to sea and eradicate the scoundrels, he was met by *huzzas*. No doubt similar alcohol-fueled bravado was given voice by men in taverns all over the Spanish Main that night. These men — the Merry Blades, Cox dubbed them — were extraordinary in that they had actually followed through.

As much as their story flabbergasted Cox, Ringrose, and Sharp, it troubled them, especially the "news of the English pirates." What did the Spaniards know? How far had the news spread? The buccaneers put the question to the captain the Merry Blades had hired, Thomas d'Argandona, who seemed an authoritative source. Not only was he a former governor of Guayaquil, he also came from a long line of accomplished commanders, including a brother recently appointed admiral of the sea armada

Plotting in a tavern

to replace Don Jacinto de Barahona, who had died in the Battle of Panama Bay.

"Gentlemen, I am now your prisoner at war by the over-ruling providence of fortune," Argandona told the buccaneers, adding that he was "very well satisfied that no money whatsoever can procure my ransom, at least for the present at your hands. Hence I am persuaded, it is not my interest to tell you a lie, which if I do, I desire you to punish me as severely as you shall think fit."

He struck Sharp, Ringrose, and Cox as a "gentleman" and a "person of quality." Sharp instructed him to continue. Back in June, Argandona said, a pair of Spanish barques had arrived in Guayaquil to bring news of the pirates' defeat of the Barcos de la

Armadilla in Panama Bay and to rally reinforcements. And then, only the day before they encountered the buccaneers, he and his crew were prompted to go pirate hunting themselves on hearing that a Spanish lookout post had spotted the *Santísima Trinidad*, which was well known throughout the South Sea. The last detail confirmed that Sharp's pursuit of the pair of abandoned rafts had been foolish — though inconsequential if the Merry Blades were the extent of the fallout.

Argandona went on to explain, however, that the Merry Blades were the least of the buccaneers' worries. Upon receiving the news of Panama Bay, the viceroy of Peru, Melchor Liñán y Cisneros, had constructed two new forts in Guayaquil to guard against the pirates. Next, he deployed several men-of-war with a plan to defeat the Englishmen he'd based on information provided to him by one of their own. That contention smacked of artifice, a claim designed merely to deter the company from further attempts at plundering the Spanish Main. It also seemed implausible. Other than a covert meeting with the Spanish families on the island of Gorgonilla, what opportunity had any of the Englishmen had to share information with the Spaniards?

The answer, Sharp and company learned, lay in the fate of the smaller of the two barques the fleet had lost on the voyage from Panama to Pueblo Nuevo: during the storm, that barque's commander, Morris Connoway, sought refuge for himself and his six-man crew at Isla Gallo, in the Pearl Islands. Venturing ashore, they found a small Spanish settlement, which they proceeded to plunder — until the settlers were reinforced by fifty armed men they'd summoned from the mainland. The Spaniards killed Connoway and five of his men, offered quarter to the lone survivor, and then took their time examining him, learning the extent of the buccaneers' plans. As a result, Viceroy Liñán had built the new forts in Guayaquil and dispatched the men-of-war to hunt for the buccaneers.

In addition, Argandona said, Liñán had two other, bigger men-of-war anchored at Lima, waiting for word of the pirates' whereabouts before setting sail in pursuit. Liñán had also diverted a third man-of-war that had been bound for Arica to pick up freshly minted silver. Instead the twenty-four-gun *Patache* would join the pirate-hunting armada.

To the buccaneers, none of this was bad news. Viceroy Liñán's fleet would soon arrive in Panama, learn that its quarry was long since gone, then have to battle the southeast trade wind and the Peru Current on the way back to Lima. As for the recall of the *Patache,* which had been bound for Arica to collect the freshly minted pieces of eight, might that mean the pieces of eight were left sitting in Arica? Argandona confirmed that that was the case. He cautioned the buccaneers, though, that the *Patache* now lay at the Callao, an outport of Lima, ready to sail on the first news of their presence.

Ringrose, Cox, and Sharp must have regarded one another in disbelief. To claim the silver in Arica, all they had to do was steer clear of Lima. That revelation was punctuated by the shouts of their comrades charged with rummaging through the captured galleon; they had found more than three thousand pieces of eight. All at once, the buccaneers' stars seemed, at last, to have aligned.

Then, out of the blue, Sharp fired a gun and splattered the blood of the Spanish friar across the deck in plain sight of his shipmates. The Merry Blades and the buccaneers alike were stupefied, and the next thing they knew, Sharp had thrown the still-breathing man overboard. The shooting had been the friar's punishment, Ringrose later wrote, as much of an explanation as any of the chroniclers provided; Sharp himself wrote nothing at all. "Such cruelties though I abhorred very much in my heart,"

Ringrose added, "yet here was I forced to hold my tongue and contradict them not, as having not authority to oversway them."

Sharp's action may not have been the random act of homicidal mania that both crews took it for but rather part of what amounted to the Brethren of the Coast's public relations campaign. Countless merchant crews surrendered at the sight of buccaneer vessels solely because of things they'd heard — for example, the famous story of French buccaneer captain François l'Olonais drawing his cutlass, cutting open the breast of a Spaniard, plucking out the man's beating heart, and gnawing on it like a ravenous wolf. In reality, buccaneer captains were far more likely to follow the precept that a skillful leader breaks the enemy's resistance and secures victory without fighting. Sharp may also have been trying to intimidate the Merry Blades and their crew, all of whom he subsequently took prisoner aboard the *Trinity*, sinking their galleon.

But if shooting the friar had indeed been calculated, Sharp would have done well to let his own men in on it. Instead, he left many of them grumbling about his fitness for command — misgivings that soon would mushroom into mutiny. Those who also believed that an unprovoked killing of a man of God risked divine retribution found validation two days later, on August 26, when, with the *Mayflower* in tow, the *Trinity* collided with her, snapping the smaller ship's bowsprit apart as if it were a dry twig, turning much of her bow to kindling, and otherwise damaging her beyond salvage.

With resignation, Cox and his crew transferred their possessions and provisions to the *Trinity* and left the *Mayflower* to sink. Their disappointment turned to relief, however, on the night of September 1, when the lookout on the masthead sighted a ship. If she were one of Viceroy Liñán's, Cox and his men now had a prayer of escaping.

20

Water, Water

ALL THE MEN could see, on the night of September 1, was a glow that, if it hadn't been leagues out to sea, they would have pegged as a streetlight or a lantern in a house. It might be another abandoned raft, or it might be a six-hundred-ton Spanish man-of-war bristling with cannons. The only thing they could rule out was a merchantman, because, as their prisoners from the galleon had told them, the news of English pirates in the area had resulted in an embargo preventing Spanish commercial ships from leaving port.

The following morning, September 2, Ringrose spied a sail where the glow had been, six leagues windward, he estimated. To have a better idea of the vessel's identity, Ringrose and company needed to get close enough to see her colors; Spaniards flew the red Cross of Burgundy on a white background. But pennants were not definitive. To veil their identity, the buccaneers often flew the Cross of Burgundy themselves. Merchant and naval vessels, too, commonly flew false flags to deceive their enemies. In this case, the buccaneers might not find out the truth until the *Trinity* was close enough to be shot to matchsticks.

But soon prisoner Nicolas Moreno, who had been the Merry

Blades' pilot (the officer who superintends the navigation) was able to identify the ship. As he told the buccaneers, she was a rich merchantman laden with rigging, woolen and cotton cloth, and other commodities made in Quito. She had set forth from Guayaquil on August 13, he added, but along the way needed to put in at Paita, around three hundred miles south, to have her mast refitted. That explained her violation of the embargo on commercial vessels: she would have set sail before it was put in place — if Moreno was on the level, that is, rather than trying to direct his captors toward a Spanish warship.

The buccaneers weighed going after the unknown ship. The risks aside, pursuing her meant deviating from their course to Arica, the cost of which could be measured in time and, more critically, water. Yet as was often the case on pirate ships, the deliberation over whether to chase after an unidentified sail was almost a foregone conclusion, the prospect of a prize a siren song.

The pursuit that ensued was, in some respects, breathtaking — the pinnacle of high-seas adventure. At the same time, it resembled a race between garden slugs. The *Trinity* was outpacing the merchantman by half a knot (.57 miles per hour), but six leagues separated them; at best it would take the *Trinity* a day and a half to close the gap. Consequently the buccaneers did not rush to prepare for battle as they had the night before. Those on watch moved around a little more than usual, but only because they were cold — Ringrose likened it to England in November.

He was glad, meanwhile, to again have the company of Captain Peralta, who was never at a loss for a yarn. The old Andalusian seized on their proximity to Tumbes — the first place the Spaniards had settled in Peru — to tell his English friend a story that, he felt, justified Spanish imperialism: the Spaniard who discovered Tumbes was a priest, and as he first landed there, carrying a cross, ten thousand Natives looked on. No sooner did he set foot on shore than two tigers sprang from the woods. The priest gently placed the cross onto the back of one of the tigers. causing both to prostrate themselves, as though worshipping it. In conclusion, Peralta said, "These animals gave to the Indians to understand the excellency of the Christian religion, which they soon after embraced." He failed to sway Ringrose, who, despite his regard for the captain, would write of the Spaniards: "Their insupportable cruelties to these poor natives I hope in due time will reach the Almighty's ear who will open the heart of a more Christian prince to deliver this people and drive away these caterpillars."

By day's end, the buccaneers had narrowed the gap between them and their quarry from six leagues to four. But then a thick mist fell, hiding her from view and giving rise to concern that she would escape during the night. When it grew dark, however, she reappeared, thanks to lights burning on her deck. Negligence, Ringrose suspected, rather than any sort of guile. The buccaneers were thus able to steer directly toward her, and by the next morning they were within three leagues, her sailors seemingly unaware that they were being pursued. Had they suspected anything, not only would they have extinguished every last flame aboard their ship during the night, they also would probably have sailed inland and run her aground so as to have a chance of defending themselves.

By the end of the second day of the chase, the buccaneers were within two leagues, and at dawn on the third day, the gap was just a league. Finally spying the *Trinity*, the commander of the merchantman tacked immediately. Such evasive action was standard operating procedure for a merchantman commander when sighting a potential predator. If he could keep away from them until dark, he would have more avenues of escape.

Sharp tacked after him and continued to close in. The merchantman might now turn back and attack or merely feign attack in the hope of scaring the buccaneers away. Sharp also had to consider the possibility that he was being led toward a Spanish warship. He studied the merchantman for tells. The choice to sail close to the wind, for example, would suggest that the ship was deeply laden with cargo. On the other hand, she might in fact be deeply laden with cargo but trying to deceive him by sailing away from the wind, as though her holds were empty. The day wore on in this fashion, and the merchantman yielded no more clues. Nevertheless, Sharp had his men clear the decks and prepare for battle. At four in the afternoon, the *Trinity* had sailed within a hundred yards of the merchantman, close enough for her crewmen to apprehend that they were being pursued by pirates. They lowered all their sails at once.

Ringrose and his shipmates cast dice to see which of the two watches would have the privilege of going aboard her first. The larboard watch won. Twenty of them then bounded onto the merchantman's deck and into her holds, where they helped themselves to, among other things, a great deal of cacao nuts and raw silk. It was a nice prize, but nothing in comparison to what they hoped for in Arica.

Sharp and company examined the merchantman's crew and chose as prisoners those they believed would be of the greatest use during the voyage, two Spaniards and twelve enslaved men. The rest they left aboard the merchantman, minus her mizzen and mainmast to delay her return to port and, thereby, a report of their whereabouts. To make sure those men were sufficiently provisioned for the extra time they would spend at sea, the buccaneers provided them with flour from the *Trinity* and ample water. It was a humanitarian gesture, one that would prove disastrous.

* * *

By tacking five hundred miles out to sea instead of continuing down the coast, Sharp could circumvent the buccaneers' three greatest obstacles: the southeast trade wind, the Peru Current, and Spanish warships. But there would be a trade-off. His navigation relied on landmasses for reference, and in this stretch of the South Sea, there were virtually none. The same dearth of land would also preclude the crew from reprovisioning—and their food and water stores were already dangerously low. If they lost their way or were delayed for any reason, their only means of slaking their thirst would be by drinking seawater, which would kill them sooner and in far more gruesome fashion than drinking nothing. In spite of their meager provisions, the South Sea experts among their Spanish prisoners—who stood to be at least as thirsty as the buccaneers if anything went wrong—unanimously recommended tacking. Sharp would be more than rewarded, they maintained, by "great gusts of wind" on the return leg.

On September 12, one week into the tack, the buccaneers had indeed lost track of their position. Using the astrolabe, Ringrose determined that they were on the eleventh parallel—660 nautical miles, or 759 statute miles, below the equator. Lacking a means of gauging longitude, though, he couldn't say where they were along the eleventh parallel, which, at 21,624 nautical miles, is one of the longest latitudinal lines on earth, crossing not only the Pacific but also the Atlantic and Indian Oceans as well as Africa, Australia, and South America. Without a landmass for reference, a seventeenth-century sailor placed blindly on the eleventh parallel would have no means of determining where in the world he was.

Unless there happened to be an eclipse. Ringrose had read in a ship's almanac that on that day—September 12, 1680—the moon would cover the center of the sun, giving the sun's outer edges the appearance of a ring of fire. The almanac also gave him the precise time this "annular eclipse" would be visible from Ile de Fer, in the Canary Islands. At one o'clock that afternoon, when the sun dipped behind the moon over the South Sea, Ringrose multiplied the difference between Canary Islands time and local time by fifteen — since the earth rotates fifteen degrees of longitude per hour — and derived the company's longitude: 285°35' east of the Canaries' Ile de Fer (now known as El Hiero), or 92°19' west of the Greenwich meridian. The *Trinity* was on course.

That left her crew to focus on the frightening rate that her stores were being depleted relative to her speed — or, rather, her torpor, a function of extraordinarily light winds. A week later, on September 19, the company instituted water rations: each man was constrained to four pints per day. To be adequately hydrated, the average sedentary adult male requires five pints of water a day. Of course, the buccaneers were hardly sedentary, constantly wrestling with ropes, furling and unfurling tons of canvas, and working the pumps. The salty air, which can also contribute to dehydration, made things no easier, though the relatively cool September weather — highs in the midsixties — was a boon.

The next day, September 13, Sharp determined that they had sailed far enough southwest to turn back toward the continent. That night, the heavens presented them with a view of the Magellanic Clouds, the pair of spiral galaxies orbiting the Milky Way that are visible in the Southern Hemisphere. The spectacle had a way of convincing mariners that they were not, as it often seemed, adrift in infinite darkness but were rather guided by a divine hand.

Sharp would have preferred wind. Over the next two weeks, there was far less of it than he'd banked on, and on September 29, the men's daily water ration was further reduced, to three and a half pints, with their daily food ration set at "one cake of boyled bread." Dehydration began to wither the company. In the early stages, its primary symptom is dry mouth, a tightening of the skin in and around the mouth resulting from the salivary glands' inability to wash away food particles. The food particles, in turn, eat into the teeth and gums, resulting in tongue sticking to the mouth, difficulty swallowing, and bad breath. The crew's oral hygiene regimen, the occasional "chew stick" twig, likely had no effect.

Dehydration also meant fewer diversions — a tongue sticking to the roof of one's mouth hindered chanteys and storytelling — and cost the buccaneers their favorite escape of all, alcohol. While brandy might have seemed the perfect remedy across the board, even the most hard-bitten among them knew it would only exacerbate their condition. The water situation steadily deteriorated over the next two weeks, intensified by the constant reminder of the deficit all about them. As the sailor in Samuel Taylor Coleridge's "The Rime of the Ancient Mariner" put it, "Water, water, every where, / Nor any drop to drink."

The journal of the ordinarily wordy Cox during this period offers a counterweight to the popular notion of a pirate ship as a floating fraternity party: ten straight days of entries consisting of nothing but recordings of the ship's position, the poor winds, and the company's minimal progress. For example:

28. Tuesd. 21 Leag. East lat. 22 deg. 35 min. wind South with rain. East 134 leag.

To Ringrose, or to any seaman with a grasp of basic math, Cox's spartan entries constituted an epic tragedy — if his distance measurements were accurate. To measure distance traveled, like most seventeenth-century seamen, Cox used a reel of tough cord, knotted every forty-four feet, which he dropped into the water from the moving ship. Because forty-four feet is 1/120th of a mile, the number of knots that unspooled over thirty seconds allowed him to calculate the *Trinity*'s speed. From September 20 to 30, he had her covering just 180 leagues, or fifty-five miles per day. Ringrose's measurements, recorded less often, were generally higher, but not significantly so. At most, the *Trinity* was averaging just two knots, or 2.3 conventional miles, per hour. A decent walker, at around three miles per hour, would have outpaced her. On October 1, each man's water ration had to be reduced again, this time to two and a half pints per day. The next four days brought neither wind nor hope.

On October 6, at long last, came the great gusts of wind. But as the company's recent run of luck would have it, the gusts were too great. The ringbolts — heavy iron rings bolting the mainstay to the deck, keeping the mainmast from toppling when the wind hit the sails on the forward side — gave way. Lest the wind send the mainmast crashing down onto them, the buccaneers had to sail downwind until the ringbolts could be repaired. Downwind, in this case, meant heading west when they needed to be heading east. They completed the repairs in "three or four glasses," as Ringrose recorded it — an hour and a half to two hours — just in time for the gusts to disappear.

The next day the *Trinity* sailed just seven leagues, the dehydration no doubt making the pace seem even slower. By now the spate of symptoms would have expanded to include muscle cramps, headaches, dizziness, insomnia, irritability, and dark yellow urine reeking of ammonia.

The *Trinity* managed to grind out fifty leagues between October 7 and 9, and on the tenth, Ringrose wrote, "We spied floating upon the sea several tufts of sea-grass, which gave us good hopes that we were not far from shore." The following day brought another good sign — a hazy sky: "Our pilot told us that the sky is always hazy nigh the shore upon these coasts where we now were." But the day after that, the sky cleared, revealing that the haze had just been haze. On October 13, the men saw a whale, according to Ringrose "an infallible token that we were not far distant from land, which now we hoped to see in a few days." And on the fourteenth appeared "several land-fowls, being but small birds, concerning which our pilot said, that they use to appear about one or two days' sail from the land." But what land, no one knew. The continent? All that mattered was the prospect of fresh water.

It took another three seemingly infinite days before Ringrose and his shipmates heard the hoarse cry of *"Land!"* from the masthead. They held off celebrating on account of the haze, which caused them to question whether what their hoarse shipmate had sighted, eight leagues away, was in fact land. To Ringrose, it looked like a sugar loaf. But by evening, as the *Trinity* advanced to within five leagues, it revealed itself to be a high, steep shore — too high and too steep for them to land.

Another five full days of sailing along the coast was required before the company came upon a suitable landing spot, a barren point set aglow by the sunrise of October 22. According to Moreno, the Merry Blades' pilot, they were now looking at the Point of Ilo, seventy-five miles north of Arica, or far too close to Lima for comfort. Stealing ashore for water, given the Spanish coastal lookouts, would jeopardize the Arica mission, not to mention the buccaneers' lives. But not going ashore for water might place their lives in greater peril. The crew was tormented by "the huge want of water we were now under," wrote Ringrose, who himself "could not sleep all night long through the greatness of my drought."

Though it was hardly the ideal time to grapple once more with the southeast trade wind and the Peru Current by sailing down the coast, the buccaneers felt they had no choice. The water allowance was reduced to a mere half pint per day. The wind blew no more than six hours a day, Ringrose reported on October 23, and "very great was our affliction now for want of water." The ration was reduced even further, by "one measure" — from eight ounces to six, perhaps — and the chroniclers' journal entries became curt or nonexistent. Admiral Sharp covered the bulk of October with "There was nothing occurred but bare sailing," and Dick reported only "many days infinite hunger and thirst."

On the morning of October 24, misty clouds shrouding the coast prevented the sailors familiar with the region, including Peralta, from determining whether the *Trinity* had reached a safe landing spot. In the afternoon, however, the clouds dissipated, revealing a score of tall cliffs, the faces of which were coated in chalk-white seabird excrement, giving them a singular appearance and enabling the Spanish prisoners to orient themselves. Known as Morro de Sama, they said, it was an ideal place to go ashore because of its proximity to the Río de Juan Díaz, a source of fresh water located just below what is today the Peru-Chile border, forty miles north of Arica. The prisoners told their captors that they could also expect to find local fishermen there who might yield intelligence on Spanish defenses at Arica.

The buccaneers sailed out to sea until nightfall to stay out of sight of any Spanish lookouts. At eight o'clock, for the first time in sixty-five days, men left the *Trinity*, eighty of them in four canoes towing a launch — essentially, a troop transport craft — that they'd captured a month earlier. But they returned the next morning having failed to find either the fishermen or the river, their thirst more agonizing than ever. A hallmark of the late stages of dehydration is an acute confusion bordering on delirium, which might have played a role in the buccaneers' next move, later that day: rather than gathering water and intelligence, they decided to skip straight to attacking Arica.

21

Ransom

THE FOLLOWING EVENING, October 25, despite their blazing thirst and its deleterious effects on their bodies and minds — or perhaps as a direct consequence of those effects — Ringrose and III other buccaneers left the *Trinity* to raid Arica. Eighteen miles of sea stood between them and a clandestine landing spot three miles from the city. They rowed their canoes all night long, reaching the landing spot shortly before sunrise, only to find, "to our great sorrow and vexation," as Ringrose wrote, "that we were descried, and that all along the shoar, and through the country they had certain news of our arrival."

On the beach ringing the bay and on the high ground atop the surrounding cliffs, men and horses stood poised to repel the invaders. Sharp was undaunted: these men were amateurs, from the look of them, probably locals. Soldiers would have been another story, since the attack had been predicated on the buccaneers' intelligence that Arica was lightly defended and that the nearest Spanish troops were in Lima, seven hundred miles away. As it stood, Sharp figured, all the buccaneers had to do now was land. They could then easily dispatch this militia, march without opposition to Arica, and help themselves to the piles of newly minted pieces of eight. At the very least, they would get some water to drink.

Landing was the hard part. The sea was running so high and explosively against the rocks that the buccaneers risked their boats being, as Ringrose put it, "staved into one thousand pieces." And almost certainly their gunpowder would be soaked beyond utility. As they searched for a hospitable stretch of shore, the sun peeked over the horizon, revealing a small island a mile off the coast as well as a brand-new threat: six ships at anchor there. Four lacked sails as well as yards, but the other two appeared ready to sail. Pilot Nicolas Moreno recognized both. One, he told the buccaneers, was mounted with six cannons, the other with four.

As if on cue, the cannons fired — thunderous discharges that, a mile away, Ringrose and company could feel in their bones. The cannonballs splashed down well short of the canoes. Evidently the Spaniards' intent had been to intimidate, which, to the buccaneers, was laughable. In the Battle of Panama Bay, with half their present number, they'd made themselves masters of far more potent ships. In Arica, though, they would have to fight on multiple fronts, a point that was raised a moment later by a shot fired by a horseman on shore. It, too, fell well short of the buccaneers, disappearing into a wave top, but it forced them to a reckoning. They would be better off, Sharp conceded, "giving over this enterprize until a fairer opportunity."

They turned and retreated to the *Trinity,* resolving to regroup in Ilo, a village seventy miles up the coast. They weighed anchor, expecting a day's sail at most now that they had the trade wind at their backs. During the night, however, the wind died altogether. "At this time," Cox reported, "water was worth 30 pieces of eight per pint to those that could spare their allowance, and he that bought it thought he had a great penny-worth."

* * *

They finally reached Ilo two days later, on October 28. Late that night, Sharp and fifty other men climbed into a quartet of canoes and headed for shore, thinking not of gold and silver but rather water, which flowed into Ilo in abundance from the snowy peaks of the surrounding Andes. Because the Spaniards had no reason to protect water, the buccaneers expected no opposition. The party rowed two miles through a calm sea. The sky was clear, the air cool. Before long the first rays of the new day showed them a placid shore, where they landed without difficulty. Not far into their march to Ilo, however, a horseman burst out of the shadows and raced toward the village. A lookout, clearly.

"No whit discouraged," as he put it, Sharp ordered his men onward. As they climbed the hill atop which the village was perched, a formidable breastwork came into view, a new construction rendered in clay and banks of sand, around seventy-five feet long. Waiting there were sixty cavalry and infantrymen in battle formation. Such an organized resistance at this backwater was astounding; it made it seem comical in retrospect that any of the buccaneers had believed pieces of eight could be gathered in the South Sea as easily as pears from a tree.

Having left eight of his men behind to guard the canoes, Sharp had a force of just forty-two. He shrugged off the opposition, advanced, and engaged them. The result? "With little resistance they yielded to the privilege of filling our water and cutting our wood," he reported.

As the Spaniards continued to do chores for them, he and his men helped themselves to Ilo's ample supply of wine and a variety of other provisions. But while the sanguine commander enjoyed the spoils, several of his men, including Ringrose, remained on edge. Since the Spaniards had continually been wise to the company's every move, it stood to reason that Spanish troops were at least on the way from Lima, if not on the verge of pouring into Ilo. That fear was substantiated by the buccaneers' examination of the cowed Iloans. A dying — which is to say, credible — defender told Ringrose's group that nine days ago the village had received word of the pirates. And yesterday a messenger had arrived from Arica to report the confrontation there.

With the eventual goal of defending Ilo against the troops from Lima, the buccaneers hurried back to their landing place and planted two flags. The first signaled the *Trinity* that the raid had succeeded; the second exhorted all the men the ship could spare to row ashore. Those men, on their sixth day of being limited to just six ounces of water, may well have rowed at record speed. Once the company was reunited, they "refreshed and feasted" for three or four days, which Sharp covered in his diary with a single word: "Jollity."

At the same time, Ringrose and the more circumspect members of the crew, such as his friends Dampier and Wafer, were continually looking over their shoulders, bracing for a Spanish onslaught. Ringrose joined a party of sixty who went to conduct reconnaissance in the valley adjacent to the town. In contrast to the barren cinder-black mountains of the surrounding Atacama Desert, the valley was in full bloom with orange, lemon, lime, fig, and olive trees. (In the sixteenth century, Ilo had been chosen by the Spaniards as the ideal site for growing olives.)

Ringrose thought it all "very pleasant" — until Spaniards appeared on the hilltops, that is, and began rolling boulders toward the buccaneers. The Spanish effort to deter them instead spurred them to further explore the valley, leading them to discover a large sugar factory. Most of the sugar had been evacuated and hidden, but it occurred to Ringrose that the Spaniards might be willing to pay a ransom for the factory's safety, perhaps in the form of cows, which the company needed for meat to fuel their return to Arica. Along with Cox and an interpreter, Ringrose carried a flag of truce to the Spaniards, who met them civilly and promised to pay a ransom of "fourscore beeves" — cows — on the condition that the sugar works not be harmed. Ringrose and company agreed, with the provision that the cows be delivered to them at the port by noon the next day.

The next day, under his own flag of truce, a Spanish official approached Sharp in Ilo and reported that sixteen cows had already been sent down to the port, with the rest due the following morning. An elated Sharp ordered his men to march back to the port in preparation to return to the *Trinity*. Ringrose thought the move premature. By relinquishing control of the sugar factory, the buccaneers would lose their leverage. He took his concerns to Sharp, who dismissed them. But sure enough, when the buccaneers reached the port, as Ringrose reported, "we found no beeves had been brought down at all."

Rather than put to sea now, Sharp returned to Ilo to complain to the Spaniards. It seemed to work. They promised him the cattle by nighttime. But nighttime came and went. The Spaniards' excuse, wrote an exasperated Ringrose, was "that the winds were so high, that they could not drive the cattle." They promised the ransom by the following noon, but when the hour arrived, the cattle did not.

His patience now exhausted, the old Sharp reemerged, ordering sixty men to march back up the valley. "We burnt both the house, the canes, and the mill," Ringrose related with relish. "We broke likewise the coppers, coggs, and multitudes of great jars of oil that we found in the house." It was much more gratifying than herding cows.

In the process, though, the party spied more than three hundred Spanish horsemen riding at full gallop toward the port, where seventy-odd buccaneers were whiling away the afternoon, entirely unaware that they were about to be, as Ringrose put it, "torn in pieces." He and the other members of the wrecking crew left the nearly demolished sugar factory and sprinted down to shore, arriving just in time to rally their shipmates into "a posture of defence."

"The enemy came riding at full speed toward us," related Cox, who expected to be driven into the sea. He and his cohorts on shore countered with "small shot," or shotgun loads, loosing a swarm of pellets as soon as the Spaniards came within firing range, and dismounting most of the lead riders, which, as Cox wrote, "put a stop to their careers and courage." At once, the Spaniards rethought their attack, wheeled off, and sought shelter in the hills. As Cox wrote, "This confirmed [to] us that we should get no other beefs." Ever again, if the Spaniards could help it.

Meanwhile, Ringrose reported, "Their forces increased hourly to considerable numbers." Rider after rider appeared. At any moment, an order would be given, and the Spaniards would commence driving the buccaneers into the sea. Sharp beat them to it, ordering his men into the canoes.

They returned safely to the *Trinity,* where Ringrose delighted in their haul, which included a "great plenty of all sorts of garden herbs, roots, and most excellent fruit." Not all his shipmates shared his interest in the fruit. If they had known about its role in preventing the scurvy about to beset them, however, they would have thrown punches for it.

22

Eighty-Five Stout Fellows

U NDER IDEAL CONDITIONS, the *Trinity* could sail eighty-five
miles in half a day. But because the eighty-five miles of
coastline between Ilo and Arica were fraught with the southeast
trade wind, the Peru Current, and Spanish men-of-war, the buccaneers were forced to follow a circuitous route to Arica, requiring
them again to tack five hundred miles to sea before looping back.
Unfortunately, on the way out to sea, the conditions were also not
ideal — especially the wind, which was virtually nonexistent —
and in the seven days following their November 3 departure from
Ilo, the company averaged just nineteen miles per day, a speed only
slightly faster than a tortoise's rate of 0.6 miles per hour. It became
an issue when the men began coming to Wafer with complaints of
weakness, lethargy, and malaise as well as bleeding from the hair
follicles on their arms and thighs.

The diagnosis was easy. The medical profession had been
aware of scurvy — the name is derived from the word *scurf,* meaning scaly skin or lesions — since the fifteenth century, when sailors started going to sea for months at a time. It has since been
estimated that scurvy killed more sailors than storms, shipwrecks, and combat combined. *The Surgions Mate* — a 1617 book by

East India Company doctor John Woodall that was as prevalent aboard seventeenth-century ships as anchors — advised administering orange, lime, and lemon juices "to prevent the disease, as also to helpe when it comes." But while at sea, surgeons such as Wafer found Woodall's treatment impractical because it also called for "wine, spices, sugar, and the yolke of an egge," among other ingredients. Despite the shipboard immunity of Ringrose and others who partook of the captured fruit, it was not until 1796 that the Royal Navy would home in on citrus as the solution to scurvy, resulting in a prescribed midjourney daily ration of lime juice sweetened with an ounce and a half of sugar. And yet another 141 years would pass before Hungarian biochemist Albert Szent-Györgyi earned a Nobel Prize with his discovery of the underlying reason for citrus's efficacy — the correlation between the affliction and vitamin C deprivation. In the seventeenth century, since scurvy disappeared upon sailors' return to shore, the prevailing view was that escaping a ship's salty, dank confines was the only real remedy.

When scurvy dug into the *Trinity*, the buccaneers had sailed only about thirty of the 150 leagues — one hundred of the five hundred miles — required before they could double back to the continent. Because turning any sooner risked running smack into the Spanish warships hunting them, they stayed the course. The scorbutic crewmen were left to convalesce in their sleeping quarters belowdecks, which were blighted by filth, cockroaches, and the wooden-ship reality that no matter the quality of the caulking, the planks comprising the overhead decking were never truly watertight. Even in good weather, seawater leaked into the lower decks through the scuppers (drains on the deck); in bad weather, it poured in through the gun-deck ports, meanwhile permeating the oakum and seams, which never quite dried. Clothes stayed wet as well, for days on end. When it was cold, there was no getting warm, and a buccaneer's lone refuge was to dangle in the lower deck's putrid, inky darkness on a sopping hammock he might share with a drowned rat — or, worse, a live one.

Cox's journal entries from this period, like those of the other chroniclers, paint a bleak picture of a crew focused solely on its abysmal knots-per-day tally in the race against scurvy. The men now faced the second stage of the disease, in which gums turn purple and soften to the consistency of a sponge, causing teeth to loosen. If the disease persisted for two more weeks, the symptoms would also include ecchymoses, enormous purple-blue bruises on skin that develop into open sores and ulcers. At the same time, "ground substance" — the gelatinous matrix that fills the spaces between tissue and cells — begins to deteriorate, leaving the body like a brick building suddenly without mortar. Blood vessels tear, bones easily break, and wounds cannot heal. The treatment, however, was almost as bad, as Dampier related: "The natives say that the best remedy they can find for it, is the stone or cod of an allegator (of which they have four, one near each leg, within the flesh) pulverized and drunk in water."

Fortunately for the buccaneers, on November 11 a gale sprang up and over the next two days propelled the *Trinity* more than fifty leagues. Cox recorded thirty-two leagues on the eleventh alone, more than the ship had traveled in total since departing Ilo. On November 13, the *Trinity*'s pace doubled to 6.4 knots, nearly that of a trotting horse, exhilarating the entire crew. That day, the company sailed an expedition-record fifty leagues, and over the course of each of the next two days, it sailed forty leagues more.

But on November 16, a heavy rain seemingly extinguished the wind, reducing the *Trinity*'s speed to that of a statue of a horse. "Very little wind" was as much as Ringrose wrote about that day. He also provided the chroniclers' lone health update that week: "Captain Peralta, our prisoner, was taken very much frantick, his distemper being occasioned, as we thought, through too much hardship and melancholy." The melancholy seems to have been pervasive. Even the appearance of the Great Comet of 1680, which streaked overhead shortly before dawn on November 19, barely caused a ripple on board. Among the chroniclers, only Ringrose mentioned it — scarcely, given his enthusiasm for astronomy: "The body thereof seemed dull," he wrote, "and its tail extended itself eighteen or twenty degrees in length, being of a pale colour, and pointing directly N.N.W."

He was also alone in reporting one of the expedition's strangest sights. On the night of November 30, nearly a week after the *Trinity* had begun tacking back toward the continent, the men on watch noted what appeared to be a mile-long sandbank — but that was impossible so far out to sea, where depths averaged two miles. As they sailed closer, the bank moved — roiling, rippling, like a serpent, with what appeared to be scales winking in the moonlight. Without question it was alive. No doubt everyone swallowed hard at the realization that the tales of giant sea serpents were not only true but also understated. As Ringrose discovered on closer inspection, however, it was not a sea serpent at all but only a school of anchovies, albeit a preternaturally large one.

On December 2, a full thirty days after leaving Ilo, the buccaneers sighted land. After dropping anchor late that evening, Sharp chose eighty-five "stout fellows," including Ringrose, to row ashore and attack the city of La Serena. The company originally had intended to land nearer to Arica, a thousand miles up the coast. But following a scurvy-ridden month at sea, the navigational error had the potential to be a happy accident, given La Serena's abundance of fruit orchards, vineyards, and farms: a pictographic map of the town would have resembled a cornucopia brimming with lemons, oranges, and preposterously large strawberries at their peak now — late springtime in the Southern Hemisphere. In addition, according to the reliable sources among the buccaneers' prisoners, the Spaniards' warnings of pirates were unlikely to have reached so far south.

Ringrose was one of fifty-three men packed into the launch, far too many, and as a result, the craft moved so slowly that Sharp and the men in canoes shot ahead and quickly disappeared. The canoe party landed to find 150 Spanish horsemen on the lookout for pirates, immediately making them regret that they hadn't slowed to wait for the launch.

"Deriving courage from their advantage in numbers," related Cox, who was in the party of canoes, "[the Spaniards] hemmed us in a ring, not doubting but to have an easie conquest over so few men." But because most of the horsemen were armed only with lances, Sharp figured a steady spray of shot could keep them at bay until the launch arrived. He divided his men into six groups — of five or six men apiece — and ordered the groups to fire in succession. "Scarce a shot flew in vain," Cox wrote of the initial volley. In addition, the first group's reloading speed exceeded Sharp's expectations: the six men were prepared to fire their second volley before the fourth group had fired its first. While sustaining only one injury of their own, the buccaneers quickly killed three Spanish officers and wounded four other men. The Spaniards kept up the fight only long enough to recover their dead, after which they retreated in disorder toward the town. Sharp and company ran after them, hoping to prevent them from warning the townspeople. But rather than head for town, the horsemen veered off the road and into a swamp.

At the same time, the launch reached shore. Ringrose and his fifty-two companions followed the trail inadvertently left by their comrades, a line of scattered paper cartridges the men had bitten off and spat to the ground while reloading. When the launch crew caught up to the canoe party at the swamp, the Spanish horsemen again bolted. And again, the buccaneers followed, until they perceived that the riders were not retreating but rather leading them on a wild-goose chase, buying time for the townspeople to evacuate their valuables.

Sharp ordered the buccaneers to reverse course at once and head for the town. Unfortunately, they couldn't find the town, not until eight the next morning, when they realized they had a new problem: La Serena was much bigger than they had been led to believe — at least three-quarters of a mile square, with eight or nine churches, businesses belonging to all manner of wealthy tradesmen and merchants, and, as Ringrose recorded, "houses and gardens being as well and as neatly furnished as those in England." In other words, La Serena was the sort of town that could mount a formidable defense even without its cavalry, and by spending half the night wandering around the countryside, the buccaneers had given the townspeople plenty of time to prepare.

But although La Serena was never mentioned among the concerns of the Spanish merchants whose letters the buccaneers had intercepted in Portobelo, the city was their argument in microcosm, if not a textbook case of what happens when a colonial empire spreads itself too thin. La Serena had long since outgrown its fortifications, and during that time, some combination of wear, neglect, and having too many other places in need of protection had transformed those fortifications into doorways. Similarly, the city still had soldiers, but they lacked training, numbers, and the latest weapons — the citizens had had ample reason to send them to delay rather than engage the invaders.

As though able to hear the La Serenans' quivering, Sharp confidently ordered his men to advance on the city. They were met by defenders who, augmented by their returning cavalry, had overwhelming numerical superiority to go with the advantage of knowing where best to station themselves in the city's cloisters, back alleys, and early morning shadows. And yet the resulting clash was not just one-sided but also so devoid of conflict as to deprive the chroniclers of a narrative. Cox's was the most extensive. "In a short time," he wrote of La Serena, "we made our selves masters of it, with little or no loss on our side."

The plunder included five hundred pounds of silver as well as a wealth of hogs, fowl, mutton, salads, wine, grain, and fruit. "We found strawberries as big as walnuts, and very delicious to the taste," wrote Ringrose. "In a word, everything in this city of la Serena was most excellent and delicate, and far beyond what we could expect in so remote a place." Many of the crew relished the opportunity for rest, relaxation, and "good fellowship" — one of Sharp's favorite terms for drinking. (Other popular euphemisms of the time included "to be well to live" and "to have a piece of bread and cheese in your head.")

Ringrose, however, could not relax. He and several of his shipmates were dogged by the question of whether the run-in with the cavalry upon landing had been bad luck or part of a disturbing trend. If "so remote a place" had been on guard against the buccaneers, what could they expect from an obvious target like Arica? In questioning the new prisoners from La Serena, Ringrose learned that several days earlier, the townspeople had been alerted to the possibility of pirates by a contingent of sixty soldiers sent overland from Arica to bolster the town's defenses. In addition, while the cavalry was waylaying Sharp and company the night before, most of the townspeople had fled, and almost certainly they would go to Coquimbo, the nearby port city, to rally more Spanish soldiers to come to La Serena's aid. Nevertheless, most of the buccaneers continued to party. One of them, William Cammock, literally drank himself to death.

Ringrose and his like-minded shipmates attempted to formulate a plan, and it seems Sharp and the good-fellowship contingent, if they even noticed, were happy to let them try. As a first order of business, Ringrose and company set up a base of operations in La Serena's Church of San Juan. (In Spanish cities, churches made good bases because of their central locations, room for large numbers of prisoners, and the devout Spaniards' reluctance to attack a house of God.)

No sooner had the buccaneers settled in than six Spanish gentlemen approached the church under a flag of truce. The reason for the visit, they said, was a request for wine for their governor, who had none in the fields to which he'd fled. To ascertain the Spaniards' true objective, Ringrose and company gave them wine and some fowls, along with a message from Sharp stating that if either the governor or his lady wanted anything else that they'd left behind — gold, silver, and jewels excepted — they simply had to ask. The same delegation returned later with a response. Seeing that the Englishmen were "such sociable enemies and so good-natured victors," the governor was inviting Admiral Sharp to drink a glass of wine with him at the top of a hill adjacent to the city. If Sharp came unarmed and with just one subordinate, the governor would reciprocate.

Perhaps less circumspect than he should have been, Sharp consented. At the meeting, he and the governor "drank and were merry together." The townspeople, Sharp gleaned in the process, feared that he and his men, "having found no considerable booty or pillage" in La Serena, would set the town afire. Suddenly seeing an opportunity to make months' worth of suffering pay off, he kept to himself the fact that his men were enamored with La Serena and would prefer to preserve it. To that end, he agreed to a ransom of 95,000 pieces of eight to be paid at ten the following morning. Upon his return to town, Sharp received a volley of small arms in tribute from his men — "Our fancies being filled with the expectation of so much money," explained Cox, "we were at a pitch of mirth higher than ordinary."

The following morning, the Spanish delegation, much like their counterparts who'd promised beeves in Ilo, arrived empty-handed but promising to pay if given a little more time. Sharp gave them until eight the next morning. An incident in the harbor that night, however, caused him to reappraise the Spaniards' reliability, not to mention the chances that he would ever see a single one of the 95,000 pieces of eight. It began when Spanish saboteurs inflated a horse's hide — as though it were a raft — and loaded it with oakum, pitch, sulfur, and other combustible materials. Next, one of them swam the hide out to the *Trinity*, wedged it between the rudder and the sternpost, and, before fleeing, set its contents on fire. Flames quickly engulfed the rudder, and putrid black smoke shrouded the ship. The men on watch ran all over the ship, desperate to find the source of the smoke, but to no avail. They initially believed that their Spanish prisoners were responsible for the fire, but the ensuing interrogation of the Spaniards failed to net actionable intelligence. Only when one of the buccaneers happened to glimpse the bloated horsehide floating past — and somehow discerned its dark purpose — did they locate the fire.

A ship is "fired"

On shore, watching the Englishmen douse the fire and save the ship, the saboteurs enacted what amounted to their backup plan, opening a sluice gate in the aqueducts serving as La Serena's irrigation system. Water flooded the town. The saboteurs' intent, Ringrose divined, was "that they might the easier quench the flame, in case we should fire the town." As if to oblige them, in the morning the buccaneers set fire to the town—"As nigh as we could, every house in the whole town," Ringrose reported with satisfaction. Once La Serena had been reduced to ashes, the buccaneers took up their plunder and marched back to the *Trinity* — directly into an ambush of 250 Spaniards on horseback. Refreshed by their four days in La Serena, the company "began to pink some of their jackets," as Cox put it, and drove the Spaniards off.

But only for the buccaneers to face a more persistent enemy: themselves. Once aboard the *Trinity*, they bickered over several issues, not least of which was their next move. All the while, in lieu of leading, Sharp, who was still fuming over the governor's deception, ranted about the "treacherous Spaniards," which, ironically, settled his men on their next move: mutiny.

23

Robinson Crusoe

I N 1966, THE Chilean island of Más a Tierra was renamed Rob-
inson Crusoe Island to celebrate its history: from 1704 to 1709,
Scottish sailor Alexander Selkirk was marooned there, inspiring
Daniel Defoe's 1719 novel. As it happens, Selkirk was the second
man to be stranded there long-term. The first, predating Selkirk
by nearly a quarter century, was a member of the *Trinity* crew.

The story began on December 7, 1680, with the buccaneers
rushing to weigh anchor in La Serena, meanwhile deliberating
about what to do with their Spanish prisoners, who, they feared,
would be inspired by the saboteurs to "plot our destruction in
earnest," as Ringrose put it. Without the Spaniards, he and his
shipmates knew, they would be the blind leading the blind. Nevertheless, they judged it expedient to put Peralta, Argandona,
Juan Moreno, the old Moor, and the rest of the prisoners ashore,
at last giving them their liberty.

Because the buccaneers' hasty departure from La Serena
had precluded reprovisioning, they set a course for Más a Tierra,
450 miles southwest, even farther away from Arica. So low were
their stores that they were forced to reinstitute water rations just
two days into a voyage that would take three weeks — if fortune

Alexander Selkirk on Más a Tierra

smiled on them. For a change, she did. On Friday, December 24, a hot summer day, they sighted Más a Tierra, which they knew by yet another of its names, Isla de Juan Fernández. At eighteen square miles, it was the largest of three islands in the Archipiélago Juan Fernández, named for the first Spanish explorer to land there, in 1574. All the islands were still uninhabited, but as the buccaneers were about to discover, Spanish men-of-war routinely sailed past on patrol.

Aboard the *Trinity*, a ravenous Ringrose studied the archipelago in the hope of spotting fowl or fish. To his dismay, he found nothing more than "a heap of rocks." Dampier was more optimistic. Goats had been brought there a century earlier by Fernández, he knew, and had proliferated.

The next day, December 25, the crew celebrated Christmas with three volleys of shot before anchoring in a bay on Isla de Juan Fernández's southern end. They planned to go ashore to obtain Christmas dinner, but the way was blocked by "multitudes of seals," as Ringrose reported, so many that "we were forced to kill them to set our feet on shoar."

Once on the island, Dampier was impressed by the scenery, including mountainsides that were "part savannahs, part wood land" and soaring cabbage trees that he felt merited several pages of description. On the beaches he was astonished to find a massive creature, twelve to fourteen feet long, "shaped like a seal, but six times as big," with a head "like a lion's" and "a broad face with many long hairs growing about its lips like a cat." The name Dampier came up with for the animal would stick: sea lion. He also discovered that its "lean flesh is black, and of a coarse grain; yet indifferent good food."

Wafer and some of his shipmates, meanwhile, found the descendants of Fernández's goats. Having learned to use the steep mountainside savannahs and woodland to their advantage, the animals presented nearly impossible moving targets. To corral them, the men harnessed another animal roaming the island, one they described as a strange sort of sheep. "His mouth is like that of a hare," wrote Wafer, adding that "his head is much like an antelope, but they had no horns... His ears resemble those of an ass, his neck small, and resembling a camel's. He carries his head bending, and very stately, like a swan." The docile animals — Wafer called them *cornera de terra,* but they are now best known as llamas — consented to being bridled and ridden as though they were horses, allowing the buccaneers to herd and kill sixty of the goats.

Now all the men needed was fresh water. On the morning of December 28, Ringrose was part of an eleven-man team that sailed a pair of canoes to search the island's north side. Quickly finding a source, they filled two hundred jars and returned to their canoes, but violent southerly gusts prevented them from sailing back to the *Trinity*. Without much choice but to wait for the wind to die down, they stayed on shore. While waiting, they were shocked to see the *Trinity* weigh anchor and set sail out of the bay. Possibly the crewmen had spotted a Spanish warship and were now either engaging her or attempting to escape — in both cases, it would be necessary to leave the canoe party behind. Ringrose speculated that the truth was more mundane, that the crew was seeking an anchorage farther from shore, lest the gale thrust the *Trinity* aground. The ship left the bay altogether, though, and from there disappeared.

In hope of a vantage allowing him to figure out what had prompted her flight, Ringrose ventured away from shore in one of the canoes, but the increasingly potent wind and a furious sea forced him back onto the island. He waited until evening before going out for another look, this time along with the entire team, in both canoes. Not only did they fail to sight the *Trinity*, they were also mauled by high winds and a furious sea; it was clear that their very survival hinged on returning to the island at once. The jars of water they'd collected were weighing down the canoes, however. Only after throwing all the jars overboard were they able to reach shore.

With no better option, they banked their canoes for the night and made camp. But to have any hope of sleep, they realized, they would need to distance themselves from the seals. Each of the animals' vocal interactions, however playful, sounded as though they were yelling at one another while jostling for position. Ringrose and his companions did not escape the clamor until they had hiked half a mile inland. Making a new camp, they kindled a fire, dried their clothes, constructed beds of fern, and rested — or tried to. Their hunger and uncertainty, it turned out, were an even greater impediment to sleep than the barking seals.

Then, from seemingly nowhere, a shearwater — a small black-and-white seabird — toppled directly into their fire and burned to death. Ordinarily, hungry men would consider this extraordinary good luck. Seamen, though, ever superstitious, imbued seabirds with a measure of divinity. When birds were in the sky, sailors believed, they communed with angels and thus were privy to future events, such as upcoming storms — the evidence was clear in birds' practice of fleeing in advance of any discernible atmospheric changes. Sailors also maintained that seabirds were the spirits of people lost at sea and that their visits were an excellent omen — even being struck by their droppings was considered a stroke of luck. The killing of such a bird, on the other hand, presaged impending disaster.

With the first spark of sunrise on December 29, Ringrose and his fellow castaways sailed their canoes back to the bay on the off chance that they had been mistaken, that in fact the *Trinity* had not left Isla de Juan Fernández. They soon spotted her — sailing away from the island. Frantically, they raced back to shore to build a bonfire in the hope of signaling their comrades. It worked, and in response a canoe arrived from the *Trinity*, which, it turned out, had indeed been shifting to a safer anchorage on account of the high winds. But to the dismay of the famished castaways, there would be no return to the ship until the winds eased. Fortunately, having anticipated that foul weather might delay the return, the rescue party had brought provisions.

When Ringrose and his companions finally made it back to the *Trinity* the next morning, they found their shipmates in a temperament that matched the foul weather. Ostensibly the trouble was the wind, which had pummeled the rigging and snapped the anchor cable, necessitating difficult repairs. But a deeper problem quickly revealed itself: the crew's long-simmering resentment of

Sharp had reached a boiling point. His seven months as admiral had yielded no significant prizes, much less the £1,000 he'd promised each man. And now he was maintaining that the South Sea jig was up: the Spaniards' general state of readiness negated the element of surprise that had been the company's greatest weapon, he argued. He and his followers sought to cut their losses and return to England via the Strait of Magellan — the 350-mile natural sea channel through Chile, between the South Sea and the Atlantic.

Most of the men wanted to continue pirating, though. The problem, as they saw it, was that Sharp had grown too wealthy by playing dice. He'd won three thousand pieces of eight, according to Cox, his vice admiral and sometime friend. Regarding the debate over continuing the expedition, Cox, who was now opposed to Sharp, wrote, "This fewd was carried on so fiercely that it was very near coming to a civil war, had not some prudent men a little moderated the thing." The "prudent" view, as Cox and two-thirds of the company believed, was to continue pirating. On January 6, they voted to depose Sharp. Next they clapped him into irons and held him prisoner while they voted on his successor. Feeling betrayed, the dethroned admiral would write in his journal that Cox was simply a "dissembling New England man" who "merely for old acquaintance-sake, I had taken... and made my vice-admiral; and not for any valour or knowledge he was possessed of, for of that his share was but small."

The last of the expedition's original five captains, Edmond Cooke, stood to be the new admiral based upon seniority, but likely his brief and troubled tenure as commander of the *Mayflower* weighed against him. In addition, at Isla de Juan Fernández, he was accused by his servant, William Cook (no relation), of sexual misdeeds: Cook said that his master had "oft times buggered him in England, leaving his wife and coming to bed to him," an act that the servant maintained had continued in Jamaica and in the South Sea, before the raid on Panama. Although it varied from crew to crew, pirates tended to be more tolerant of homosexuality than society in general and vastly more tolerant than the Royal Navy, where "if any person in the fleet shall commit the unnatural and detestable sin of buggery or sodomy with man or beast, he shall be punished with death by the sentence of a court-martial." Aboard the *Trinity*, it was not Cooke's buggery but his treachery — which came to light during the company's investigation of him — that was viewed as the greater transgression. As Ringrose related: "Searching his writing, we found a paper with all our names written in it, the which it was suspected he designed to have given unto the Spanish prisoners." Consequently, Cooke was also clapped in irons.

Another candidate for the position of admiral was John Watling, a veteran privateer with a reputation as a rugged and stout seaman. Perhaps foremost among his qualifications was his conviction that the company could still take Arica. In addition, as a religious man, he represented a sorely needed antidote to Sharp. The company voted Watling in, and he immediately set to work straightening them out, casting dice overboard and instituting the weekly observance of the Sabbath, beginning that day, a Sunday. Although they countenanced stealing and killing, a surprising number of buccaneers were Christians, and more than a few were Jewish. Most, though, had no use for God until they were on the gallows. All the men on the *Trinity*, however, were fine with Watling's beliefs — as long as his prayers for a mountain of silver were answered.

On January 12, three days into his tenure as admiral, Watling was put to the test by three large Spanish men-of-war on patrol.

A hunting party on Isla de Juan Fernández first spotted the ships. They instantly dismounted their llamas, raced to their canoes, and shoved off, whipping the sea to froth in their rush to warn the other men. At the same time, they fired their guns into the air — the company's distress signal — spurring a crowd of their shipmates from shore, where they had been cutting wood and washing clothes, back to the anchored *Trinity*.

In half an hour, the Spanish warships were within sight of the bay, at least with the aid of a spyglass, enabling Watling to determine that the biggest of the three was the eight-hundred-ton *El Santo Christo,* mounted with a dozen or more great guns. The second, the six-hundred-ton *San Francisco,* carried at least ten cannons. The buccaneers didn't recognize the third ship, but at 350 tons, although she was slightly smaller than the *Trinity,* she outgunned her eight to none. Watling knew the *Trinity* could sail circles around the Spaniards, allowing the buccaneers to replicate their Panama Bay success. But to do so, they would need to be at sea. If the Spaniards penned the *Trinity* into the bay, she would be unable to outmaneuver them. Accordingly, Watling gave the orders to hoist up the canoes and boats and get under sail as soon as possible.

Because weighing anchor — dislodging the anchor from the sea floor and then hoisting the two- or three-thousand-pound iron bulk onto the vessel to be stowed — could burn half an hour, the crew opted to release the cable, leaving the anchor behind. By necessity, they also left behind the Miskito crewman known as William the Striker. He was hunting goats, it turned out, and had not heard the gunfire signal of his comrades, nor could they find him. As he emerged from the woods and saw, to his horror, the receding silhouette of the *Trinity,* the Spaniards caught sight of him from the decks of their men-of-war and began devising a plan to capture him.

Little is known about William the Striker — not his age, not even his name before the English dubbed him William, if he'd had a name at all. According to Dampier, the Miskito "had no names among themselves and they take it as a great favour to be named by any of us." Now, abandoned on an uninhabited island three thousand miles from home and four hundred miles from the nearest civilization, William's only hope was to survive until his shipmates returned to rescue him. If they returned. And if the Spaniards didn't get to him first.

He began by building himself a hut, choosing a location a mile inland that, he hoped, would be hidden from the view of the Spaniards, who had begun combing the island for him. If they found him, they would kill him — once they had extracted what they could of the buccaneers' Arica plan. William chose a good spot. The Spaniards passed him by and eventually left the island. But they would be back, he was sure.

In the meantime, he turned to home improvements, using goatskin to insulate his hut, upholster a wood-framed couch and bed, and sew blankets, subsisting on goat meat all the while. Once he had used up his musket balls, necessitating that he hunt something else, he carved a series of notches into his knife blade, thereby transforming it into a crude saw, which he used to cut the four-foot-long iron barrel of his musket into smaller pieces. These he heated in his fire until they were malleable, and, hammering them with stones, he forged harpoons, lances, hooks, and a new and longer knife. This arsenal allowed him to hunt seals, whose meat was decidedly not good but whose skins provided the material for new clothing and from whose innards he was able to fashion the fishing line he used to catch the abundant red snappers and groupers he'd seen. The fish were so plentiful, as it happened, that he was able to catch them with a line and hook alone, absent any bait. In an hour, he later figured, he could catch enough to feed fifty men.

More than three years later, on March 23, 1684, William the Striker would prepare such a meal, adding three goats to the menu, when a number of his shipmates indeed returned for him.

The rescue of William the Striker

For now, on January 12, 1681, as soon as the *Trinity* sailed out of the bay, the three Spanish men-of-war ran up their red flags, signifying that no quarter would be given and eliminating the buccaneers' hope that the Spaniards hadn't seen them. To show he was undaunted, Watling responded by hoisting his own red flag. Meanwhile he kept the *Trinity* as close to windward as possible, trying to separate the eight-hundred-ton *Santo Christo* from the others so as to board her without their interference. Clearly wise to this tactic, the men-of-war clung together so that if the *Trinity* were to try to single one of them out, the other two would turn her to flotsam.

Invigorated by the likelihood of a fight and the resulting plunder, the buccaneers looked to Watling in eager anticipation of his revised plan of attack. Their new admiral, however, wanted to advance on Arica — or, per Dick's interpretation, "run for it." Watling, in the interest of at least the semblance of a democratic process, put the matter to the whole crew. Everyone agreed that engaging the Spaniards would at best imperil Arica. And as it transpired, the Spaniards in the warships were similarly "cowardly," in the analysis of the increasingly hawkish Ringrose, who believed they were "as unwilling to engage us as we were to engage them." Rather than pursue the buccaneers, the Spaniards anchored by Isla de Juan Fernández.

Still, as the *Trinity* sailed toward Arica, the crew came to feel that Watling had blinked, a far greater transgression for a pirate captain than wantonly murdering a friar, as Sharp had done. As Ringrose charitably put it, Watling had showed himself to be "faint-hearted." And of greater concern, because Watling was aware that a second such offense would jeopardize his command, he might now be inclined to place valor ahead of discretion. Two weeks later in Arica, that scenario would play out to the letter, when a third of the buccaneers Watling sent into battle wound up as either prisoners or corpses.

24

The Very Illustrious and Royal City of Saint Mark of Arica

THE NATIVES OF the island of Iquique were best known for their bright green teeth, the result of continually chewing on the leaves of the coca plant, the source of cocaine and a minor stimulant in and of itself. The Iquiquans were also known to have excellent intelligence about the Spaniards in Arica, 120 miles north. For that reason, on the afternoon of January 24, Watling and twenty-five of his men left the *Trinity* twelve leagues off the Chilean coast, where she might avoid Spanish detection, and went by canoe to Iquique. Or, rather, they tried to. They couldn't find it, as they reported upon their return to the *Trinity* the next day.

That evening, a second canoe party set out for Iquique. At four the following afternoon, they reappeared with four men they'd taken prisoner on the island — "two old white men and two Indians," according to Ringrose. With the crew gathered around the *Trinity*'s deck, Watling interrogated the prisoners one at a time, beginning with the first of the old men, who described the ways in which Arica had been greatly fortified since the pirates' visit the previous October.

Lies, declared Watling, ordering that the man be shot. The new admiral may have been taking a page from Sharp's book of intimidation tactics. Ironically it was Sharp — freed from his irons now and serving as a mere rank-and-file crewman — who protested most vehemently. Shooting the old man would be cruel, he said, and, on a pragmatic level, rash. The company needed to gather as much information as possible about Arica to formulate a plan to —

A gunshot interrupted Sharp. Quartermaster John Fall lowered his smoking pistol, having carried out Watling's order. The old man fell dead to the deck boards. Turning back to the crew, Sharp said, "Gentlemen, I am clear of the blood of this old man." He stormed across the deck to a water bucket and made a show of washing his hands. "And I will warrant you a hot day for this piece of cruelty, whenever we come to fight at Arica."

Ignoring him, Watling proceeded to interview the second old man, who came off as a better source than the first. The overseer of the governor of Arica's expansive fishing enterprise in Iquique, he was in regular contact with his fellow Spaniards in Arica, the buccaneers learned, and well attuned to the goings-on there. It was true, he told them, that the city had undertaken extensive fortifications since the Englishmen's visit in October, including the placement of twelve copper guns atop the fortress, the addition of three ships and a barque to the port's defenses, and the installation of seven companies of the king's soldiers to man them. The Ariqueños also had taken the precaution of evacuating all their silver, gold, and jewels.

At that point, it would have been reasonable to expect Watling to have the quartermaster dispense another musket ball. The old man implied, however, that he knew where the silver, gold, and jewels had been cached. Intrigued, Watling let him continue. The man told of the two great caches — one ten leagues from Arica, the other twenty-five — before going on to detail exactly how the buccaneers might access them. "All of these things pleased us mighty well to hear," Ringrose wrote in an entry notable for its giddy musings on "rich mines of silver" and "plate, gold, and jewels" and the absence of his old misgivings and anxieties.

Apart from Sharp, whose recalcitrance was written off to his demotion, the rest of the crew shared Ringrose's enthusiasm. Yes, they were aware that the second old man's testimony had been colored by his aversion to having his own blood splattered alongside that of his countryman. But Arica looked to be the buccaneers' last shot at the South Sea and, by extension, the last shot at the wealth necessary to achieve their dreams back in England or abroad. For once, the crew's disparate elements were united into a whole that was greater than the sum of its parts, making the impossible seem possible — a feeling more intoxicating than any coca-plant derivative.

Their conviction was articulated by Watling after he gave the order to "bear up the helm" — to make the *Trinity* run before the wind to Arica. He would have Arica, he swore, or it would have him.

Arica

* * *

At midnight on January 28, several miles off the Chilean coast, Watling, Ringrose, Wafer, Sharp, and 104 more buccaneers boarded the launch, four canoes, and a barque that they had acquired at Iquique, then left the *Trinity* to plunder La Muy Ilustre y Real Ciudad San Marcos de Arica (the very illustrious and royal city of Saint Mark of Arica), as Arica was officially known.

Because their attack plan hinged on seizing Arica's fort, they had taken great care to keep their freshly fabricated hand grenades dry, all but mummifying them in canvas and then waxing the canvas down not once but twice. Beyond that, neither Ringrose nor the other chroniclers described their grenades. The best at the time were cast-iron balls packed with slow-burning gunpowder and topped by a wick. More often, buccaneers used bottles filled with gunpowder and musket balls or other bits of metal. A tin or wooden box or even a gourd could also work as the container. Sometimes, lacking a container, they made grenades by adding musket balls to a handful of pitch and, once the tarlike resin was dry enough, inserting a gunpowder core. Whatever the case, after rowing and sailing through waves and darkness for seven hours, the buccaneers would have no way of knowing whether their waterproofing had been successful until they lobbed the grenades into the fort.

The party landed just before sunrise on the jagged coast of Caleta Vítor, fifteen miles south of Arica, and concealed themselves and their boats among the rocks, which were the size of cathedrals. They stayed there all day, resting as much as they could. At nightfall they returned to the water and headed up the coast as far as the Bay of Chacota, landing on its rocky coast at sunrise the following day, January 30, a date that was especially meaningful to the Englishmen. As Ringrose wrote in the opening of his journal entry, it was "the day that is consecrated in our English calendar unto the martyrdom of the glorious King Charles the first." Thirty-two years earlier, Charles I had been beheaded after a series of struggles following his marriage to a Catholic. The appropriate observance of the anniversary of his martyrdom, Ringrose and company thought, was to wreak havoc on as many Catholics as possible.

From the Bay of Chacota, Watling and ninety-one men — including Ringrose, Sharp, Cox, Povey, and Dick — proceeded on foot toward Arica, which was four miles north. Dampier, currently ascending the Chilean coast aboard the *Trinity,* would play a key role later that day in the company's getaway from Arica. So, too, would Wafer, who was among the fifteen men chosen to stay behind at the Bay of Chacota to guard the boats. If necessary, Wafer's group would also serve as an emergency rescue unit. If they saw a single column of smoke rising from the city or the adjoining fields, they were to send one of the canoes up the coast to Arica. Should they see two columns of smoke, all four canoes and the launch were to go. The code was proprietary — or it should have been. Unfortunately for the buccaneers, the Spaniards would learn of it and use it to wreak havoc of their own.

Watling and his infantry quickly found themselves in a brick-red desertscape topographically reminiscent of a rough sea. Their march was hindered by mountainous sand dunes, dust-clotted air, and fiery solar rays unimpeded by so much as a wisp of a cloud. This was the Atacama, which ranks as the driest nonpolar desert on Earth and would qualify as the driest desert of any sort if not for Antarctica's McMurdo Dry Valleys. Had Ringrose or anyone else in the company known that, he would have brought water along. If old Captain Peralta were still with the company, surely he would have advised taking a calabash or two, the extra weight notwithstanding. As it stood, the deficit would prove critical.

Although difficult to climb, the tall dunes were beneficial insofar as the view they afforded the buccaneers. "We saw from thence no men nor forces of the enemy," wrote Ringrose, "which caused us to hope we were not as yet descryed, and that we should utterly surprize them." Two draining miles later, however, the company spied a lookout post — a trio of sentinels on horseback perched atop a high precipice. If he and his men could capture the sentinels, Watling thought, they could both prevent Arica from being alerted and pick up intelligence on the state of the city's defenses. The problem was, to keep the sentinels from galloping off and alarming the city, the buccaneers would need to shoot them, and the gunshots themselves would alarm the city. The best bet, Watling decided, was to loop around the lookout post.

As the buccaneers proceeded, the barren sierra offered them little in the way of cover. They hoped, though, that the sea of shadows between the dunes would conceal them. But only a few steps into the loop, the three sentinels spotted the party and launched into a full gallop down their dune and toward the city. Watling was undaunted, at least as far as his men could tell. He simply modified the attack plan. Rather than concentrate his full force on the city, he had forty of the ninety-two men branch off to attack the fort directly, hoping they would be able to take it before the sentinels' alert routed so many reinforcements there that the sheer quantity of Spanish musket balls would render the buccaneer grenades inconsequential.

Cox was among the fifty-two-man infantry continuing with Watling into Arica, which proved to be a sixteen-square-block bayside city beautified by willows, fruit trees, and the verdant fields of the Azapa Valley oasis. Perhaps Arica's most striking feature was its backdrop, a sky seemingly too blue to be real, an effect of the utter absence of clouds. Cox was more interested in the city's inhabitants, who, as the invaders neared the town, were milling about outside the breastworks. Why, he wondered, were these Ariqueños standing around outside the fortifications rather than behind them? Had the sentinels failed to warn them? The answer came when the Ariqueños started toward him, not only fully prepared but also possessing an overwhelming numerical superiority. There were hundreds of them. Cox, who'd had the misfortune of participating in Sawkins's failed raid of Pueblo Nuevo, must have felt a sense of déjà vu.

Ringrose, meanwhile, was part of the unit tasked with attacking the fort, which stood adjacent to the city at the base of the Morro de Arica, a 450-foot-high trapezoidal rock overlooking the port. Glinting on top of the rock were the dozen copper cannons the supposedly mendacious old man from Iquique had warned of. With them, the Ariqueños would have no difficulty reducing to toothpicks the barque from Iquique, now on her way up the coast to rendezvous with the invasion force after the raid and haul their plunder out to the *Trinity*. Taking the fort, therefore, was crucial for the buccaneers.

The fort ought to have been a small, crumbling adobe building, like so many other defensive installations on the coast of the Spanish Main. In fact, that was exactly what it had been before a wealthy Portuguese civilian, Manuel Rodríguez, met, fell in love with, and married a Spanish woman. In 1643, in exchange for Spanish citizenship, Rodríguez agreed to pay eighteen thousand pieces of eight to replace Arica's old adobe fort with a new one made of stone. If the buccaneers were to breach Rodríguez's construction, their grenadiers first needed to get close enough to lob their grenades through its crenels, the squared notches in the parapet. The explosions would clear away defenders, allowing the raiders to climb over the parapet and access the roof.

The hard part was getting close enough to the fort through the tempest of Spanish musket balls and, potentially, grenades. (The job of grenadier was so risky that the articles for Morgan's Panama raid had promised five pieces of eight to each man who so much as threw a grenade at the enemy.) When the buccaneers did manage to toss their grenades through the crenels and into the fort, the devices failed to explode, either on account of dampness or poor construction or simply because the enemy defused them. Consequently, Ringrose and his cohorts were left in a firefight with Spanish soldiers who were shooting down from high stone walls that, unlike the Santa Maria garrison's palisades, could not simply be wrenched apart.

The buccaneers' attempt to formulate an alternative plan was interrupted by distant gunshots, so many and so frequent that the reports blended into a continuous thunderclap. Through a haze of gun smoke, Ringrose saw Watling's force not only being repelled from the city but also on the verge of being annihilated by as many as five hundred Ariqueños. Abandoning the attack on the fort, Ringrose and company sprinted downhill toward the city to help their comrades, meanwhile firing their muskets into the enemy's flank. They succeeded in driving the attacking Ariqueños back to their breastworks. The retreat proved fortuitous for those Ariqueños, because they were able to regroup and incorporate the influx of reinforcements before returning, emboldened, to the fray.

At the base of the hill, Ringrose found himself in the midst of a smoky, bloody, and "very desperate" battle. The Ariqueños, he gathered, had not only halted the advance, they had also killed three of the buccaneers and wounded two more. And that was just the beginning of the bad news. A man who surrendered to the buccaneers during the fighting told them that the Ariqueños had been girding for this battle for three days, ever since hearing of the Englishmen's appearance on Iquique. Immediately, the Ariqueños had assigned six hundred Spanish soldiers to guard the city proper and three hundred more to the fort. And in the days since, they had mustered another four hundred soldiers from Lima, who brought along arms for seven hundred Ariqueños. If those figures were accurate — and they seemed to be, based on what Ringrose had already witnessed — the buccaneers were now outnumbered twenty to one.

But whereas their infantry, a moment earlier, had been an incoming musket ball away from turning and running into the Atacama for their lives, now, with the infusion of the forty men from the fort, Watling was able to avail himself of their world-class marksmanship, and, as a result, the buccaneers advanced, steadily. Until suddenly given pause by a series of distant deep-throated booms that was in turn drowned out, an instant later, by the singularly stomach-turning raspy buzz of twenty-something-pound cast-iron balls descending at speeds in excess of a hundred miles per hour. Each ball was able to turn a man to pulp if it struck him — and, even if it landed a dozen feet away from him, still able to kill him by driving enough kinetic energy into the ground to transform rocks or shards of clay into bullets.

The balls came from the twelve copper cannons atop the Morro de Arica — the very guns the forty reinforcements had been originally tasked with neutralizing. If the buccaneers were to retreat toward the Atacama now, they would provide the cannoneers clear shots. If they attempted to maintain their position, they would be pummeled. The city, however, was out of the cannoneers' range. So the buccaneers had all the more reason to advance, as soon as possible.

Plunging into a cloud of bitter gun smoke buzzing with musket balls, they reached the breastworks. But, as Ringrose reported, "The enemy made several retreats unto several places, from one breastwork to another." Ringrose and his companions found themselves under fire from every angle, too many angles to cover. They tried anyway, but no sooner did they drive the defenders away from one section than fresh defenders sprang up in their place, in greater number. The same dynamic repeated itself for several hours, during which the sun, sand, and thirst ravaged the buccaneers. The Ariqueño gunfire was worse, killing as many as seven of the company. "But our rage increasing with our wounds, we still advanced," said Ringrose, "and at last beat the enemy out of all, and filled every street in the city with dead bodies."

Indeed, a postmortem written by an anonymous Ariqueño described the Englishmen "advancing with superhuman vigour, with the ferocity and fury of lions, fighting with feigned contempt for all risks and mocking death." Many of the Ariqueños cried for quarter. Some were denied it vindictively, thanks to the belief, expressed by Cox, that they were "men that never give it themselves." But most cries for quarter "our unwary commander too readily granted." Cox worried that having so many prisoners would prove unmanageable.

As the buccaneers advanced farther, the gunfire quieted and the air cleared enough to give them an unobstructed view of the stunning city that, against all odds, they now controlled. Only mastery of the fort stood between them and total victory.

With the fighting in the city tapering, the men turned their attention to Arica's hidden treasure caches. "Gentlemen, I know you are men come to seek a fortune," they were told by one of their prisoners, a Spanish captain seeking to curry their favor. "If you want money or plate, come along with me, I will show you where there is more than you all can carry away." Watling already knew where the money was, thanks to the old man from Iquique whose life he'd spared. But if the old man had been either mistaken or dissembling, or if the money had since been relocated, this Spaniard could be worth his weight in silver, provided he was telling the truth.

Before Watling could entertain the offer, though, he needed to neutralize the fort, lest he and his men load their barque with silver only to have the cannoneers sink it. He sent word to the fort demanding that the soldiers there surrender. No response came, suggesting to Cox that the soldiers were stalling for reinforcements. If that were the case, then by waiting any longer Watling would be playing into their hands. But to Cox's frustration, Watling not only continued to wait but also wasted time securing prisoners and assigning guards. With more prisoners than men of their own, Cox saw an administrative nightmare, at best.

Not until a full hour had passed without word from the Spaniards did Watling go in person to the fort, bringing the men he hadn't assigned to guard duty, including Cox, who was at once grateful to finally be advancing on the fort and furious that the company had waited so long to do so. His ire grew as the fort came into view, brimming with Spanish musketeers.

The buccaneers were hardly in any condition to take on even half as many Spaniards, having had nothing to eat or drink since early that morning. From the high vantage of the fortress grounds, however, they could see that the surrounding Azapa Valley was alive with Spanish reinforcements on their way into the city. The attack of the fort had to happen now or never.

Watling used the glut of prisoners to the buccaneers' advantage. As Dick explained, "We placed some of these prisoners before the front of our men, when we assaulted the castle, just as Sir Henry Morgan did the nuns and friars at Portobelo." To repel the buccaneers, the musketeers in the fort would have to shoot through their own countrymen — likely friends, in many cases, and possibly family. To the buccaneers' surprise, the musketeers in the fort fired indiscriminately. Still the prisoners, as human shields, provided the buccaneers cover, allowing them to get close enough to the fort to lob their second round of hand grenades. It was no more effective than the first round, though. Again, not a single grenade exploded.

To remove the parapet from the equation, Watling had his men climb onto the flat roof of a nearby house, which gave them the height to fire down into the crowded fortress. From it, the buccaneer sharpshooters felled Spaniard after Spaniard, soon placing victory within their grasp — until the four-hundred-man detachment of Spanish soldiers from Lima poured into the city. Swarming the house, the soldiers forced Watling and company to postpone their assault of the fort in order to defend themselves. Although the roof gave the buccaneers the high ground, like most residential roofs it lacked a parapet, making them open targets.

With the enemy's "numbers and vigour increasing every moment," Watling ordered a retreat — to the downtown church he had repurposed as the company's field hospital. Once there, he felt, he and his men might shore up their control of the city and regroup. Providing cover fire for one another, they descended the roof and reached the ground safely. But the route to the church, along which unseen enemies fired from within buildings, was more perilous. By now dehydration also impeded the buccaneers, significantly: a two-hundred-pound man who sweats away ten pounds over five hours of typical marching and fighting, much less in the Atacama desert, can expect a 30 percent reduction in foot speed as well as muscle cramps, diminished reaction time, and dangerous balance deficits.

During this scramble, Watling was shot "in the reins," as Cox put it — an archaic expression for the loins predicated on the notion that they controlled human passions — and fell dead short of the church. Another buccaneer, a Black slave whom Watling had freed in Jamaica, had one of his legs shot out from beneath him. The Ariqueños swarmed the man, offering him quarter on the spot. By way of refusal, he shot and killed four or five of them before a Spanish musket ball ended his life, and not in vain, judging by the inspiration his heroic stand provided his comrades.

Cox and Ringrose were among the seventy who made it to the church — just in time for the cannon crews up on the Morro to upend the notion that Spaniards were averse to firing at their own churches. In the city streets, meanwhile, more than a thousand armed Ariqueños and soldiers added to a rain of projectiles that blew out the church's windowpanes and forced the buccaneers to dive for cover, blindly, since the air was so thick with plaster dust and gun smoke that they could scarcely see one another.

The buccaneers' three battlefield surgeons, meanwhile, were unable to manage all the wounded, less a result of the influx of casualties than an influx of the church's communion wine, with which the trio had celebrated the buccaneers' victory, prematurely. And unfortunately, they'd drunk all of it, because their comrades now were, like Ringrose, "extream faint for want of water and victuals, whereof we had had none all that day." Added Povey, "So many of our party being almost choked for water made use of their owne." In other words, they drank their own urine, which is inadvisable: urine's salinity is comparable to seawater's, and it carries waste products that can cause low blood pressure and organ failure. On balance, though, those men were fortunate. At least ten of the company were dead, including both quartermasters and the boatswain, leaving the company without leadership. Another eighteen men lay, in Ringrose's words, "desperately wounded."

Smelling blood, the Spanish soldiers streamed out of the fort and into the city, joining the mob closing in on the church. As what amounted to a human noose tightened around the building, Ringrose, who reflected that Sharp's warning of a hot day in Arica had been prophetic, was among several buccaneers to turn to their former admiral. Sharp was a natural, if flawed, leader and a capable tactician. Also, as they saw it, he was their lone chance of escaping this cataclysm alive. But initially he ignored their entreaties, in part because he was preoccupied with returning Spanish fire and mostly because he was still stung by their mutiny. The men redoubled their supplications.

Sharp said nothing for a long time, then began issuing orders. His plan was simple: retreat. He divided the forty-seven healthy men into an advance guard, flankers, supports, and a rear guard, and he ordered the three surgeons to evacuate the wounded. The surgeons refused not only to help but also to leave; they were too drunk. In Sharp's experience, this was not entirely unusual. When Henry Morgan's ship the *Oxford* caught fire, in 1669, several of the three hundred fatalities were buccaneers who might have disembarked but were simply too inebriated.

Leaving behind the surgeons — and, by necessity, some of the wounded — Sharp and the advance guard shot their way out of the church. The other units hurried into the street behind them, the rear guard with muskets blazing, keeping the Ariqueños back. Fire continued to pelt the retreating buccaneers — musket balls bored channels through the dusty air around them as they shot and slashed their way out of Arica — but the onslaught was not enough to adequately suppress their own fire. Their objective was to reach the savannah at the city's edge, where they could position themselves with the sea to their backs and, using trees and rises in the land as protection, keep the enemy at bay long enough for Wafer and the boat party — with the launch and four canoes — to come to the rescue.

In a measure of either their extraordinary luck or their enemy's poor marksmanship, they emerged from the city without sustaining a single gunshot wound. The Ariqueño mob followed them onto the savannah, shooting incessantly. Although off target, the efforts necessary to rebuff the deluge prevented the buccaneers from starting a fire to summon the boats. But someone else had already lit a fire to summon the boats, Ringrose realized, stricken with horror at the sight of twin columns of smoke rising from the city. The only conclusion was that the drunken surgeons, under duress or otherwise, had relayed the distress signals to the Spaniards, who would now ambush the rescue party.

Aboard the *Trinity,* well offshore, Dampier read the two ribbons of smoke from Arica as the distress signal, but something seemed odd — the spacing between them, perhaps. Suspecting that the Spaniards themselves had set the fires, he advocated for the *Trinity* to sit tight rather than enter the port. In the boats, however, Wafer and company suspected nothing and raced into their own hell.

Back on the outskirts of the city, a fresh company of Spanish horsemen thundered across the savannah toward the forty-seven buccaneers — and, oddly, past them. The reason soon became gut-wrenchingly clear to Sharp and company: the horsemen sought to block the buccaneers' way to the shore, forcing them onto the open field to face an onslaught of soldiers, all 1,200 of whom were fighting together now, under the direction of a Spanish general. According to Povey, the general sat on a horse atop the Morro de Arica, where, with a perfect view of the entire city, he waved his handkerchief to position his troops, all the while crying out, "Valiente soldados, buina valienta soldados." Added Povey, "Some of our peopple passed a shott att him but could not have the fortune to hitt him."

Sharp was now out of tactical gambits. Still, he saw a path forward: go out in a blaze of glory, taking along as many Spaniards as possible. The prospect galvanized Cox, Povey, Dick, and even Ringrose, who burned "to revenge the defeat and disappointment we had received." The onetime straitlaced purser was now a stalwart member of the band he'd initially scorned as "wild men." Placing a higher value on their brotherhood than on any amount of silver, gold, and jewels, or even the prospect of his own survival, he joined them in "resolving to die one by another."

The forty-seven men formed a circle around their wounded, turned to face the sea of soldiers, and, one last time, raised their muskets and fired with hellish precision. Everywhere, Spaniards fell, dispersing the survivors, but only for a few seconds before they regrouped and renewed their charge. In those seconds, the buccaneers reloaded and delivered a second volley, sending several more of the enemy into the next world and staggering the remainder.

The Spaniards began to retreat, taking shelter behind their breastworks. This presented an escape route, as though the sea had parted. Sharp ordered the men to take it — quickly, because the company of horsemen was racing to block them. The buccaneers sprinted, and as they neared the bay, Sharp directed them onto a boulder-strewn stretch of coastline that the men on horses would be unable to navigate.

Upon reaching the narrow sandy beach, Ringrose realized that the Spaniards' counterfeit distress signal had been a stroke of luck: Wafer and the rest of the boat party were now waiting at the water's edge.

25

The Itch

I HOPE IT WILL not be esteemed a vanity in me," Sharp wrote after returning to the *Trinity*, "to say that I was mighty helpful to facilitate this retreat, which brought my men to recollect a better temper, and unanimously on getting to our ship, to restore me to my command again." On January 31, he began his second stint as admiral by sailing the *Trinity* to and fro in plain view of the Ariqueños, with the objective of baiting them to "send out the three ships we had seen in the harbour to fight us," according to Ringrose, who, like Sharp, burned for retribution. Damnably, the ships stayed put.

Cooler heads, including Dampier and Wafer, were relieved. As they saw it, the South Sea was about to be brought to a boil with Spanish men-of-war seeking to finish the company off. They wanted to get out while there was still a chance. (Ringrose's thoughts on these and other topics over the following few months are largely unknown, because he fell ill on February 1 and ceased journaling almost completely for a time.) The matter of next steps was decided in council, where the majority declared themselves satisfied with the amount of plunder taken. Traditionally, such a declaration marked the end point of a pirate cruise. The men decided to reprovision at — i.e., raid — the small port town of Huasco, 650 miles south of Arica, before returning to the North Sea via the Darien.

Faring reasonably well against their familiar foes the southeast trade wind and the Peru Current, they landed at Huasco six weeks later, on March 12, and faced little resistance there, garnering fruit, vegetables, 120 sheep, eighty goats, and five hundred jars of fresh water. The sailing on their return north was their best to date: for once the southeast trade wind and Peru Current were working for them. At the rate they were traveling — nearly 150 miles per day — they would reach the Darien Isthmus in less than three weeks.

As the wounds from Arica healed, however, they felt an itch to repeat their Huasco success. On March 17, when they had traveled seven hundred miles up the South American coast without seeing so much as a glint of a man-of-war's sail, the itch intensified, and one of the buccaneers floated the idea of stopping at Ilo to "reprovision" once again. Why Ilo, of all places? his shipmates wondered. Wouldn't the town be especially on guard against pirates, having been raided just a few months ago? But after discussion, everyone agreed that Ilo was the perfect choice. Who would ever expect them to raid it a second time?

Not the Iloans, as it transpired. Sharp and company attacked them on the night of March 27, literally catching the town asleep and taking it without having to fire a single shot. The victory only exacerbated the buccaneers' itch and increased their appetite for plunder. It also led them to question the rumors they'd heard — of the viceroy of Peru's new pirate-hunting armada, of gallows being erected with their names on them, and of soldiers from all corners of the Spanish Empire streaming into the South Sea to capture them.

They put the question to the Iloans, who reported hearing that many of the buccaneers captured in Arica had been, as Cox put it, "knockt on the head" — a euphemism for executed. But not, evidently, the three surgeons. Prized for their medical skill, they were given quarter in exchange for telling their captors everything they knew, including that the company was planning to leave the South Sea via the Strait of Magellan (which, at the time of the battle, was accurate). The bloodied buccaneers had indeed sailed south from Arica, evidently leading the Spaniards to conclude that their pirate problem was solved and, as a result, to let down their guard. The Iloans had heard absolutely nothing of a concerted Spanish antipirate effort since then. To Sharp's way of thinking, the South Sea was again open for business. Most of his men remained circumspect, though; if he were to alter the *Trinity*'s course, he would risk another mutiny.

The next thirty days, during which the *Trinity* traveled more than a thousand miles, were completely free of Spanish warship sightings. Their absence won Sharp several converts, including Dick and Cox. From their perspective, even if the Spaniards deployed every last one of their warships and *avisos* — reconnaissance boats — the *Trinity* was still a moving target in a stretch of sea the size of Europe. Worst-case scenario, if the Spaniards found her, she could always outrun them. A group Dampier characterized as "the abler and more experienced men" disagreed. The worst-case scenario, they maintained, was another Arica, in which the Spanish force would zero in on them while they were on land.

Arica had been a miscalculation, admitted Sharp's supporters, whom Dampier described as "the meaner sort." To Captain Sharp's credit, they said, he had argued vociferously against raiding Arica. By paying greater heed to intelligence going forward, this faction maintained, the buccaneers could home in on the right — i.e., lightly guarded — Spanish target. A single score of 100,000 pieces of eight, hardly a stretch, would mean a share of a thousand pieces of eight for each of the remaining men. But there was no evidence to support this hope, the experienced men argued. The company's presence in the South Sea for nearly a year now had resulted in every single piece of eight being evacuated or hidden in caches. Exactly, came the retort, and those caches were opportunities.

And so the debate roiled on, dominating every otherwise uneventful waking moment. On April 17, with the ship again on the brink of civil war, Cox assembled all the men and laid out Captain Sharp's proposal that the company continue the cruise, striking at Spanish ships until each and every man was satisfied with his share. Povey, impressed with Sharp's sworn promise — to "doe the uttmost of his power to gett money enough" and not to leave "till every man is willing" — was among those persuaded to stay in the South Sea. Dampier and Wafer, too, had come around to the idea of continuing, but not with Sharp as captain. Yes, he was a capable tactician — his orchestration of the escape from Arica was a good example — but he was a poor leader. Consequently, the pair gravitated toward the experienced men who were "altogether dissatisfied with Sharp's former conduct." At the same time, Dampier marveled at the fact that, just a short while earlier, the meaner sorts now backing Sharp had been the loudest in calling for his ouster.

The two factions could not be reconciled. They agreed, though, to take a vote: Whoever had the majority would keep the ship, and the others would depart in the longboat and canoes. The result was a victory for the Sharp party, placing Dampier and Wafer among the forty-seven men who would leave the *Trinity.*

"This was a great weakning to our party, and a hindrance to our designs," wrote Cox, one of the fifty-four to sixty men remaining. "Nevertheless we bore our loss as chearfully as we could, and resolved not to quit those coasts till we had got the booty we expected." Those men "did fully resolve, and faithfully promise to each other, they would stick close together," added Ringrose, who was now among them.

Their persistence was about to pay off.

Part III

Straits

26

Expect to Be Shot to Death

THE BREAKAWAY PARTY had one notable rule: "If any man faultred in the journey over land, he must expect to be shot to death." The reason, Dampier explained, was that the Spaniards were sure to track them into the jungle, and "one man falling into their hands might be the ruin of us all." He agreed to abide by the rule. As did the young and hale Wafer, never imagining that he might come to regret it.

As their leader, the "abler and more experienced men" comprising the party chose John Cook (unrelated to William Cook, the servant who had accused Edmond Cooke of sodomy), a Caribbean native born to English parents on the island of St. Christopher. Originally a respectable merchant captain, Cook had been forced to abandon his ship in 1679 near Curaçao (off the Venezuelan coast) in order to escape Spanish *guardacosta* cruisers. Dampier, who was typically sparing with praise, wrote that Cook was "very intelligent" and "sensible."

Twelve leagues northwest of Isla de la Plata (near the equator), on the morning of April 17, 1681, the Cook party prepared to leave the *Trinity*. In parting amicably from the contingent remaining aboard the ship, the forty-seven members of the breakaway party secured ample provisions, including flour, chocolate, and sugar. They also took five of the enslaved men — a portion of their expedition share. To attempt to cross the Darien Isthmus, they first needed to travel two hundred leagues by sea in a motley fleet consisting of a longboat and two canoes, one of which had recently been sawed in half so that it could be repurposed as bumkins, "vessels for carrying water" — this according to Dampier, who was the lone man to chronicle the saga of the breakaway party. At ten o'clock that morning, having patched the second canoe into watertightness and rigged it with sails, those men boarded their dubious craft and shoved off.

At first there was too little wind to sail, but at noon, when it was already too late for them to return to the *Trinity*, the wind grew strong enough to demonstrate the folly of attempting two hundred leagues of high seas in patchwork canoes. The launch, too, was threatening to founder. To keep her afloat, the men cut up an old dry hide and strategically wrapped it around the hull. It worked, and by nightfall the fleet had covered some fifty miles.

A harrowing, tempestuous night gave way to another too-calm day that brought into view an even greater peril, a Spanish barque. Determining that the ship was sitting at anchor — near Cape Pasado, about twenty miles below the equator — Cook began to see her as an opportunity. He sailed into the bay for a better look, establishing that she was carrying timber and that most of her crew had gone ashore — without accounting for the possibility of pirates drifting past. An attempt to take her carried risks beyond those of fighting her remaining crew — another of the breakaway party's guiding principles was to steer clear of Spaniards whenever possible. But the barque could provide a significant fleet upgrade as well as excellent cover for the duration of the sea voyage: to outward appearances, the buccaneers would be humdrum Spanish timber merchants. They attacked and boarded the vessel, coming away with not only their desired upgrade but also several Spanish prisoners who could provide them with vital intelligence.

Over the next six days, they sailed the new barque 250 miles before stopping at their former haunt, the island of Gorgona, for water and some necessary maintenance. As ever, the island was a snake-infested hellhole, for which reason they were astounded to find a newly constructed house large enough to accommodate a hundred people. Spaniards, the buccaneers assumed, based on the great cross hanging over the entrance. The buccaneers' prisoners, meanwhile, knew exactly what the house was: a barracks for Spanish soldiers. No doubt hoping that the soldiers would appear and hang the Englishmen, the prisoners said nothing.

Only after Cook and company established that the house was vacant and the information became capital did the prisoners "happen to remember" that Spanish soldiers had recently begun coming to Gorgona from the mainland every two or three days with the expectation that the Englishmen would, at some point, return to careen. Upon sighting them, the soldiers were to carry the news with all haste to Panama, where a trio of pirate-hunting warships lay at the ready.

The buccaneers consequently cut their Gorgona stay short, leaving the next day, April 25, which brought heavy rain. With it came a reminder that the region was entering the rainy season, which would make the trek across the Darien highly problematic. For now, though, between the weather and the Spaniards, they would be happy just to reach the Darien. Over the following few days, "excessive showers of rain" soaked them. On April 28, the rain gave way to a haze through which they sighted a pair of vessels five miles west. According to the prisoners, these were

Spanish warships on patrol between Gorgona and the Gulf of Panama, with 350 men and thirty guns between them.

Should the warships give chase, the buccaneers resolved to run their barque ashore and take to the mountains; they would be plunging into an unfamiliar and particularly inhospitable stretch of jungle, but at least they would have a chance of survival. Luckily, they didn't have to follow through on their escape plan; the Spanish warships continued ahead. Either the haze had veiled their barque or their Spanish-merchantman cover had worked. Whatever the reason, they were profoundly relieved.

On April 30, thirteen days after departing the *Trinity*, they came within sight of the Gulf of San Miguel, where they had emerged from the Santa Maria River after their successful raid of the town of Santa Maria a year earlier. Now the river was their escape route. Unfortunately, as their scouting party discovered, the mouth of the river was guarded by a Spanish ship brimming with soldiers. When the scouts returned to the barque and delivered the news, the rest of the men were, predictably, disheartened. They clung to the hope, however, that the Spanish ship would move on.

This time with Dampier along, the scouting party canoed back to the river mouth. Not only were the Spaniards still there, they also spotted the buccaneers, as became clear to Dampier and the other scouts when three men leaped into a canoe and raced toward them. The scouts fled at once, rounding a small island to escape their trackers' view, then banking the canoe and finding places to hide on shore. To their pursuers, the buccaneers hoped, it would appear that they had continued into the gulf. Their pursuers headed straight for the island, however, and hurried ashore. Dampier and the others waited breathlessly in the hiding spots as the three Spaniards crunched their way through the underbrush, as if they knew exactly where to find their quarry. In moments they were within seventy-five yards — pistol range for the buccaneers, who ambushed them, taking all three men without having to fire a shot.

Hoping to learn the Spaniards' plans, the scouts set to examining their new captives. The Spanish ship and her 150 men had been stationed at the mouth of the river for six months, the captives said, for the express purpose of intercepting English pirates returning to the North Sea. And another three hundred men would be joining them within a day. Worse, from the standpoint of a party in desperate need of guides to help them cross the isthmus, the Natives in the area were now cooperating with the Spaniards. In sum, the breakaway party would not be taking the Santa Maria River.

When the scouts returned to the barque with this news, the company quarreled over where to go instead. Dampier proposed the Río Congo, just ten miles west, at the cusp of the gulf. None of his shipmates had heard of it. Its mouth was near Point San Lorenzo, he reminded them, where Baz Ringrose's canoe had been captured and then released by Spanish soldiers. By taking the Río Congo, Dampier went on, they could canoe across much of the isthmus rather than fight the jungle. To his extreme frustration, he not only failed to persuade the others to take the route, he couldn't convince them that such a river existed.

The group compromised, deciding to cross the isthmus by land farther up the coast. After sailing overnight — passing the mile-wide mouth of the Río Congo, to Dampier's consternation — they landed four miles past Point San Lorenzo, where the jungle was so formidable that, a year earlier, the buccaneers had judged leaving the Spaniards there tantamount to marooning them. Now, having packed up their clothes and provisions, Cook and company began a jungle trek that was fifty miles longer than the route Dampier had proposed. And it would make their last two weeks at sea seem like a pleasure cruise.

Aware that they stood no chance of reaching the North Sea without a guide, the Cook party's immediate aim was to spot a hut, even though they could not be certain they wouldn't be greeted with poisoned blow darts or arrows. But they encountered nothing other than trees and torrential rain, falling as though the storm clouds had split in half. Tree limbs shaken loose by the high winds dropped all around them. At the same time, the slower men fretted over the company's agreement to execute anyone unable to keep pace. As it transpired, after a year aboard a ship, on a starvation diet much of the time, all the men lacked the physical conditioning for any kind of extended foray, much less a trek through some of the most difficult jungle terrain on the planet. They were better off, Cook decided, building huts and waiting out the storm.

They did so, and the next morning the skies cleared enough for them to resume their search for a guide. Happening on a path, they followed it and were brought to a small Native village. (As usual, the chroniclers gave no more specificity than "Indian," but likely it was Kuna.) The villagers seemed hospitable, the women welcoming the buccaneers with calabashes brimming with the beerlike chicha co-pah and the men forthcoming with details of a capable guide. One of the men offered, in exchange for a hatchet, to show the buccaneers the way to the guide's house. They accepted, and the following morning, the party set out on a hilly eight-mile march.

Again, some of the men lagged, and the slowest decided he

would be better off left to his own devices in the jungle; there, at least, he had a chance of survival. As Dampier related, he "gave us the slip." The party could only hope that a jaguar found him before the Spaniards did.

It took the remaining men the better part of the day to reach the guide's house, which sat on a bank of the Río Congo. Unlike the villagers, the guide spoke "very good Spanish," but unfortunately he claimed to know of no way from there to the North Sea. This raised Dampier's suspicion, which was validated when the man offered to lead the party instead to Santa Maria, where, he no doubt knew, the Spaniards would pay him handsomely for delivering the Englishmen. But while the buccaneers weren't about to head to Santa Maria, they had no other option for a guide, so they attempted to win him over. They succeeded only in angering him. He was "not their friend," he declared.

Hoping his friendship was for sale, they offered him a combination of beads, money, hatchets, machetes, and cutlasses — almost everything in their possession — yet he was unmoved. His wife, however, had taken a fancy to a sky-colored petticoat in one of the buccaneer's bags. Following a heated discussion with her husband, the woman obtained a new petticoat and the Cook party a guide — who suddenly remembered a way north across the isthmus. He also remembered, however, that he had a foot injury precluding so long a trek. But if he could keep the petticoat, he said, he would give the Indian who'd brought them instructions for a two-day march to the home of yet another guide. This man, he assured them, would be able to take them to the North Sea.

It was hard to imagine a more dubious proposition, but as the buccaneers saw it, their only other option was to turn back to the South Sea, which could mean running smack into the enemy, now almost certainly on their trail. Although they had sunk their barque at Point San Lorenzo, given the rampant opportunism they had so far witnessed in this part of the Darien, it was hard to imagine their story had not been sold to the Spaniards. They paid their original guide in the form of another hatchet and, eager to distance themselves from the Spaniards, once again followed him into the jungle.

The next morning, which was clear, became a rainy afternoon, but the men barely noticed, because every fifteen minutes they needed to cross a river in order to advance. The next day, the breakaway party's fourth in the Darien, the rain was more noticeable, lashing the men all afternoon and most of the night. Meanwhile, the mud either slowed or, far worse, during steep descents, accelerated their pace. The small crude huts they built to sleep in failed to keep out the water, turning the act of kindling even a small fire into an ordeal and making it impossible to dry their clothes or warm themselves. This might have been tolerable if not for the painful emptiness of their bellies. The downpour did have one upside, as Dampier related: "The Spaniards were seldom in our thoughts."

The conditions also made it difficult to keep gunpowder dry, ordinarily a minor problem but in this instance one that drastically altered the course of Lionel Wafer's life. He happened to be sitting on the ground near a buccaneer who was drying out gunpowder on a silver plate. When another man passed by with a lit pipe, a bit of smoldering tobacco fell from its bowl, just a crumb, but enough that, on impact, the gunpowder blew up and the resulting fireball leaped at Wafer, engulfing his knee and devouring so much of the tissue that the kneecap was not just exposed but also left bare. By the time he escaped the flames, much of his thigh was severely burned as well, and up and down his leg the flesh was decimated.

Wafer's medical kit contained salves and disinfectants, allowing him to treat the wound. But even walking was excruciating, as was the prospect of continuing for days on end through harsh jungle. Reflecting on the rule of the expedition, he was forced to confront the very real possibility that one of his companions might prescribe a bullet for him. With that in mind, he wrote, "I made hard shift to jog on." But, ironically, it was the accident that made him indispensable to the company, because it reminded the men that they needed a doctor.

To aid Wafer's trekking, Dampier recorded, the company "allowed him a slave to carry his things." Each enslaved man was already carrying the belongings of at least one buccaneer, which made advancing through the jungle — hard in the best of circumstances — a torment. The cataracts of rain and sucking mud made the task even more difficult, and the additional weight of the medical kit worse still. During the night, as Dampier wrote, "We always kept two men on the watch; otherwise our own slaves might have knockt the head while we slept." Little wonder.

Despite the men on watch, that night four of the company's five slaves managed to elude detection and run away, taking with them Wafer's musket, the pieces of eight constituting his entire expedition share, and, as he realized when it came time to change his bandages, his medical kit, which, as he wrote, "thereby left me deprived of the wherewithal to dress my sore" and treat the pain. One way or another, it seemed, he would be leaving the party. For the time being, he forced himself onward, keeping pace with the two other stragglers: Robert Spratlin, a mariner, and William Bowman, a onetime tailor considered a "weakly man."

While an improvised cane could help Wafer keep his weight off the injured leg, it could also be an impediment — for example, during the repeated crossings of the potent Río Congo, when he needed to plant the implement in unsteady silt while withstanding the onslaught of the current. During one such river crossing, on the party's eighth day in the jungle, the current bowled over buccaneer George Gayny, and the brown water swallowed him entirely. His companions couldn't find him, and, with no other choice, they trudged on, speculating that he had been held underwater by his heavy backpack, the contents of which included three hundred pieces of eight, a weight of nearly twenty pounds. The theft of Wafer's own share of the plunder had at least relieved him of the concern that he would meet the same fate.

Finally, the buccaneers met and hired their new guide — remarkably, without a hitch — an old man who seemed capable yet knew no way of circumventing the river. So the buccaneers gritted their teeth and slogged on, with no real idea of where they were or how far they had to go, spending much of that day and the next in rivers, all the time in rain — "extraordinary hard rain," as Dampier put it, "with much lightning and terrible claps of thunder." There was no point keeping watch. No one could sleep.

On the tenth day of the isthmus crossing, on the bank of an especially violent stretch of river, Wafer and his fellow stragglers, Spratlin and Bowman, watched the guide and the rest of the party cross without incident. Wafer attempted to go next. No sooner did he wade in, however, than the current hit him like a stampede, plunging him into blackness and firing him downriver, seemingly toward oblivion. Meanwhile his gaping wound and exposed kneecap were stabbed by fallen tree branches and the jagged rocky river bottom.

An eddy at a bend in the river enabled him to regain enough control to winch himself ashore. He didn't complain afterward, however, writing only, "I got over." Just witnessing the incident, however, was horrific enough for Spratlin and Bowman to decide to stay put and abandon the party, an option afforded them only by the raging river between them and the men who would otherwise have shot them as deserters. Wafer, now utterly incapable of proceeding, was not so fortunate.

27

The Pyre

THE SIXTY BUCCANEERS still at sea in May of 1681 were faring somewhat better than those in the Darien. "Our company and forces were extremely weakened," Dick wrote of the *Trinity* crew, "but our hearts as yet were good; and though we had met with many disappointments in several places, yet we hoped that at last, by some means or other, we should attain the ends of our desires, which was to enrich ourselves."

In Ringrose's analysis, "The greatest part of our attempts on land had proved hitherto very unsuccessful." Sharp concurred. He proposed shifting their attention to merchant vessels, allowing them to maintain their strategic advantages and avoid ambush. The rest of the men agreed, and the company decided to focus on the commercial shipping zone just south of the equator.

First, though, they needed to careen; it had been nearly a year, and the *Trinity*'s hull was in shambles. They also wanted to "fit up" the ship, to transform her deck into an unobstructed fighting and boarding platform, in this case by dismantling the forecastle and lowering the quarterdeck. Unfortunately, such modifications required greater carpentry know-how than they had among the remaining crew. But as luck would have it, on May 8, while scouting for a careenage in the Gulf of Nicoya (a dogleg inlet halfway up the coast of what is now Costa Rica), they learned about a busy Spanish shipbuilding yard nearby.

Sharp took twenty-three men to the yard and issued, as Cox put it, a "friendly" invitation to the chief carpenter to join them. In Sharp's version, the recruitment wasn't as friendly: he and his men marched in, dragged the carpenters out of bed, then left with them as well as their tools, ironworks, and other "necessaries," as he put it. Those necessaries included six jars of wine and brandy, and as a result of drinking too much of the latter, Scottish buccaneer John Alexander horribly overloaded his dory with the tools and ironworks. On the way back to the *Trinity,* the craft sank, and he drowned. Nevertheless, over the next two weeks, the Spanish carpenters were able to alter the *Trinity* to Sharp's specifications. They also stabilized the masts, among other modifications designed to boost the ship's speed and agility. In gratitude, Sharp set them free and, as a bonus, gave them a barque the company had recently captured.

The alterations had an unexpected cost, though. Dutch buccaneer James Marquis, who spoke fluent Spanish, had evidently enjoyed the carpenters' company so much that he ran off to join them, taking along a local woman with whom he had become enamored. He left behind his share from the expedition, a total of 2,200 pieces of eight, but it was small compensation to his ex-shipmates, given the likelihood that he would betray their plans to the Spaniards. In addition, Marquis had been their interpreter — an excellent one. Fortunately, wrote Cox, "we had one Mr. Ringrose with us, who was both an ingenious man, and spake very well several languages."

Although fitted up now, the *Trinity* still needed careening, which would have been a relatively straightforward process if not for the need to clear out of the Gulf of Nicoya posthaste to avoid any Spanish soldiers tipped off by Marquis. The buccaneers careened instead 140 miles down the coast, in the Golfo Dulce. After surviving a scare when a tornado snapped the *Trinity*'s anchor cable and flung the ship onto the shore — which, luckily for them, was flooded — they finally put to sea on June 28. And the hunt was on.

Nearly two weeks later, at noon on July 10, around a hundred miles north of the equator, one of the men spied a sail. Clearing the decks that they had just spent a month retrofitting for such a moment, the buccaneers gave chase. Over the course of the afternoon, they closed the gap enough to recognize their quarry as the *San Pedro,* the barque Sharp had seized in Panama Bay fourteen months earlier and plundered for wine, gunpowder, and fifty thousand pieces of eight.

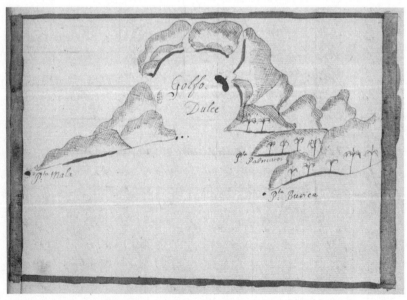

Map of the Golfo Dulce by Basil Ringrose

This time, the *San Pedro* "was so deeply laden," as Ringrose noted, "that she seemed clearly to be buried in the water." The problem was, she now had ample personnel to take on the depleted buccaneer crew, including as many as forty fighting men. But those men had no reason to think the buccaneers were in any way diminished, what with the shrill blast of the boatswain's whistle signaling all hands to quarters, pirates pounding a hasty path on the *Trinity's* deck to reach their appointed stations, and the rigging suddenly alive with top-fighters. And, as the *Trinity* drew within firing range, likely the forty Spaniards on the *San Pedro* didn't stand and watch; the sight of one of the pirates' deadeye marksmen atop a mast would be enough to send them all lunging for the nearest cover.

Of the ensuing engagement, Ringrose wrote, "Our great ship got up with her, and at about eight o'clock at night made her a prize." The other chroniclers said much the same thing in fewer words, suggesting that, as had been the case in Panama Bay, Sharp ordered the Spaniards to strike, and they complied, allowing his men to board.

In the *San Pedro's* holds, the buccaneers found high-end cargo: coconuts, silk, cloth, stockings, and eight chests full of pieces of eight — 21,000 in total — and another sixteen thousand pieces of eight in bags. The money alone would net each man five hundred pieces of eight, or as much as he might have earned in five years on the straight and narrow. In light of this prize, the buccaneers' "many disappointments" could now be viewed as hard work and persistence rewarded, and it steeled their resolve to stay the course.

Back in the Darien, recalling the rule that anyone who lagged would be killed, Wafer reflected on his decision to join the breakaway party, if not to abandon his medical practice in Port Royal and turn pirate in the first place. What had he been thinking? For one thing, he'd been a habitual risk taker, a trait that had been ingrained in him during a childhood that was nothing if not peripatetic. Born in Scotland to itinerant parents in 1660, he had spent his youth bouncing between the Scottish Highlands, Wales, and Ireland before going to sea in his late teens, on trading voyages to Java, Sumatra, and Borneo. He served primarily as a surgeon's assistant, called a loblolly boy, the name derived from one of the job's central duties: serving patients a gruel known as loblolly.

In 1679, when he was nineteen, he again sailed in the service of a barber-surgeon — typically the jobs were one and the same — this time on a trading voyage to Jamaica. The ship was commanded by a Captain Buckenham, who had a reputation in London as a "gentleman" and a "trusted shipmaster," because of which the Lords of Trade and Plantations trusted him to carry their correspondence to colonists in the West Indies. Buckenham, Wafer, and company reached Jamaica before their objective — sugar — was ready for milling, giving them time to sail to the Bay of Campeche to add logwood to their cargo. Wafer passed on the chance to see the Yucatán in favor of visiting his older brother, who worked in Jamaica on a sugar plantation. The choice was providential, because during the voyage, Buckenham was arrested by the Spanish navy for trafficking in stolen logwood and sold into servitude, to a baker in Mexico. Another captured crewman, who had managed to escape the Spaniards, told Wafer that each morning, the baker chained a log to Buckenham's leg and then left him in the streets all day to sell bread. Certainly Buckenham's was a cautionary tale for anyone trying to make a living at sea.

Wafer decided to put down roots for a change; with his

brother's help he settled into a house in Port Royal and secured work as a surgeon. But just a few months later he found himself in what amounted to a job interview with a pair of buccaneers ("privateers" was the less incriminating term Wafer used when writing of the meeting), Edmond Cooke and another captain named Lynch. Surgeons were in constant demand by buccaneer captains, given piracy's occupational hazards on top of the usual "sailors' diseases," such as scurvy and syphilis. Not surprisingly, a pirate captain had greater difficulty signing on surgeons than he did the usual indebted ne'er-do-wells, vagrants, and scoundrels, who had a lot less to lose. Yet if a captain left port without a barber-surgeon, crew morale immediately declined, because the job fell to the ship's carpenter — whose methods and tools were somewhat comparable, or at least more so than the cook's — meaning that limbs would be amputated with the same ripping saw that had just been used to cut away a shipworm-ridden chunk of hull. As a result, when pirates decided to liberate the entire crew of a captured ship, that often did not include the surgeon. And upon meeting a surgeon in port, pirate captains often gave him no choice but to take a position with them. In his writing, Wafer implied that he was the victim of such a circumstance, claiming that Cooke and Lynch "took me along with them." This was more judicious than a confession to running off with pirates in search of adventure. Either way, during his isthmus crossing with the breakaway party, he surely regretted having ever stepped out of his office that day.

It's difficult to pinpoint how far the party had traveled by April 10, 1681, when he found himself "not able to trudge it further." The buccaneers had little idea themselves. But it was far enough, they decided, to nullify the risk of his falling into Spanish hands and compromising the party's chances of reaching the

A recruitment

North Sea. Consequently, they allowed him to remain behind at a Kuna village, along with two other stragglers: John Hingson, a career mariner, and Richard Gopson, a scholar who had left academics to apprentice as a druggist in London before finding his way into piracy.

It was far from an ideal scenario for the three Englishmen, left indefinitely in the bowels of a dark and hostile jungle, dependent on the good graces of villagers who were anything but hospitable. "Some of them look'd on us very scurvily," Wafer wrote, "throwing green plantains to us, as we sat cringing and shivering, as you would bones to a dog." It was possible that the story of John Gret — the Kuna boy who sailed with privateer William Wright's crew before his untimely death at the hands of

English slavers — had reached this neck of the Darien. Whatever the case, for Wafer, Hingson, and Gopson, a stay in hostile conditions was safer than continuing. They resolved to resume the trek to the North Sea once the rainy season ended, four months hence.

For Wafer, however, there was no certainty that he would live that long. Lacking the means either to treat his wounds or to alleviate his agony, he turned himself over to the Kuna healers, who, fortunately, took him in and applied herbs — which they had chewed into a paste — to the wound on his knee, covering it with a plantain leaf.

None of the villagers spoke English, but one young man spoke Spanish, which he'd learned as a boy after being taken prisoner by Spaniards (he eventually escaped). Wafer and his two countrymen had only a smattering of the language between them, but it was enough to develop a rapport with the young Kuna measurable in the extra plantains he snuck to them in the middle of the night. Without him, they would have starved.

He was also able to shed light on why they hadn't received a warmer reception from the rest of the Kuna. Apparently, upon embarking from the village for the North Sea, the Cook party had forced two villagers to serve as guides. Having received no news of the two guides since, the villagers had come to suspect that Cook and company had murdered them, perhaps to keep them from reporting to the Spaniards. Yet despite their clear contempt for Wafer, the villagers continued to take care of him, applying a fresh poultice every day for nearly three weeks after his arrival. At the end of that time, save for a slight weakness in his knee, he was, to his amazement, "perfectly cured."

But since their men had yet to return from the North Sea, the Kuna "seem'd resolved to revenge on us the injuries which they suppos'd our friends had done to theirs." Some of the villagers wanted the Englishmen to be put to death. Others called for turning them over to Spanish soldiers in order to curry the Spaniards' favor. Fortunately for the buccaneers, the majority of the Natives despised the Spaniards even more than they did murderous Englishmen, quashing the latter option. The Kuna still liked the first option, though. Killing the Englishmen, they thought, would be just retribution. Even slowed by the Cook party, the guides' trip to the North Sea couldn't possibly have taken longer than the twenty days that had elapsed. Reckoning that the return leg would take ten days at most, the villagers decided that if the two guides hadn't returned in that time, they would execute Wafer, Hingson, and Gopson, and they began constructing a large wooden pyre for that purpose.

Two men did stagger into the village a few days later, but not the guides. It was Bowman and Spratlin, the members of the breakaway party who had fled rather than risk crossing the Río Congo. But as they had since come to appreciate, fording a raging river was pleasant in comparison to walking unguided through the Darien jungle for twenty days. Having barely survived, they saw the Kuna village as their salvation.

The villagers accommodated them by adding more wood to the pyre. No record exists of Bowman's or Spratlin's reactions, but it's safe to say that, like their three countrymen, they spent the next days in the grip of icy, abject terror, ruing the life choices that had brought them to this point. When the tenth day arrived with no news of the two guides, the villagers announced that, at sundown, they would set the woodpile ablaze with the five Englishmen atop it.

28

Bloodletting

THE BEST-KNOWN EPISODE of the buccaneers' South Sea expedition, at least among numismatists, was entirely lost to history until 2003, when Florida-based treasure hunters pieced together the story of the company's encounter with the *Santa María de la Consolación,* a Spanish treasure galleon "bloated with silver, gold, and gems mined from the mountains of Peru." That story, as reported by the *Orlando Sentinel,* began sometime in 1681, when the *Consolación* was poised to sail from Lima to Panama and offload her precious cargo to the Spanish treasure fleet, which would convey it to Spain. But because of reports of English pirates in the vicinity, the galleon's captain, Juan de Lerma, was reluctant to weigh anchor. Pointing out that the *Consolación* had twenty-six iron and brass cannons, whereas the pirate ship — the *Trinity* — had none, Viceroy Liñán dismissed Lerma's concern and ordered him to sea.

Against his better judgment, Lerma complied, and, sure enough, the *Consolación* ran into the "devil pirates," as he called them. His effort to elude them ended off the coast of Guayaquil when the *Consolación* struck either rocks or a reef and began to sink, irreparably. As he and his 350 men scrambled to their small boats, Lerma ordered the ship set on fire so that the treasure would not fall into the pirates' hands. He quickly came to regret the choice. Infuriated at having lost the treasure, Sharp and his men followed the Spanish boats to Isla Santa Clara, a tiny island in the Bay of Guayaquil, and "retaliated by beheading the crew and passengers — an estimated 350 people." As a result, the island has since been called La Isla de Muerto, or the Island of the Dead.

Or so goes the *Orlando Sentinel* story, its primary source being the Florida treasure hunters, who at that time were selling the cache of seventeenth-century silver coins they'd found in the Bay of Guayaquil. "The story and history behind it is what makes it valuable," one of them told the paper.

But Sharp and company are likely innocent — of this crime, at least. Isla Santa Clara had been known as La Isla de Muerto long before he and his crew entered the Pacific because, as Dampier wrote, "it appears like a dead man stretched out in a shroud." Further, none of the chroniclers aboard the *Trinity* mentioned the incident, which would be odd, given their relish in recounting their many other crimes. Ringrose's August 29 journal entry includes their only reference whatsoever to the *Consolación*:

> This day our pilot told us, that since we were to windward, a certain ship that was coming from Lima, bound for Guayaquil, ran ashoar at Santa Clara, loosing there in money, to the value of one hundred thousand pieces of eight; which otherwise, peradventure, we might very fortunately have met withal.

Moreover, Spanish records from the time of the *Consolación* wreck — likely May or June of 1681 — place the company in the Gulf of Nicoya, nearly a thousand miles north of Isla Santa Clara. To make the case that the buccaneers nevertheless engaged the

Consolación and then covered up the incident, the treasure hunters used deduction predicated on a map of the Bay of Guayaquil produced between 1682 and 1689 by English cartographer and close Bartholomew Sharp associate William Hacke. The map includes the notation "In the year 1681 Capt Sharpe gave chace to a ship in this sea and shee was lost on fowle ground near St. Clara in her was 100,000 ps 8/8 besides plate and other goods of value." Given the dearth of evidence, however, it seems that Hacke simply received misinformation, perhaps from Sharp himself.

In reality, Ringrose and company were fortunate not to have crossed paths with the *Consolación,* because Liñán was probably right; given the treasure ship's prodigious firepower, the *Trinity* would have been the likelier of the two vessels to wind up on the ocean bottom, and the buccaneers would have missed out on the far greater prize they indisputably did encounter that summer: the *Santo Rosario.*

Chief Lacenta and other Kuna

Back in the Darien, in mid-May, on the day that Wafer and the four other Englishmen were to be burned to death, Lacenta, a regional Kuna prince, happened to pass through the village and see the pyre. Absent confirmation of the fate of the two guides, Lacenta thought that executing the Englishmen was excessive. He instructed the villagers to first take them up the isthmus to a Kuna community whose residents were privy to the North Sea coast comings and goings.

The Englishmen, who would have been elated to leave the village under any circumstances, happily marched north in spite of "nothing but swamps, having great rains, with much thunder and lightning," as Wafer recorded. Their cheerfulness was put to the test over the next two days. They had no provisions save a handful of dry corn provided by their guides, and they slept on the cold ground. They might have taken comfort from the trees shielding them from the rain, except that whenever the wind shook the trees, branches were loosed onto the men. And after failing to find any food during the third day of the march, they spent a rainy night on a small hill that, by morning, had become an island surrounded by floodwater. It seemed that the five Englishmen and two Kuna would be stuck until the water receded, and no one could say when that might happen. Likely satisfied that the Englishmen were now as good as dead, the two Kuna swam off and did not reappear.

Wafer and company chose to wait out the flooding rather than enter the coffee-brown water themselves; the Darien was challenging enough when they could actually see the snakes, caimans, and so forth. Instead they sat and watched the water level, hoping it would drop. Over the course of the day, it didn't budge. For diversion, they had the Greek edition of the Bible, which Gopson was fond of reading and translating extemporaneously "to such of the company as were dispos'd to hear him," as Wafer put it.

By the next day, to their surprise and relief, the floodwater had receded enough for them to resume their march. Without their guides to lead them, the small party headed north using their pocket compasses, in spite of what they had learned from the Kuna. On previous occasions when buccaneers had taken compass readings and showed them to a Kuna, invariably he would shake his head and point in a different direction. The compasses were pretty things, the Kuna maintained, but useless. Only now, while trying to follow a compass line through broken country, did Wafer fully understand why. He did have some knowledge of Kuna navigational techniques: they guided themselves by the sun, when it was visible, and otherwise by reading the wind's effect on the trees. But neither he nor his companions knew how to use the Kuna methods themselves.

At the end of the day, they came to a river that was forty feet wide and far too deep and turbulent to ford — a dead end, it seemed, until it dawned on them: the river's sudden rise and fall must have been responsible for the flash flood and the water's equally rapid decline a day later. Since no amount of rain could have accounted for that over so brief a span, the tide had to be the culprit. Therefore, they determined, the North Sea had to be close by.

Another positive sign was the tree trunk lying across the river. It had been strategically placed there, they believed, by the rest of the Cook party on their way north weeks earlier. Wafer and his companions determined to cross it themselves in the hope of picking up the other Englishmen's trail on the far side. Unfortunately, the rain had made the bark so slick that walking across it appeared impossible; Wafer resorted to sitting astride the trunk to pull himself across. Hingson, Spratlin, and Gopson followed suit, all succeeding. But Bowman, the former tailor, slipped and fell into the water. The current shot him downriver and dragged him under the surface of the water, after which there was no trace of him. Drowned, his sickened companions soon concluded.

Worse, they realized, they had forced him into the crossing for nothing. The far bank was muddy to the point of impassable, and the terrain was so treacherous otherwise that if Cook and company had indeed crossed the tree trunk, they would have been forced, only moments later, to return the way they'd come.

Wafer and his three remaining companions recrossed the trunk themselves, utterly despondent, until midway they spotted Bowman. A quarter of a mile downriver, a bough hanging over an eddy had enabled him to hoist himself ashore. If the others hadn't turned back, they would never have found him. A joyous reunion ensued, tempered by the reality that, once again, they were lost — inextricably, it seemed — and that "hunger and weariness had brought us even to death's door," as Wafer wrote.

A berry tree afforded them their first meal in five days, enabling them to march onward — or, rather, to inch onward, the flood having transformed the earth underneath them to "mud and ooze." Their progress was further hampered by their blistered feet and the chafed skin on the insides of their thighs, which had been abraded to pulp by their torn, perpetually wet clothing. The rest of their bodies, meanwhile, were riddled by mosquito bites that had transformed into large open sores by the jagged underbrush.

Wouldn't it be nice, one of the men mused, to float down the river instead? The others laughed at first, yet the more they discussed the idea, the less far-fetched it seemed. The river did appear to run toward the North Sea. What if they constructed a raft? In the woods they found hollow bamboo stalks seemingly designed for that purpose. Having hewed the stalks into uniform lengths, they bound them together with vines. The process took an entire day, at the end of which they used their excess wood for a fire, took up lodging beside it, and dreamed of cruising downriver.

But not long after the sun went down, rain began to fall, and it seemed to Wafer that heaven and earth and the space between them would soon merge into a single body of water — or tar, as it would appear in the smothering darkness. The men came to appreciate that darkness a moment later when lightning tore into the jungle, accompanied by "horrid claps of thunder," bolt after percussive bolt that perfused the air with the stifling stench of sulfur. The lightning ceased at midnight, and Wafer soon missed it, because he and his comrades could hear rivers raging on either side of them that they could not see. They managed to light a small fire, but a surge of floodwater carried it away.

Fearing that a greater surge might at any moment snatch them up, they climbed the nearest hill. A flash of lightning illuminated flooding that was even worse than they'd feared. The rivers to either side of them were now conjoined, swelling by the minute and sweeping up everything not rooted to the jungle floor. Even atop the hill, they, too, would be carried off. There was now no other option than every man for himself.

Wafer found refuge four feet off the ground in a cavity within the rotted trunk of a cotton tree. Floodwater surged all around him, creating a ferocious river that toppled one nearby tree after the next. He spent the night freezing, trying and failing to put his hunger out of mind and appealing to God to spare his life.

Improbable as it may have seemed during the night, morning eventually came, and with it the trill of the jungle, in which Wafer could distinguish the voices of frogs, toads, mosquitoes, and the "hissing or shrieking of snakes and other insects, loud and unpleasant, some like the quacking of ducks." The rising sun seemingly dispersed the floodwater, enough for him to venture out of his tree trunk. His limbs were so stiff and the ground so slippery that he could barely stand. Nevertheless, in the hope of finding his companions, he returned to the spot where they had made their fire. It was deserted. He called out to them and was uplifted upon receiving an identical greeting in response, only to realize in the same instant that it was his echo. He took this as confirmation of his solitude, and all at once terror inundated him, and in that state, his hunger and grief weighed on him to the point that standing no longer seemed worth the effort. He collapsed and lay on the ground as though dead, which, it seemed, he soon would be.

As he waited, he heard a voice. It belonged to Hingson, who had saved himself by climbing a tree. As had the rest of the men, who soon found Wafer and Hingson. All eyes were moist as they greeted one another and thanked God for their deliverance.

Next they raced to check on their newly built rafts, which they had secured to a tree the night before. The tree still stood, and the rafts remained in place, but despite being constructed of bamboo, they were underwater and would no longer float. Frustrated, weary, and cored by hunger — the berries were all they had eaten in the seven days since leaving the Kuna village — the men weighed returning to the village. They would again need to contend with the villagers' antipathy and the possibility of being burned alive, but at least there would be a chance of survival — provided, of course, that they could find their way back.

Seeing no other option, they tried following the river in the opposite direction in the hope that it would lead them to the village. It did, in just a single day — giving them a newfound appreciation for the severity of the previous week's impediments. As the five men came within sight of the Kuna huts, however, fear made them think better of proceeding. But if they did not seek the assistance of the villagers immediately, Wafer knew, they would die of starvation.

While the others waited behind, he went in by himself. He found a number of the villagers in a house, presumably the common war house, or fort. They were not at all put off by his sudden appearance, as he had anticipated, but rather amazed by it, and they peppered him with questions. He wanted to answer, but a combination of the delicious warmth inside the house and the rich aroma of the meat boiling over the fire consumed his thoughts and, eventually, his consciousness — he was only vaguely aware of falling into a swoon.

The next thing he knew he was being revived, then introduced to a pair of villagers — the same men who, weeks earlier, had been forced into service as the Cook party's guides; they had recently returned home.

On May 24, following an especially arduous twelve-day jungle trek, the Cook party had reached the North Sea, leading them to a decision that would shape the fates of Wafer and the four other Englishmen back in the village. "At our first landing in this country, we were told that the Indians were our enemies," Dampier wrote before acknowledging, "I must confess the Indians did assist us very much." He went on to question whether they would have survived without the Kuna. The answer was obvious. Accordingly, after finding a crew of French buccaneers just off the North Sea coast at LaSound's Key, the very first thing the members of Cook's party did was trade for the goods their Kuna guides wanted most, to reward them, as Dampier put it, "to their hearts' content." In addition to beads, knives, scissors, and mirrors, each man in the party gave the guides a half-dollar. The two Kuna guides were more than gratified. On returning to their village, they shared "large commendations of the kindness and generosity of our men," according to Wafer. Thanks to the Cook party's largesse, the same Kuna villagers who the other week had planned to immolate Wafer and his four companions were now "very good friends."

After a week of rest and refreshment with these new friends, the five Englishmen set out again for the North Sea, this time led by four able guides. The party reached the river in one day, whereas it had previously taken three, and they embarked in a canoe — upriver. Had they succeeded in their attempt to float downriver on bamboo rafts the week before, Wafer realized, they would have wound up in Panama Bay, squarely in the hands of the waiting Spaniards.

In mid-June, six days into their second river effort, they reached the settlement ruled by Lacenta, the Kuna prince responsible for having stalled their execution. He greeted them at his palace, which sat high on a hill overlooking the confluence of two rivers, likely the upper Río Chepo and the Río Cañazas. Surrounding the palace were the homes of fifty of his administrators as well as the stateliest grove of cotton trees Wafer had ever seen — each tree, he reckoned, was six to eleven feet in diameter.

It would be impossible to reach the North Sea until the conclusion of the rainy season, the prince told the Englishmen — Cook and company had made it only just in time. In the interim, he said, they were to be his guests. Although reluctant to spend several additional months in the jungle, they saw no choice but to acquiesce. Besides, to men who had been trekking through Darien swamps for weeks, the village seemed a paradise. Almost immediately, however, Wafer enraged Lacenta, and once again their lives were in jeopardy.

The trouble started when Wafer observed a bloodletting. The patient, who happened to be one of Lacenta's seven wives, had been suffering from a fever and recurring fits. A healer sat her down on a stone in the river and used a miniature bow — about two feet long — to fire ten-inch-long arrows up and down her naked body. Wafer told Lacenta of "a better way," a way of letting blood "without putting the patient to so much torment."

The bloodletting of one of Lacenta's wives

The prince requested that Wafer perform the treatment. After binding the woman's arm with a strip of bark, the Englishman prodded with his lancet and breathed a vein, causing the blood to issue in a steady stream, exactly as he had intended. "But this rash attempt," he would reflect afterward, "had like to have cost me my life." Accustomed to seeing blood let drop by drop, Lacenta was apoplectic. Begging his patience, Wafer continued, drawing twelve additional ounces of blood before binding up the woman's arm and prescribing a day of rest. Lacenta took up his lance and swore that if his wife failed to recover, he would bleed Wafer's heart.

Wafer spent the ensuing twenty-four hours awaiting the outcome and the verdict, which was delivered by Lacenta, who, in the presence of his attendants, bowed to the English surgeon and kissed his hand. His wife's fever had broken, he said, and her fits were no more. As he went on to extol Wafer's medical know-how, his attendants swarmed the Englishman, planting kisses wherever they could find a spot — his hands, his knees, his feet — before taking him up in a hammock and parading him on their shoulders. "Thus I was carried from plantation to plantation," Wafer would recount, "and lived in great splendor and repute, administring both physick and phlebotomy to those that wanted."

He also began accompanying Lacenta on hunting trips, and a friendship blossomed. Soon the prince refused to go anywhere without him. At the same time, the Englishman immersed himself in Kuna culture, learning their language and adopting their simple attire. He allowed them not only to paint his skin but also to install a golden half-moon plate that dangled from his septum. He also began to develop a fondness for the Darien, the characteristics of which were nicely embodied by a prickly, forbidding fruit he encountered there that was "as big as a man's head" and, to his surprise, had "the taste of all the most delicious fruits one can imagine mixed together." Because of its resemblance to a pine cone, it would become known as pineapple.

In summation of his new life, Wafer wrote, "I lived thus some months among the Indians, who in a manner ador'd me." They adored him too much, though, given his hope of returning to England. After Lacenta offered one of his daughters to Wafer in marriage, the Englishman wrote, "I plainly perceiv'd he intended to keep me in this country all the days of my life."

He and the other buccaneers began plotting their escape.

29

A Warm Deck

WILLIAM DICK, NOT one for hyperbole, summed up the events of Friday, July 29, 1681, as "one of the greatest adventures of this whole voyage, if not the greatest of all." It began on a gray, drizzly morning, about twelve leagues from Cape Pasado, when a man climbing one of the *Trinity*'s masts glanced windward, into the mist. His cry — "A sail!" — electrified the crew, as ever. But that sentiment was fleeting, because, as the buccaneers discerned in the first steps of their rush to glimpse the prospective prize themselves, she was enormous, and she was heading directly toward them. One of the Spaniards' chief men-of-war, Ringrose thought, sent to destroy them.

With an eye toward capitalizing on the weather gage position, Sharp gave orders to fight. While he and his shipmates scrambled to clear the deck, Ringrose couldn't help wondering if they were capable of capturing a vessel so large. If Sharp's gambit failed, the *Trinity* would be taken — at best. As the other ship drew closer, however, the buccaneers perceived that she was not a man-of-war but rather a merchantman and, better still, riding quite low in the water beneath the weight of her cargo — sailing beautifully, from a pirate's standpoint.

In a short time the two crafts met, and "the Spaniard began to fire some small arms at us," Cox wrote, words that would become pivotal in the piracy trial that would result from the encounter. The buccaneers replied with a torrent of small shot: as Cox put it, "We warmed their decks." The volley felled four of the Spaniards, two of them permanently, including the ship's captain, Don Diego López. The remainder, daunted by the loss of their commander, cried out for quarter.

Sharp, Ringrose, and eleven other buccaneers boarded the ship, the *Santo Rosario,* which had been bound from Lima to Panama. Her crew was "about the number of forty, more or less," according to Ringrose, whose reporting was unusually imprecise, perhaps because he was distracted by one of the passengers, whom he described as "the beautifullest woman that I ever did see in all the South Sea." He wasn't alone in his appraisal. After providing an uncharacteristically brief summation of the wine and brandy taken from the *Santo Rosario,* Sharp wrote, "We took also a prize of the lady called Donna Joanna Constanta, about 18 years of age." He meant "prize" literally, as in a captured commodity, with the potential to bring a sizable ransom given her title, social status, and comeliness. His description was similar to Ringrose's: "the beautifullest creature that my eyes ever beheld in the South Seas." It is unknown whether he or any of his men "presented their services" to her, though there is no reason to speculate that this raid was the exception wherein they behaved with a modicum of virtue. The men of the *Trinity* would end up giving Constanta and much of the *Santo Rosario*'s crew their liberty, but it was only because the company lacked the manpower and provisions to keep them as prisoners.

In any case, the buccaneers' preoccupation with her may have cost them as much as a million pieces of eight. The boarding party did take coins and plate worth ten thousand pieces of eight from the *Santo Rosario*, but as Cox would later learn, they overlooked "670 piggs of metal, which we (such was our dullness) supposed to be tin." (The term *pigs*, meaning one-hundred-pound-plus metal bars, is derived from the resemblance of their molds and the molten metal feeder to a litter of suckling pigs around a sow.) Cox tried several times to convince Sharp that they should transport the pigs to the *Trinity*, but the captain simply wasn't interested. Before leaving the *Santo Rosario*, the party did take one pig, but only to melt it down for bullets. Later in the expedition, when a crewman tried to sell off the seventy-five pounds that remained of it, he discovered that it was in fact silver, worth 1,200 pieces of eight. "Thus we parted with the richest booty we had gotten in the whole voyage, through our own ignorance and laziness," Dick grumbled.

They did take something that would prove to be of even greater value, however — a book that they would probably have overlooked as well if the Spaniards hadn't tried to cast it overboard. "But by good luck I saved it," wrote Sharp. "The Spaniards cryed out when I gott the book." It contained 315 pages of South Sea charts, maps, sailing directions, and extensive descriptions of all the Spanish ports. Such a book — known in Spanish as a *derrotero* — was priceless as military intelligence, for which reason Spain severely prohibited the production of a printed or mass-produced edition and took great pains to secure the few hand-written versions. In England, where the South Sea was essentially uncharted, a Spanish *derrotero* would be worth a king's ransom, at least. Consequently, the buccaneers decided to return home.

Given the difficulty of transporting their loot overland, the most expedient route was via the Strait of Magellan. They left the *Santo Rosario* behind with only her foremast standing and her passengers and all but two of her crew aboard. They did take a Biscayer who had proclaimed himself the best pilot in those seas as well as eighteen slaves and a fifteen-year-old boy named Simón Calderón, who became Sharp's servant. Nothing is known about Calderón's performance in the role, but the buccaneers would come to regret their decision to take him when he became a key witness for the prosecution in the ensuing piracy trial.

After buying their two Kuna guides beads, knives, scissors, and mirrors from the French buccaneers at LaSound's Key, Dampier and the thirty-nine other members of the Cook party abandoned their plans to return home. Instead they cast their lot with the Frenchmen in a fleet consisting of eight buccaneer crews, including one with a hundred men led by their former admiral John Coxon, who had left the original company thirteen months earlier, following the Battle of Panama Bay, losing several of his seventy-man party during the isthmus crossing. On their return to Golden Island, he and the survivors had resumed pirating in the North Sea.

Setting aside any lingering animus, his onetime subordinates now joined him in plying the Caribbean for the rest of summer — with some success. In August, they returned to the Kuna community near LaSound's Key in the hope of obtaining word of the five Englishmen they had left behind in the Darien. The Kuna not only had word of them, they also had the Englishmen themselves. Spratlin, Bowman, Gopson, and Hingson were brought aboard one of the buccaneer sloops.

The raucous reunion that ensued was blunted for Dampier, however, by the absence of his friend Wafer until, an hour later, one of his shipmates exclaimed, "Here's our doctor!" He pointed at the group of Kuna sitting on the fringe of the celebration, haunches resting on the backs of their heels in the typical Indian fashion. Typical of the Kuna as well, all were naked except for their waistbands and striped with body paint. The one with the nosepiece dangling over his mouth looked familiar to Dampier. It was Wafer! The other crewmen soon came to the same realization and, reprising their earlier welcome, congratulated him on his arrival, one for the ages.

Thus the Kuna's leading practitioner of "physick and phlebotomy" left his adopted home in the Darien to go on a trip to England to acquire hunting dogs for his hunts with Lacenta — or so he had told Lacenta to gain the prince's leave. Really, Wafer planned to return to England for good. That plan changed, though, as soon as Dampier told him about the new and improved buccaneer fleet. The pair would go on to rove the West Indies together under the French captain Jean Tristian (or Tristan), their first of many new adventures in pirating — or, as Dampier liked to call it, "privateering."

30

The Horn

ALL THE BUCCANEERS' previous sailing was smooth in comparison to their attempt to get out of the South Sea. On August 4, five days after taking the *Santo Rosario,* Sharp set a course for the Peruvian town of Paita, 350 miles south, where the company could resupply before crossing the Strait of Magellan into the Atlantic. Sailing into fresh gales that day, the *Trinity* gained fewer than five miles. The next two days were also abysmal, until viewed in hindsight over the following two days. On August 7, Cox wrote of the company's progress, "We have got nothing." And on August 8: "We could get nothing." In fact, by Ringrose's tally, the *Trinity*'s distance traveled was worse than nothing; he recorded the ship as having lost three leagues.

And that was far from the most disturbing news. Reading through letters taken from the *Santo Rosario,* Ringrose gleaned that the Spaniards' intelligence on the buccaneers had been extraordinarily thorough and accurate, a realization that lent credence to the *Santo Rosario* prisoners' claims that Liñán, the viceroy of Peru, was now personally gunning for the *Trinity* with a seventeen-ship armada. Liñán had also ratcheted up the pressure on his soldiers to find and engage the pirates. According to the *Santo Rosario*'s pilot, the viceroy had beheaded one of the Spanish navy's most distinguished admirals for his failure to attack the Englishmen while they were careening at Gorgona. Meanwhile, as Ringrose read, there was now a general peace in Europe. Consequently, if they were caught, he and his shipmates could expect no lifeline from an England intent on keeping that peace. On one side was an armada determined to obliterate them. On the other were gallows. In short, it was possibly the worst time in history to be an English buccaneer in the South Sea.

In the days that followed, Ringrose reported, "What we got in the day by the help of the wind, we lost in the night by the current." It was frustrating, and as usual the buccaneers took out their frustrations on one another: tempers flared at the slightest perceived offenses, and petty affronts resulted in duels. Even the mild-mannered Ringrose found himself embroiled in a duel — a measure of the shipboard tension or, perhaps, the continuing change within the Englishman. No record exists of the circumstances other than that the duel was set to be fought at the next landfall. (Because duels divided the crew, they were not permitted at sea.)

When the *Trinity* reached Isla de la Plata, on August 12, having covered a mere twenty-three leagues in eight days, the duel was fought, likely "at sword and pistol," with the duelists standing back-to-back until instructed to turn and fire their weapons. In such a contest, if both parties were still standing afterward, they continued the fight with cutlasses, and the first man to draw blood was declared the winner. Ringrose's journal entry for that day constitutes the sole coverage of the duel, about which all he said was, "Our quarter-master, James Chappel, and myself fought a duel together on shoar." Otherwise, all that's known is that both Ringrose and Chappel survived.

Any further attention that might have been given to the duel was preempted by the threat of a slave revolt aboard the *Trinity*. As one of the enslaved men had confided to Sharp, the others were waiting for a night when their captors were "all in drink." As soon as the buccaneers fell asleep, they would be cut in pieces, no one receiving quarter. Charging onto the deck, the commander confronted the ringleader, a man named Santiago, whom the company had taken from Iquique. In response, Santiago leaped overboard to escape. Sharp took aim and shot him to death, terrifying the rest of the conspirators into submission, at least for the time being.

Next, to keep the viceroy of Peru's forces from succeeding where the conspirators had failed, the crew decided to give the *Trinity* "a pair of boots and tops," as Ringrose reported. Boot-topping — cleaning the part of a ship's bottom that lies immediately under the surface of the water — is a version of careening undertaken when haste renders it inconvenient to treat the whole ship. Although quicker than careening, boot-topping could still require several strenuous days, and, in this case, heighten the anxiety of a crew expecting to find seventeen sets of sails on the horizon at any moment. Yet even though the *Trinity*'s boot-topping took four days, and they desperately needed to distance themselves from the Spaniards, the buccaneers were "very merry all the while," according to Ringrose. He credited the wine and brandy taken from the *Santo Rosario*. When the company weighed anchor, on August 16, it seemed as though Mother Nature had joined the party, bringing wind and current that, over the next twelve days, propelled the *Trinity* all the way to Paita.

Like much of coastal Peru, Paita was mountainous and barren. The town itself was unimposing — just seventy-five or eighty poorly built low-slung brick houses and a pair of churches set on a small bay — hardly the sort of place the buccaneers expected the Spaniards to waste many musket balls protecting. On the cool, clear night of August 28, Sharp and thirty-two of the men piled into two canoes with high hopes of taking Paita undetected. Instead they found Spanish musketeers waiting behind breastworks on a hilltop overlooking the bay.

It was clear to Ringrose that the Paitians had received word that the *Trinity* was coming, or at least that she'd been seen along the coast. Paita had also received supplemental forces, including three companies of cavalry and infantry, everyone with guns, for a total of 750 defenders, 150 of whom took aim and fired at the buccaneer canoes. With an explosion of incandescent muzzle flashes and percussive reports, the fusillade produced no shortage of shock and awe. But if the Spaniards had sought to physically harm the buccaneers, they would have been better served by waiting until the canoes were within effective firing range. "This preposterous firing was the preservation of our people," wrote Ringrose. Had the Spaniards instead held their fire until the buccaneers reached shore, they would have undoubtedly killed every one of them.

Sharp ordered the *Trinity* to retreat, his easiest decision of the entire expedition, and the company sailed south once more. As Ringrose related, "All our hopes of doing any farther good upon the coasts of the South Sea being now frustrated, seeing we were descried before our arrival wherever we came, we resolved unanimously to quit all other attempts, and bear away for the Strait of Magellan."

The entrance to the Strait of Magellan was due south of Paita, three thousand miles as the crow flies. Such a course would mean sailing against the southeast trade wind and the Peru Current yet again. While Sharp and the crew could reach their destination sooner by circumventing their old nemeses — sailing southwest as far as the thirtieth parallel would save more than a month — the problem was provisions, the shortage of which had prompted the raid on Paita in the first place. Because of the dearth of landmasses on the way to the thirtieth parallel, the buccaneers would have no opportunity for procuring any more food or water. In charting such a course, Sharp would be betting that they could survive on what little they had — a fool's bet, he knew, but one with better odds than they would have against the seventeen-ship armada.

Forty-five arduous days later, on October 12, 1681, the lookout atop the *Trinity*'s mainmast spied land. The ship was now on the eastern leg of a voyage that had been unremarkable save for perilous winter weather and near starvation, both of which had been expected. The cloudlike mass of land sharpened, as the *Trinity* drew nearer, into one of several towering snow-blanketed islands that, as far as Sharp knew, he had just discovered.

While he searched the bay for the best place to anchor, a buccaneer named Henry Shergall, who was climbing to the spritsail top, slipped, crashed into the icy water, and drowned before his shipmates could reach him. Several of the buccaneers regarded the incident as an omen warning them away from the island, spurring a debate over whether to land. Hunger won, and the men went ashore.

Although seemingly barren, the island sated them with mussels, limpets, and various kinds of fowl, including geese, an eagle, and a penguin. The men also turned up a six-foot-long cord made of braided grass, knotted at the end, which was enough for them to conclude that they were not the island's first visitors. Nevertheless, Sharp claimed the discovery, naming it and the surrounding isles His Royal Highness the Duke of York's Islands, in honor of King Charles II's brother James, who would become king himself when Charles died without a legitimate heir, in 1685.

Known to this day as Isla Duque de York, the two-hundred-square-mile island sat a hundred miles northwest of the Strait of Magellan, Ringrose determined by taking observations. It was as much as he could do at the time, because, along with a number of his shipmates, he was confined to the *Trinity* by "the gripes," bouts of sharp abdominal pains that persisted for days. The outbreak was the first of several events that the superstitious could point to as validation of their interpretation of Shergall's drowning.

The next came that night, when rocks cut through the anchor cable, costing the *Trinity* her heaviest anchor and forcing the men to create an impromptu mooring out of the remainder of the severed cable, a grappling hook, and a tree on the shore. That tree turned into yet another problem two nights later, around midnight, when the wind barreled in from the south with such fury that it uprooted the tree. While the crew fought through a barrage of rain and large hailstones in an effort to fasten the ship to a new tree, she started to drift ashore. Her stern ground sickeningly through rocks, and before the men could secure her, she sustained significant damage to her pintles — the stout pins fastened to the back part of the rudder. Meanwhile the gooseneck — the iron fitting that enabled the rudder to pivot — broke altogether. The sum of the damaged parts was that Sharp and company could no longer control the ship's direction; until they could find or capture another shipwright, they were permanent residents of His Royal Highness the Duke of York's Islands. "Great was now our extremity," Ringrose wrote, "and greater it will be, if God send not better weather."

He did not. Over the next two weeks, "scarce a minute" passed without rain, sleet, snow, or hail barraging the *Trinity* and damaging one vital, specialized ship part after the next, meanwhile precluding any of the buccaneers from leaving the ship. But on October 26, as though a switch had been thrown, winter became spring, allowing them to venture out and explore the island. On November 4, having repaired the *Trinity*'s pintles, contrived a workaround for the gooseneck, and rehung the rudder, they sailed for the Strait of Magellan, covering the 125 miles to the strait's western entrance in a day.

Or so they thought. On a map, the entrance is hard to miss — a huge blue swath stretching between Chile's Pacheco Island, at latitude 52°25′ S, and Cabo Pilar, twenty-five miles southeast. But Pacheco itself is like a grain of rice within a bowl of rice; it is one of 504 islands clustered in proximity to one another, most of them hugging the continent and some of them nestled within the strait. Even on a clear, sunny day, distinguishing the strait from the continent can be a challenge. On November 6, 1681, when Ringrose determined that the *Trinity* had reached latitude 52°00′ S, where the buccaneers expected to find Pacheco Island and the entrance to the strait, it was so hazy that they lost sight of land completely. Rain and fog supplanted the haze over the next two days, with so much of the latter that the buccaneers mistook a low-lying cloud for land. The conditions prevented Ringrose from taking an observation of their latitude, on top of which he continued to be tortured by the gripes.

On November 12, when the weather finally cleared — along with the gripes — Ringrose determined that the *Trinity* was at latitude 55°25′, or 180 miles below Cabo Pilar, the southernmost point of the entrance to the Strait of Magellan. Not only had the buccaneers altogether missed their turnoff, they had also sailed a good forty miles past their contingency escape route, the Le Maire Strait, the sea passage at the continent's southern tip that had been discovered by Dutch explorer Jacob Le Maire in 1616.

On paper, reaching the Atlantic now was a simple matter of continuing east around the tip of South America. The buccaneers balked at that route, however, because it entailed contending with another of Le Maire's discoveries, Cape Horn, a cauldron of vicious currents, gale-force winds, mountainous waves, and icebergs the size of towns that turned ships into shipwrecks. Legend had it that to get through a gale off Cape Horn, a sea captain had once made a deal with the devil. By holding on to the ship's masts, the devil conducted her forward, but before long he pleaded with the captain to release him from the bargain. The moral: "The De'ill himself can't hold to a bargain if he has a Cape Horn gale against him."

Rather than take their chances with Cape Horn, seventeenth-century mariners returning from the South Sea often sailed west,

traveling all the way around the world in the other direction. As of 1681, no Englishman had ever succeeded in rounding Cape Horn from the South Sea, and Bartholomew Sharp had no intention of becoming the first. Instead he sailed southwest in the hope that the trade wind would propel the *Trinity* back up to the Strait of Magellan.

That is, he tried to sail southwest. For two days, an inordinately strong current had pushed the *Trinity* even farther south, all the way to 57°50′ S, by Ringrose's observation. If accurate, it meant the buccaneers were now more than three hundred miles below the Strait of Magellan and at least two hundred miles below the western coast of the continent.

Overnight they maintained an eastward course, expecting to sight the continent's low-lying southeastern coast in the morning. But come dawn on November 15, they saw only snow and sleet — and the sea, all around as usual but now also atop the ship, as mammoth swells began rolling across the deck. The same day, the wind hit the *Trinity* with such ferocity that it tore her theretofore stalwart sails to shreds. It must have seemed to the buccaneers that the day would never end, and in one respect that was true: in "summertime" at that latitude, the sun ceases to set, confounding the circadian rhythms of the sailors. Two days later, icebergs added to the buccaneers' troubles, including several "islands of ice," as the stupefied Sharp described them, each sixty to seventy feet high and two leagues in circumference. Which was nothing compared to the next round of ice islands the *Trinity* had to dodge, each so long that the men could barely see from one end to the other.

Ringrose's observation now put them at 58°23′ S, or closer to the Antarctic Peninsula — which had yet to be discovered — than to the Strait of Magellan. At this juncture, the company had to rule out the Strait of Magellan as an escape route. The Le Maire Strait, too. Even if they could somehow make it back, likely the viceroy of Peru's forces would by now be deeply entrenched at the entrances to both. The Spaniards wouldn't dare go near Cape Horn, though, nor would they expect the buccaneers to, no matter how crazy they deemed the Englishmen. Yet to escape from the Spaniards without first freezing or starving to death, the buccaneers saw no other choice. They continued east, toward the continent's dreaded southern tip, or, as Dick put it, "such a way as peradventure never any mortals came before us."

31

Landfall

To battle Cape Horn, the buccaneers first had to conquer the Drake Passage, the most dreaded body of water on the planet. Located between Antarctica's South Shetland Islands and the cape itself, and straddling the sixtieth parallel, the icy six-hundred-mile-wide collision of the Atlantic, Pacific, and Southern Oceans was host to the extraordinarily long, potent waves known as graybeards as well as to the notorious Shrieking Sixties gales (also known as the Screaming Sixties).

It didn't help that the buccaneers were still dressed for the tropics. Several of them simply couldn't bear the cold, resorting to lying as close as possible to one another. One enslaved man needed a frostbitten foot amputated, a procedure that only delayed his eventual death from the cold. A second of the enslaved men also died on account of the arctic conditions. Yet hunger was the greater threat, because none of the anticipated opportunities to reprovision had presented themselves since the *Trinity* left His Royal Highness the Duke of York's Islands, which itself had hardly been a bounty. "We were now kept to a very short allowance of our sorry victuals," wrote Ringrose, "our provisions growing very scanty with us."

At ten o'clock on the morning of November 18, the sea suddenly grew dead calm, which, given the tendency of calms to precede storms, was ominous. Two days later, the men woke to a fog so thick that they couldn't see from one end of the *Trinity* to the other, the visibility so poor that their first inkling of an iceberg might be the stomach-churning sounds of their bow crumpling against it. The fog cleared at noon that day, though, long enough for Ringrose to determine that the *Trinity* was now more than two hundred leagues east of His Royal Highness the Duke of York's Islands, meaning that the buccaneers had not only rounded Cape Horn, they were also as many as a hundred leagues past it.

On trial a year later in London, with his life on the line, Dick would argue that he and his shipmates had performed a public service with their historic rounding of the Horn, demonstrating that there was "a much easier passage from the North Sea unto the South Sea" than through the straits. For the time being, though, the buccaneers were far more excited by their capture of a "small and white land fowl," one of three or four they saw, giving them hope that they were close to land. "Yet none we could see," wrote Ringrose, "in all this long and tedious voyage."

The tedium was alleviated by a plot to murder Sharp. The trouble started on the afternoon of December 5, when Sharp, in an attempt to cheer up a crew depressed by fourteen consecutive days without so much as a glimpse of land, dug into the chests of money from the *Santo Rosario*. Each man's share came to 322 pieces of eight (another three years' worth of conventional wages), which was celebrated wholeheartedly. But failing to factor in the volatility of money, alcohol, and betting when mixed, Sharp went on to tap the barrels of wine taken from the *Santo Rosario* and to exempt dice from the company's gambling-at-sea prohibition. Ever the shrewd gambler, he won a staggering amount of the crew's money, causing them to quarrel with him, leading to blows.

Sharp ran to his cabin and returned to the deck with his pistol. Pointing the weapon at the head of crewman Richard Hendricks, he snapped the trigger. Perhaps indicative of the extent to which alcohol influenced the proceedings, the expert marksman's ball flew low, striking Hendricks's neck before lodging directly in the rigging behind him. Hendricks dropped to the deck, where he was taken for dead by his friends, who ran to get their own firearms and exact retribution. They would have killed Sharp, according to Povey, if not for the interference of shipmates with "more discretion in them" on account of being "soberer." Finding that Hendricks had regained consciousness and was relatively unharmed, the combatants cooled down. "Things came to an understanding," added Povey. "All was husht up."

Really, though, all was hushed up only insofar as Hendricks and his allies kept their planned response on the down-low: on Christmas Day, to comply with Sharp's decree that the holiday be merry, they would kill him. On December 7, he got wind of their plan, and, as a preemptive countermeasure, he upped the wine ration to three jars per mess. In the short term, he figured, he would win over the crew, and by Christmas the stocks of wine would be depleted, meaning that the conspirators would be sober and therefore less inclined to carry out their plot. While plundering the *Santo Rosario,* however, Sharp, in his preoccupation with the beguiling Donna Joanna Constanta, had undercounted the amount of wine taken. As a result, on Christmas Day, several full barrels remained.

Christmas of 1681 was "extremely hot," according to Ringrose. Or normal for December on the twenty-second parallel (that of Rio de Janeiro), where his calculations placed the *Trinity* after a month in which the ship had covered 2,500 increasingly warm miles.

To celebrate the holiday, the crew killed the sow that had been a diminutive three-week-old suckling pig when they brought her aboard seven months earlier, in the Gulf of Nicoya. Now she weighed ninety pounds. The dinner marked the first time in four months that the men had eaten meat, and it whetted their appetite for more. Several eyes fell on the pet spaniel belonging to the quartermaster, James Chappel. Chappel had no intention of eating his dog, but faced with the same pirate crew who had given up the chance to capture a ship carrying 100,000 pieces of eight in order to go hunting for meat, he knew he would be lucky even to come away with compensation. A group of crewmen that included Cox purchased the spaniel from Chappel for forty pieces of eight — the then average price of a horse — and enjoyed a feast of, as Cox put it, "the hogg and the dogg." As for the surplus wine from the *Santo Rosario,* Sharp, having had a change of heart, allowed it to be served "rather that my men might not mutiny." It worked, and despite the drunkenness of Hendricks and his coconspirators, the captain did not meet his demise. Christmas was, by all accounts, very merry.

The spirit carried over to the new year, augmented by the *Trinity*'s brisk pace — thirty leagues a day — and good fishing, including the catch of a 120-pound albacore tuna. It rained, but even that worked to the buccaneers' advantage, allowing them to collect what Ringrose described as "a bumpkin of water." His observation on January 2, 1682, placed them at 06°06′ S, or 420 miles below the equator. Five days later, they crossed the equator, and less than two weeks after that, on January 18, Ringrose's measurement of their latitude was 13°12′ N, the same as the Caribbean island of Barbados. The thriving English colony not only had everything they needed, it was also the world's leading producer of rum. Sharp steered west, aiming to "run down the latitude" in order to make landfall there.

Two days later, the sight of a passing seabird electrified the men. As Ringrose explained, it provided "good hopes we should e'er long see land." After agreeing that the first man to sight land would be given a piece of eight by each of his shipmates, the buccaneers began counting down the hours to the feast they would have and the drinking bout sure to follow.

On January 25, they began to look out in earnest for land, not just off the bow but also in every direction, their eyes darting back and forth, expecting each glance to fall upon a protuberance, if not a coast. They sighted only tornadoes, which they managed to avoid. The next two days brought more of the same. By now it had been nearly three months since they had set foot on solid ground, ten weeks since they had even laid eyes on terra firma, and two years since they had begun the expedition. In addition to their general need for food, they desperately required fresh fruit and vegetables. And many had an even more acute need — as they saw it — for meat. When no land was sighted that day, the crew's last remaining pet seemed destined for the same fate as Chappel's spaniel. The little shaggy dog from the *Santo Rosario* was auctioned off at the mast by his owner. With a bid of forty pieces of eight, Sharp won, intending to take the dog down to the cookroom if the crew didn't see land soon.

An hour before sunrise the next day, January 28, an irregularity appeared on the horizon — Barbados, four leagues off — and the shaggy dog was given a reprieve. Shortly thereafter, although it must have seemed like centuries, the *Trinity* sat bobbing a mile from shore, alongside a British pinnace. Ringrose wrote, "I cannot easily express the infinite joy we were possessed withal, this day to see our own countrymen again."

But to his dismay, his countrymen declined the invitation to come aboard the *Trinity*. By way of explanation, they shared two news items: first, there was now peace at home between England and Spain; second, their vessel served as a barge for His Majesty's frigate *Richmond,* which was anchored at Bridgetown, Barbados's principal city. In other words, on account of the improved Anglo-Spanish relations, if the *Trinity* were to go any farther, the *Richmond*'s crew would be obligated to clap the buccaneers in irons. There could be neither a landing at Barbados nor even time to procure so much as a chicken. To a man, the buccaneers feared that once the *Richmond* received word of them, she would chase after them, inevitably meaning that her crew would seize them for pirating and strip them of every last piece of eight they had amassed on the expedition. At once they heaved up their topgallant sails, studding sails, and everything else that might hasten their departure.

At eight o'clock on the morning of January 30, 1682, having sailed three hundred miles from Barbados in two days, the buccaneers spied an object on the horizon that resembled a giant sea serpent: a tall protuberance followed by three smaller rounded rises. It turned out to be Antigua, as they had hoped. Although the 108-square-mile island had been occupied as early as 2400 BCE by the Siboney, or stone people, Christopher Columbus is credited — at least in the annals of European history — with discovering it, in 1493. He also named it, after the Santa Maria de la Antigua (St. Mary of the Old), an icon in the Seville Cathedral.

By 1682 Antigua had become one of the most prosperous British colonies on the strength of its sugar industry, which is to say on the strength of the 37,500 enslaved Africans who accounted for 94 percent of the island's population. That industry had largely been established by one man, Colonel Christopher Codrington II, a prominent planter in Barbados who expanded his operation to Antigua in 1668 before relocating there in 1677. Codrington was now the governor of Antigua, and, from the buccaneers' point of view, God: their lives hinged on landing at his island. They were on the brink of starvation; the *Trinity*'s sails and rigging were in tatters, and her hull was seemingly held together only by the mollusks.

The Antiguans who came aboard to greet them, gentry and common people alike, welcomed them heartily and were eager to receive them on the island. But their position wasn't necessarily the same as Codrington's. Before the buccaneers could be received, they needed to request permission of the governor to come into the port. Sharp sent a letter to Governor Codrington that included a gift of jewels for Mrs. Codrington. The company waited on tenterhooks for word back, receiving none that day. The following day brought nothing, either, save seawater leaking into the hull. Codrington's reply finally came the day after, February 1. He refused to permit the company to come ashore, not even for refreshment. He also returned the jewels.

In council, the buccaneers discussed how they might still avail themselves of the townspeople, who remained willing and eager to trade with them. The result was a decision to disband the company: henceforth, each of the ninety or so men would fend for himself. All but seven went ashore at Antigua, refreshing themselves and then trying to find passage home.

Ringrose concluded his journal with:

Thus I myself and thirteen more of our company went on board Captain Robert Porteen's ship, called the Lisbon Merchant, and set sail from Antigua on February 11th, and landed at Dartmouth in England, March 26th, anno 1682.

Likely trying to steer clear of Codrington, Sharp sailed — on February 1 at the earliest — to Nevis, a small island fifty miles west that was not only hospitable to pirates but also produced the highest-quality sugar in the British West Indies and thus some of the region's best and most potent kill-devil, the latter perhaps factoring into his confusion over the date he landed. His final diary entry ends: "I arrived on the 30th of January at Nevis, from whence in some time I got passage for England."

"Some came into England, others went to Jamaica, New England, &c," Cox wrote from London in a final journal entry that was uncharacteristically brief and lacking in humor, perhaps because its primary subject was his arrest on charges of piracy. One of his codefendants, William Dick, completed his own narration of the expedition with "Thus we dispersed." He would go on, however, to comment on the trial in some depth.

Povey was among the seven crewmen who remained aboard the *Trinity*, by necessity: they had all gambled away their entire expedition shares. Having been gifted the ship by the rest of the company, they planned to sail 750 miles west, to Petit Goâve, the pirate haven in French Hispaniola where the buccaneers had purchased their expired logwood-cutting license in 1679. If Povey and company could buy a new license, they thought, they could earn their fares back to England. Unfortunately, "the shipp was so crewell leakey that thay hardly ha[d] the patience to keepe her above water to St. Thomases." Halfway, on perceiving that another ship was chasing them, they decided to put in at the nearby island of St. Thomas, which they hoped would be a safe haven; the Dutch colony was neutral to both warfare and jurisdiction among the Spanish, English, and French. Moreover, most of its 150 nonenslaved residents were English, and its governor, Nicolai Esmit, was the brother of the retired buccaneer Adolph Esmit.

Indeed, Povey and his companions received a warm welcome. Governor Esmit sent out extra hands to help bring the *Trinity* into a berth, and the island's residents flocked to purchase the cocoa and much of the other plunder still aboard the ship. A day later, however, the anchor cable broke, wrenching the leaky *Trinity* ashore and damaging her irreparably. Still, the anonymous chronicle believed to have been written by Edward Povey ended on a high note: "Thus the good shipp Trinity...ended her voyage, and through the blessing of god brought us amounge our cuntry men againe."

But one of those countrymen betrayed them. On March 8, Henry Morgan, acting in his capacity as both Jamaica's lieutenant governor and commandant of the regiment, sent an update on the hunt for Bartholomew Sharp's crew to Sir Leoline Jenkins, secretary of state for England's Southern Department as well as the chief law officer of the High Court of Admiralty. In that letter, Morgan reported the apprehension of four Sharp crewmen, one of whom had surrendered to him and given up the other three, who had "since been found guilty and condemned." Judges determined two of them "fit objects for mercy," whereas the third, proving "a bloody and notorious villain, and fit to be made an example of," was hanged.

The man who surrendered, hoping to obtain the favor of the court, had agreed to serve as an informant as well as to pen an account of the entire expedition for use as king's evidence. This informant is believed to be Edward Povey because of the account's caveat: "Thiss being what I can think on att present, being the true actions of our voyage as near as I can remember, my jornall being detained att St. Thomases and lost."

Cooperating earned Povey a prison cell in lieu of a trial for his life. In England, meanwhile, his former captain and shipmates had no such luck.

32

The Silver Oar

ROBERT LOUIS STEVENSON'S 1883 novel *Treasure Island* opens with an aging seaman taking up lodging at the Admiral Benbow Inn in England. The captain, as the seaman refers to himself, proceeds every evening to sit by the fire in the parlor, drinking rum and singing wild sea chanteys. Replace the fictitious Admiral Benbow Inn with the actual London riverside inn known as the Anchor on Salpeter Bank, and the description might serve as an account of Bartholomew Sharp's return to England in the spring of 1682. Even the name of the inn in *Treasure Island* has a basis in Sharp's reality: one of his most famous adversaries was Rear Admiral John Benbow, the commander in chief of the Royal Navy's antipiracy efforts in the West Indies.

While Sharp was finding his way through the Anchor's maze of small, oddly configured rooms and availing himself of the brick fireplace in the inn's Lion and Sword tavern, across town at the Court of Saint James's, Spain's ambassador to England, Don Pedro Ronquillo Briceño, was demanding that Sir Leoline Jenkins locate the South Seas pirates and arrest them posthaste.

Ronquillo, as the ambassador was known, was a stout man of fifty-two whose voluminous shoulder-length wig framed sharp, aristocratic features that were set in consternation even when he was calm. And at the Court of Saint James's, he was the opposite of calm. The pirates had gotten away with taking Spanish ships and ports for more than four million pieces of eight, he declared. Along the way they had destroyed twenty-five ships and murdered more than two hundred Spaniards, including Don Diego López, the captain of the *Santo Rosario*. And now they were in England, having sailed from Nevis aboard the *White Fox* and landed in Plymouth on March 25. How could England permit such miscreants to reenter society? Had the English forgotten the Treaty of Madrid? Had they not agreed to respect Spanish trading overseas? One could not say that King Charles II was upholding his commitment to ending piracy.

Ronquillo's rant succeeded in spurring Jenkins to have investigators search the London taverns and inns known to be pirate-friendly. At the Lion and Sword, investigator Thomas Campe learned that an Anchor on Salpeter Bank lodger, evidently while in his cups, had confided to other patrons that he had been an outlaw for sixteen years, robbing all nations — Spain in particular. The lodger's name was Bartholomew Sharp, the Anchor's landlord told Campe, adding that Sharp had said that "he had lived a wicked course of life abroad and thought that he should never dye a naturall death," but he had returned to England from the West Indies on the off chance of receiving a pardon. And then there was the loot in Sharp's room, many thousands of pounds in cash, according to the landlord, and "several portmanteaus of gold and silver coined and uncoined in medals, jewels, and other things."

It was not a crime to possess trunks full of gold, silver, and jewels. And the details of Sharp's rum-abetted yarns left Ambassador Ronquillo without ample evidence to initiate an Admiralty court case. That changed, however, when he turned up Simón

Calderón, the fifteen-year-old Chilean from the *Santo Rosario* who'd been pressed into duty as Sharp's servant on the *Trinity*. Having continued in the captain's service during the Atlantic crossing, the boy was still in London, allowing for a May 18 deposition in which he told of the *Trinity*'s attack of the *Santo Rosario*. Along with the descriptions he provided of Sharp, another pirate he thought was named Gilbert Dike, and a third man he called Scott, the High Court of Admiralty had enough to issue warrants for the arrests of Sharp, William Dick, and John Cox.

Jenkins's investigators found Dick — going by William Williams — in Shadwell, in the county of Middlesex. Cox they picked up in Lower Shadwell. Both buccaneers were promptly relocated, along with Sharp, to the Marshalsea prison, in Southwark. For fear of joining them, Basil Ringrose and the other twenty-two *Trinity* crewmen still at large in London either fled or went into hiding.

The Marshalsea would later be immortalized in the novels of Charles Dickens, whose father was imprisoned there for debt in 1824. In 1682, it consisted of a group of three-story fifteenth- and sixteenth-century houses with gabled roofs and a Jacobean-era courthouse. The compound might have passed for one of London's grander blocks if not for the chevaux-de-frise — logs atop the walls sprouting iron spikes, serving the same function as barbed wire — and the monolithic iron bar securing the gate.

The three buccaneers found themselves among three hundred wretched inmates, a mix of seamen and debtors crammed into a warren of small windowless rooms in which they slept on mounds of filthy hay or, at best, beds not much larger or softer than a plank. At all times they were forced to endure a concentration of stenches seemingly dense enough to create their own atmosphere. As nondebtors, Sharp, Cox, and Dick were given the option of paying rent for superior accommodations, "superior" being a relative term; "slightly less terrible" would have been more accurate. The best rooms were a pair of minuscule single occupancies that offered a view of the open space within the prison walls — a largely grassless lawn the inmates called the Park — from which the occupants could hear a torrent of raucous chatter, the batting of shuttlecocks, and a general ruckus that reverberated against the clapboard walls until nine or ten every night. There is no record of whether the buccaneers upgraded. Unsurprisingly, while at the Marshalsea, none of them journaled — and, luckily for them, their shipboard writings had not found their way into evidence. Almost every incriminating detail from the expedition awaited them in court, however, courtesy of their shipmate turned informant, Edward Povey.

CAROLUS STUART de II.de
Koninck van
ENGELAND, SCOTLAND en YRLAND.

King Charles II of England

* * *

In the more pleasant confines of the Palace of Whitehall, meanwhile, King Charles II was following their case closely. On May 25, 1682, four days before his fifty-second birthday, Charles instructed one of his confidants, the Earl of Conway, to send a letter to Sir Leoline Jenkins. His Majesty, the earl wrote, had learned of a Spanish book that Bartholomew Sharp had plundered from the *Santo Rosario,* and that had since been seized as evidence by Jenkins's investigators. This book, or *derrotero,* was thought to include proprietary maps and details of the South Sea. His Majesty wished Jenkins to bring it to him "with all the privacy" he could.

The king had the *derrotero* in hand by June 7. To an empire dying to get in on South Sea colonization, a copy of the book would be invaluable. Obtaining a copy, however, required literally copying it — by hand, a process that took weeks, and the original had to be returned to the Spaniards following the trial, which was set to begin in three days, on June 10, a Saturday. Likely it would conclude the same day, given the swift efficiency of Admiralty courts. Also, production of the copy would benefit tremendously from Sharp's supervision and annotation, neither of which would be possible, of course, if he were hanged.

Next the king had the Earl of Conway write Jenkins and request that the trial be put off until the following Wednesday or Thursday and, equally important, that it should be postponed in such a way that would not perturb Ronquillo, at the same time keeping His Majesty's name out of it. "When you come here," Conway added to that message before signing off, "[H]is Majesty will acquaint you with the reason of it." But despite Jenkins's efforts, Ambassador Ronquillo — the plaintiff, effectively — refused to delay the trial. King Charles hurried the *derrotero* into the hands of the country's top translator and cartographer and tasked them with completing a copy within seventy-two hours.

The trial began, as scheduled, on June 10, 1682. (At the time, it was not common practice to create transcripts of Admiralty proceedings; if one happened to have been produced in this trial, its whereabouts are unknown. But the indictments, depositions, and verdict from the case all remain in High Court of Admiralty archives and facilitate an account of the proceeding.) In the morning, the Marshalsea jailers removed the accused pirates from their cells, transported them to the nearby New Hall courthouse, a converted church, then led them into its austere, dark-paneled courtroom, where, at certain times of day, the sunlight struck the mullioned two-story windows and, as though imparting a verdict from on high, cast shadows in the shape of the cross onto the defendants.

As Sharp, Cox, and Dick were prodded toward the bar near the front of the room, it is easy to imagine the sudden buzz among the spectators, who, at the time, paid more for admission to courtroom galleries than they did to go to the theater and who now stood on their toes and strained their necks around pillars to see the faces of the accused pirates. They also held their noses. To further mitigate the "gaol air" — as well as the potential spread of "gaol fever" — courtrooms were strewn with pungent herbs and vinegar, especially in the boxy defendants' docks and, in this case, at the bar. For the same reason, the judges — who would soon enter the courtroom themselves and sit to face the defendants — brought small bouquets of flowers to their benches.

At the thick wooden slab of a bar, Sharp, Cox, and Dick must have been aware that they were mentally being fitted for nooses by everyone present, including the twelve-man petit jury seated in the stalls to either side. If the buccaneers glanced at the stalls to get a read of the jurors' dispositions, they may have had to squint against the glare: in some courtrooms, a mirrored reflector was hung overhead to direct light from the windows onto defendants' faces, affording the jurors a better view of facial expressions that might signal dissembling or guilt. For the same reason, a sounding board, placed over their heads, amplified defendants' words.

Notably absent from the bar was any sort of defense attorney. Prior to 1696, not only were defendants prohibited from employing legal counsel, they were also left unaware of the evidence against them until the trial. Spontaneous responses left less opportunity for mendacity, the thinking went, and no manner of skill was required to make "a plain and honest defence" — if the defendants needed help, the judges would look out for them. Defendants were permitted, however, to consult an attorney on matters of law, and Ronquillo's correspondence mentions a Mr. Moule advising Sharp, Cox, and Dick.

Seventeenth-century trial

The buccaneers were banking on the same anti-Spanish sentiment that had abetted Henry Morgan following his 1671 raid of Panama. But that sentiment had softened in the wake of the Anglo-Spanish peace and Morgan's own about-face. Just a year after Morgan's raid, following the seizure of a Spanish frigate in the Caribbean by buccaneer captain Peter Johnson, Jamaica's governor, Sir Thomas Lynch, sent English ships "to burn the [frigate] and make examples of all these obstinate thieves." Johnson was apprehended, tried in England, and then made to do the "marshal's dance": pirates flailed wildly on the gallows as a result of nooses tied especially for them so that the drop would strangle them instead of breaking their necks.

When the ten High Court of Admiralty judges entered the courtroom, the entire audience shot to its feet. The judges each wore a rich scarlet robe with a starched ruff at the neck and a black cincture around the waist. They may or may not have worn shoulder-length powdered wigs, increasingly popular in judicial circles in the early 1680s but not ubiquitous until 1685. The especially formidable group included five admirals, three senior lawyers, one captain, and Sir Thomas Exton, the renowned advocate-general, in place of Leoline Jenkins, who had either recused himself or otherwise could not attend. Adding menace was the ornate silver oar prominently displayed before them, the venerable mace of the Admiralty court. *Mace* in this context means a ceremonial staff of office, but the hefty oar appeared suitable as another kind of mace — the club used in the Middle Ages for smashing apart a foe's armor. It was most famously held aloft for all to see — a symbol of the authority of the High Court of Admiralty — during the post-trial processions of condemned pirates from the Marshalsea to the Thames riverbank gallows known as Execution Dock.

Pirates at Execution Dock in London

When the procession of the judges into the courtroom concluded and everyone retook his seat, the court clerk — possibly the scarlet-cloaked registrar — finally addressed the three buccaneers: "You stand here accused of pyracy and robbery. You shall speak the truth, the whole truth, and nothing but the truth, so help you God." Next came the indictment. Among its hanging offenses were "piratically and feloniously stealing" the *Trinity,* "breaking and entering" aboard the *San Pedro,* and the murder of Captain López of the *Santo Rosario.*

Looking up from the indictment, the clerk asked the prisoners, "How say you, are you guilty of the pyracy and robbery of which you stand accused, or not guilty?" When they replied,

"Not guilty," Ronquillo—aided by a proctor, the Admiralty court's version of an attorney—launched into a case that was far more detailed than even the buccaneers' journals were. He brought forth, for example, an incredibly thorough itemization of the booty they'd plundered from the *Santo Rosario,* including "40 lb. weight of sea bread worth 50 shillings," a "hamper of potatoes worth 5 shillings," and "two sails for a ship worth £6." His description of Captain López's death had even greater specificity, including the murder weapon's valuation—ten shillings—and the assertion that with it, Sharp had dealt the Spaniard "a mortal wound one inch wide and four inches deep, in and on the left side of his body, near the said left nipple." Dick and Cox, meanwhile, were accused of aiding and abetting their captain "feloniously, wilfully, and with malice."

Ronquillo piled on additional "piratical and felonious" accusations before corroborating the prosecution's story with five witnesses: the Anchor on Salpeter Bank's landlord; the fifteen-year-old former Sharp servant, Simón Calderón; a West Indian boy who went by the name Francisco Bernardo; and a pair of sailors of African descent, Domingo Fernández and Jacinto de Urbina, who claimed to have been plucked from the *San Pedro* by the pirates and enslaved aboard the *Trinity.*

What exactly the five witnesses said in court is unknown, but presumably it echoed their deposition testimonies, which were damning, especially Calderón's relation of the *Santo Rosario* crewmen's initial encounter with the *Trinity,* which they thought was a Spanish vessel until the men aboard revealed themselves to be pirates and began firing muskets, killing Captain López. The pirates proceeded to capture and loot the *Santo Rosario,* Calderón went on, and afterward they tortured the crew to find out whether there were any valuables they had missed. The boy also said the pirates had murdered a Spanish prisoner they suspected of plotting an uprising. Urbina, who had been aboard the *Trinity* during the *Rosario* encounter, corroborated Calderón's account.

With Ronquillo's case thus completed, it was incumbent upon Sharp, Cox, and Dick to disprove the evidence against them and establish their innocence. They had no right to call witnesses of their own, but they were permitted to cross-examine the prosecution's witnesses. The gist of the argument in their depositions — presumably the same case they tried to make in court — was that they had been duly commissioned "by the Indian Emperour of Darien" to fight the Spaniards in Panama. When asked by Ronquillo to show the commission, Sharp scoffed. "Everyone knew that those kings did not know how to write." The commission, the buccaneers contended, was no less legitimate for having been delivered verbally.

Going on to defend himself against the *Trinity* charge, Sharp claimed that, in Panama, a group of buccaneers were pursued by Spaniards then in command of the ship and that they had taken her "in their own defence." Skipping over the two years of pirating, he added that he subsequently sailed southward to "round the land in those parts and so to come for England, and to give an account of [the] discovery of those places to the king."

While denying outright that his crew met with the *San Pedro*, Sharp acknowledged crossing paths with the *Santo Rosario* four or five leagues from Cape Pasado, but he rejected the notion that the buccaneers attacked her. Only after she fired at the *Trinity*, he said, did he order his men to fire in return. He subsequently saw that her boatswain "was wounded in the buttock, but whether the master or any of the company of that vessel were killed in that dispute" he knew not. He also denied taking anything from her save "a small basket or two of potatoes, and some wine," and those only out of necessity, "to prevent starving."

The testimonies of Cox and Dick differed from Sharp's only in the quantity of the provisions that exigency dictated they take from the *Santo Rosario* — "300 weight of bread" and "a jar or two of brandy," according to Cox, while Dick copped to "5 or 6 jars of brandy." Like Sharp, Dick claimed that the Englishmen had tortured no one in the South Sea. As for the rest of Ronquillo's case against them, it lacked evidence save for the word of, as Dick put it, "two or three villains of our own company, among which were two negro's, who turn'd cat in the pan, and had a spleen against Capt. Sharp." The racial subtext was likely to resonate among his contemporaries in England, where, earlier in that century, while addressing national discontentment with "Negroes and blackamoors," Queen Elizabeth declared that "those kinde of people should be sente forth of the land," and until 1810 the *Encyclopaedia Britannica*'s "Negro" entry ascribed numerous vices — including idleness, treachery, revenge, cruelty, impudence, stealing, and lying — to the "unhappy race."

As it transpired, the judges could not reach the requisite unanimity to admit the testimonies of Fernández and Urbina. The court's issue, as recorded by a flabbergasted Ronquillo in his letters, was that the sailors had not been baptized; hence, they could not adequately swear to tell the truth. Ronquillo became convinced that the fix was in after overhearing one of the judges tell Sharp, "We are already insured of the business." The jurors had been bought, in other words. Yet the other three witnesses passed the court's muster, and, as Ronquillo told the jury in closing, their testimonies contained more than ample evidence of the manifold piratical, felonious, and murderous practices of the prisoners before them. For those crimes, he insisted, the three men deserved to be hanged.

Permitted no closing statement of their own, Sharp, Cox, and Dick were returned to custody while the judges summed up the case for the jury, adding their opinions. The judges then ordered the jurors to "huddle" and reach a verdict. Quickly. With an eye toward getting litigants back to sea and keeping trade ships on schedule, Admiralty courts operated at stunning speed, at least by legal standards. Entire cases such as this one could be tried within an hour.

The same day, Sharp, Cox, and Dick were returned to the courtroom and heard the following report on the jury's deliberation:

Session of Oyer and Terminer and Gaol Delivery of our lord the King for the Admiralty of England at New Hall in the parish of St. George in Southwark in the county of Surrey on Saturday, June 10, in the 34th year of King Charles II of England. Bartholomew Sharpe, John Cox, and William Williams were severally acquitted of several felonies, piracies, and murder and released.

Beyond Dick's remark that it had been "a fair trial," no other record exists of the reaction of the acquitted men, but it is safe to say they were the opposite of Ronquillo's. As the Spaniard saw it, England had rigged the case, believing the defendants to be worth more for the intelligence they had gathered than for any example their corpses might set for the citizenry. He protested the acquittal all the way to King Charles himself, who replied that he "did not meddle with matters relating to law." If he had others meddle for him, he kept it to himself.

Charles certainly had his people attempt to put out the resulting diplomatic fire. After Spain's secretary of state expressed astonishment at the English legal system, Leoline Jenkins sent a suggested response to England's ambassador in Madrid, Sir Henry Goodricke, that included a denial — "how uncontrollable the verdict of juries are with us" — and a counteraccusation of "inhuman usages" of Englishmen under the power of Spaniards in the West Indies.

Goodricke's rendition of that message led Spain's own King Charles II to complain that it wasn't enough to blame the jury — that "the damage is so great as to deserve an interposition of the King of Great Britain's power and authority," especially in light of the treaties between their nations. If the situation were reversed, the Spanish monarch went on, with Spaniards acquitted of pirating English vessels, he would personally overrule the court in the interest of the relationship between the two crowns. He added his hope that his English counterpart would do likewise.

But his English counterpart did nothing, as far as is recorded. In response, the Spaniards seized Goodricke — nominally for displaying England's royal coat of arms on the gate outside his house — and imprisoned the forty-year-old in a Hieronymite convent outside Madrid. Goodricke escaped a few months later and made it safely back to England in February of 1683, by which point the Spanish reprisal effort had run out of steam.

Two months later, England's King Charles commissioned Bartholomew Sharp as a captain in the Royal Navy.

33

The Sequel

FOLLOWING HIS ACQUITTAL, Sharp got into the publishing business, overseeing the secret production of a "waggoner" — a maritime term for a book of charts and maps, derived from the name of a Dutch cartographer, Lucas Waghenaer, who published the first such collection in 1584. In addition to hand-painted maps derived from the *Santo Rosario*'s *derrotero* and Ringrose's extensive drawings, Sharp's waggoner included both his own journal and that of Ringrose, who had escaped prosecution. Ringrose's sole punishment was the editing of his account by either Sharp himself or someone else with an almost identical style of aggrandizement. Words like *courageous* and *sea-artist* were interpolated alongside Ringrose's mentions of "Captain Sharp." The most drastic such edit appeared in Ringrose's May 22, 1680, journal entry, covering the death of Richard Sawkins. Originally Ringrose had written, "Captain Sawkins was a valiant and generous spirited man, and beloved above any other we ever had among us." After the editor's pass, Sawkins was remembered as "a man who was as valiant and courageous as any could be, and likewise next to Captain Sharp, the best beloved of all our company."

Completed on October 23, 1682, the waggoner began with the inscription:

To the high and mighty monarch Charles the Second, King of great Britaigne, France and Ireland &c. This Wagoner of the Great South Sea is humbly dedicated and presented by your own majesty's ever loyal subject, Barth. Sharp, 1682

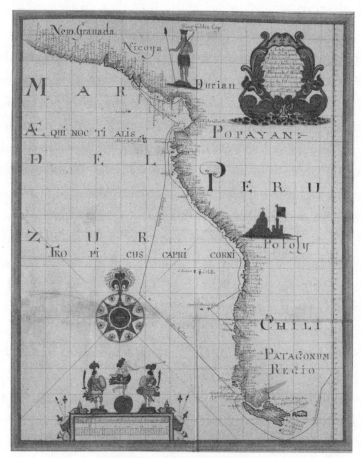

Map from Sharp's waggoner

One month and two days later, on November 25, 1682, Sharp received his captain's commission and was appointed to the command of the *Bonetta,* a sleek fifty-seven-ton sloop of war. His orders were to sail to the Caribbean in the spring and recover the contents of a Spanish treasure ship that had been wrecked off Hispaniola. The optics alone — Captain Sharp, back in the Caribbean, relieving yet another Spanish ship of silver and gold — threatened to spark an international incident.

More than anyone in the Court of St. James's, Sharp took steps to nip the Spaniards' outrage in the bud, albeit unwittingly. Seemingly allergic to his newfound respectability, he dug into his chests of gold, silver, and jewels and plunged into "good fellowship," according to Dick, to the extent "that he was soon reduced low, as most of the bucaniers used to be after their voyages." By the time the *Bonetta* set sail for the Americas, on April 13, 1683, Sharp's insobriety had cost him his captaincy as well as his fortune, and because of authorities' fears that he would return to piracy, he was also expressly forbidden aboard any of His Majesty's ships in an official capacity. On learning that Sharp had managed to book himself a passenger berth on a navy vessel bound for the Caribbean, the Admiralty court issued an additional order that "no commander should carry him into those parts of the West Indies again, fearing lest he should do more mischief unto the Spaniards."

With exactly that in mind, Sharp looked instead to merchant ships for passage, but with rumors swirling on the docks that he planned to tempt crews to mutiny and turn pirate, one merchant captain after the next refused him. Realizing that no one would even transport him out of England, he scraped together £20 and bought an old boat that had been lying around a Thames River dock near London Bridge. After provisioning her with bread, butter, cheese, and beef, he rounded up a crew of sixteen men and sailed downriver.

Forty miles later, he tacked into the North Sea. As the sails caught the wind, his crew may have observed his face and arms glistening in the sea spray and his hair flapping behind him like a black cape, in which case they were likely to have seen an over-all change in his appearance attributable to the bliss — the thrill, the whirl — of once again being at the helm, slicing through whitecaps, and distancing himself from cold, gray terra firma. Or perhaps the explanation was much simpler: he was no longer unemployed.

Soon afterward, at the confluence of the North Sea and the English Channel, Sharp sighted a French vessel that, according to Dick, "he clapt aboard, seized, and made himself master thereof." He sailed her to the nearby Romney Marsh, where there were cattle grazing, and sent some of his men ashore to "provision." They returned with enough cows to victual their Atlantic cross-ing. All that remained was to procure brandy, and they would be in business.

Sharp and company went on to capture bookstores a year later, in 1684. Following the blockbuster success of the February pub-lication of the first English edition of *The History of the Bucaniers of America,* publisher William Crooke won even more readers with a second edition, released in October, that included a journal of Sharp's exploits with the terse title "A brief account of Cap-tain Sharp and companions; their voyage from Jamaica unto the province of Darien and South Sea; with the robberies and assaults they committed therefore the space of three years, till their return for England in the year 1682. Given by one of the Bucaniers who was present at those transactions." Its author was credited only as "W. D." to protect him from self-incrimination — or, rather, further incrimination, because he almost certainly was William Dick.

Also debuting in 1684 was *The Journal and Adventures of Capt. Barth. Sharp,* which, as it happens, did not include Sharp's journal; the journal in the title was instead John Cox's, published anonymously. Cox's name would become known to the throng of pirate nonfiction readers in February of 1685, however, with the publication of a second volume of *The History of the Bucaniers of America* that included Basil Ringrose's journal. It was titled *The Dangerous Voyage and Bold Assaults of Captain Bartholomew Sharp and Others* in lieu of Ringrose's original choice, *A Journall Into ye South Sea by Baz Ringrose.* By the time of its publication, Ringrose was back in the South Sea. According to various sources, he was either compiling material for a new book, employed as a commercial shipping officer, pirating again, or some combination of the above.

In his own memoir, *A New Voyage Round the World,* not published until 1697, Dampier wrote that Ringrose was serving as the supercargo on the *Cygnet,* a 180-ton merchant ship that had set sail for the South Sea from England with a crew of thirty-six on October 1, 1683. "He had no mind to this voyage, but was necessitated to engage in it or starve," Dampier wrote of his friend, though probably that was more of his exculpatory spin. After all, Ringrose had returned to England with enough booty to do whatever he wanted. And that was before transacting the publication rights to his journal and being cast as a pirate extraordinaire by Cox, W. D., and Crooke, whose preface to the second volume of *The History of the Bucaniers of America* declared that Ringrose "not [only] fought with his sword in the most desperate engagements and battels of the bucaniers against the Spaniards, but with his pen gave us a true account of those transactions."

Ringrose went on to compile material for a sequel. Whereas Bartholomew Sharp serves as a reminder of pirates' knack for blowing fortunes and wearing out welcomes ashore, forcing a return to the sea, Ringrose's second act, notwithstanding Dampier's claim, appears to have been entirely by choice, a far cry from his desire in 1680 "to quit those hazardous adventures, and return homewards." When reflecting on the expedition in the waggoner he produced after returning to England in 1682, he wrote with relish of the buccaneers' exploits in the South Seas — or "the Spanish Seas as [the Spaniards] proudly call them; but if the sword gave them their title, it likewise gave us ours, for we were masters of these seas 22 months and might have been there to this day if we would have stayed there."

The *Cygnet* venture was entirely Baz Ringrose's idea, according to Dampier: Baz had gone to "eminent" merchants in London in 1683 and proposed fitting out a ship with £5,000 worth of goods to sell in the South Sea. But though Baz may have been "ingenious," he was off the mark in his market analysis. Once the *Cygnet* reached the South Sea, he was not able to unload the goods.

On October 2, 1684, the *Cygnet* crossed paths at Isla de la Plata with buccaneers who had formed a new South Sea fleet. With ten ships and nine hundred men, the new fleet would not suffer from the manpower shortage that had repeatedly hobbled the old one. With their commercial enterprise flagging, many of the *Cygnet* crewmen had wanted to turn pirate even before they were enticed by the prospect of joining the new buccaneer fleet.

Among the buccaneers on Isla de la Plata were Dampier and Wafer. Neither wrote of the reunion with Ringrose, and it is unknown whether they encouraged him to join the new fleet, but their sentiments may be gleaned from their actions before and after: since leaving the *Trinity*, in April of 1681, neither man had returned home — or, rather, they hadn't returned home in the traditional sense, to their families in England. Home for them now was among buccaneers, wherever adventure was in the offing.

Wafer continued buccaneering until 1688, when "some troubles," as he put it, necessitated his return to England. Those troubles were an arrest on piracy charges in Point Comfort, Virginia, landing him in a Jamestown jail before he and his codefendants — his fellow Darien straggler John Hingson and Captain Edward Davis — were transferred to Newgate Prison, in London. There the trio sought to avoid yet another relocation, to the gallows, by capitalizing on King James II's offer of amnesty to certain buccaneers. Unfortunately for their case, James had recently gone into exile in France and been replaced by the joint reign of William III and Mary II.

In 1691, however, William and Mary granted Wafer, Hingson, and Davis amnesty; they were free men. The decision also presented them with a path toward recovering the booty that had been confiscated from them in Virginia — in Wafer's case, 1,158 pieces of eight, 162 pounds of plate, and one and a half ounces of gold: they had to relinquish one-quarter of the total as well as send an additional £300 back to Virginia to help the colony start a college. The result was the 1693 founding of the College of William and Mary, today the second-oldest institution of higher learning in the United States, after Harvard.

It's highly likely that, as in the cases of Sharp, Dick, and Cox, Wafer's value to the Crown affected the outcome. He went on to become a key player in the colonization of the South Seas, beginning with his book, *A New Voyage and Description of the Isthmus of America*, a reminiscence of his time in the Darien. It was published in 1699, but while still a manuscript, its insights into the economic opportunities on the isthmus sparked the formation of a massive publicly funded effort to establish a Scottish colony in the Darien. The colony's business entity, the Company of Scotland Trading to Africa and the Indies, paid Wafer £20 to suppress publication of his book for a month so that its intelligence would remain proprietary. He subsequently received an additional £750 to serve as expert adviser for the enterprise. Dampier was hired, too.

In 1698, the colony's initial wave of 1,200 pioneers established the city of New Edinburgh just across the Bay of Darien from Golden Island. Within nine months — before Wafer even had the chance to visit — three-quarters of the settlers had died of tropical diseases and the rest had evacuated. The jungle has since erased all traces of their effort. In 1704, Wafer used the preface to the second edition of *A New Voyage and Description of the Isthmus of America* to lobby the English government to try another Darien colony, this time correcting the Company of Scotland's failure to cultivate a friendship with the Kuna. A year later, however, when Wafer died, so did enthusiasm for the project.

Like Wafer, Dampier continued "privateering." Following the first South Sea expedition, for which he escaped charges, he participated in myriad raids on the Spanish Main until 1686, when he relocated to the eastern Indian Ocean. His lone stop of any duration there was at a fort in British Bencoolen, Sumatra, where he served as a gunner until a clash with the settlement's governor necessitated an escape that routed him to London in September of 1691. This marked the first time that he had been to England, or seen his wife, in twelve years. It wasn't long before he was off to the Caribbean for more pirating.

When his first book, *A New Voyage Round the World,* was finally published, in 1697, readers still could not get enough of pirates. Seeking to "avoid needless repetitions" of the other published accounts of the South Sea expedition, he covered the famous Battle of Panama Bay with only "We were in sight of Panama by the 23d of April." Instead he spent several pages describing the betel nut, a move that was not only a judicious sidestepping of self-incrimination but also a prudent literary choice: to seventeenth-century readers, his "richly detailed account of people, places, things, plants, fishes, reptiles, birds, and mammals" was as fresh and engaging as Apollo 11 transmissions from the moon would be to viewers almost three centuries later. *A New Voyage Round the World* was an immediate bestseller, into its third printing within just nine months and available in several foreign-language editions soon thereafter. Thus Dampier became his generation's Charles Darwin as well as a great influence on Darwin himself — the father of evolutionary theory kept a copy of *A New Voyage Round the World* with him on the HMS *Beagle*.

Yet the acclaim paled in comparison with the joy of sailing a leaky vessel into the stormy unknown. In 1699, Dampier accepted command of the English Admiralty's expedition to explore New Holland, now known as Australia, resulting in a slew of discoveries, two more successful books, and the honor of having a number of Australian landmarks and flowering plants named after him. But he found that exploration lacked the exhilaration of ducking incoming musket balls, and in 1702 he returned to privateering — legitimately, for once, thanks to licenses England granted during the War of the Spanish Succession. He was still at it in 1709, at age fifty-eight, as a member of the crew that took the twenty-gun, 193-man Manila treasure galleon *Nuestra Señora de la Encarnacion Desengaño* for £150,000 worth of gold, gems, and other cargo. Only his death, in 1715, would keep him from returning to sea.

Accordingly, back on October 2, 1684, at Isla de la Plata, it is hard to imagine either William Dampier or Lionel Wafer dissuading their friend Baz Ringrose from a return to piracy. More likely, they welcomed him home. In any event, Ringrose signed on, as did the rest of the *Cygnet* crew. The new buccaneer fleet devoted much of the following year to the pursuit of a Spanish fleet carrying the king's treasure: twenty-four million pieces of eight. It was an adventure that merits its own book. In the end, Dampier, Wafer, Ringrose, and company succeeded in intercepting the Spaniards but found themselves outgunned and with no choice but to retreat.

After a narrow escape, the trio remained with the new band of buccaneers, who decided to try their luck instead on the western coast of Mexico. There, in February of 1686, Ringrose went ashore to get provisions as part of a force under the *Cygnet's* captain, Charles Swan. The party proceeded fifteen miles inland via canoe and then on foot to the small town of Santa Pecaque (now known as Sentispac, located in the western state of Nayarit, about a hundred miles north of Puerto Vallarta), which they captured without resistance. While there, as Dampier reported, Swan and company took a prisoner, who told them about a Spanish battalion of nearly a thousand men just three leagues away. It was hardly the first time in the buccaneers' experience that a prisoner tried to warn them off with details of a superior fighting force nearby. Dismissing the information as uninspired propaganda, they took their time securing supplies. But on returning to their canoes the following day, February 19, they realized that the prisoner had been spot-on. Ambushed by the Spanish battalion, fifty buccaneers died. "They were stript, and cut and mangl'd that [Swan] scarce knew one man," Dampier related, adding that among the dead was "my ingenious friend Mr. Ringrose."

Ringrose was but thirty-three years old. He certainly had not lived long. Yet in the end, he may have achieved the "merry life and a short one" to which pirates aspired. The journal he kept aboard the *Cygnet* presumably holds the answer, but it has never been found. Given the breadth of the new South Sea fleet's adventures and the paucity of available reporting, it may be the greatest pirate treasure of all time.

Acknowledgments

This book would not exist without the savvy and gumption of literary agent Richard Abate. It would be three hundred pages of pirate tropes if not for the help — intervention, really — of U.S. Naval Academy history professor Virginia Lunsford. And it would be three hundred historically sound but ponderous pages if not for the shrewd, incisive editing of Ben George. Those three need never pay for grog again.

Also due grog: Katherine Akey, perhaps the best book marketer in the Seven Seas; Ben Allen, the most diligent production editor in the known universe; proofreader Kathryn Blatt, who no doubt could spot a typo from outer space, much less from beyond the three-mile outer limit of human eyesight; the incomparable maritime historian, author, and Blackbeard-channeler, Baylus Brooks; incredibly meticulous copyeditor Barbara Clark, of whom, in the near future, authors will surely erect a statue; ridiculously talented graphic designer Kirin Diemont; the Anne Bonney of research assistants, Talia Fine; all-star muse Lucy Graves Hollis; editorial assistant Evan Hansen-Bundy, who nimbly shifted between a dozen roles on this project, not least of which was Job; Brandon Kelley, who is to marketing what the buccaneers were to musketry; first and best manuscript reader Joan Kretschmer; Basil-Ringrose-level-resourceful Hachette audio producer Michele McGonigle; Candice Millard, a sublime writer and this book's equivalent of an astrolabe; researcher Simon Neal, who, in digging through ancient municipal records in England, effectively doubled as an archeologist; maritime expert and brilliant author Jim Nelson, who for this book went so far as to make a how-to video on loading and firing a flintlock musket; publicist Alyssa Persons, whom the Brethren of the Coast would have been lucky to hire for their public relations campaign; Karen Shepard and Henry, Malcolm, Matthew, and Trouser Thomson, of course; reader and pirate authority Cindy Vallar, whose eponymous website is the subject's answer to the Library of Alexandria; gifted designer-cum-cartographer Jeffrey Ward; Jack Wareham, the Usain Bolt of research assistants; Craig Young, *Born to Be Hanged*'s admiral as well as its source of illumination — without him there would be zero illustrations; and anyone else who has read this far.

Please send questions or comments to kqthomson@gmail.com.

A Note on Sources

Born to Be Hanged was built from the chronicles of seven buccaneers who participated in the South Sea expedition: Basil Ringrose, Bartholomew Sharp, William Dampier, Lionel Wafer, John Cox, William Dick, and Edward Povey (almost certainly the member of the company who turned "cat in the pan" and wrote his account of the expedition for use as king's evidence). Their words have been reprinted herein exactly as published or transcribed three and a half centuries ago, save for minor amendments to misspellings, period conventions, and the like that hinder readability. Because the chroniclers were thieves and murderers and frequently inclined to drinking on top of a collective tendency to self-aggrandize, dispense with incriminating details, and varnish the truth, this book also relied on the men tasked with keeping them honest, principally Henry Morgan, Leoline Jenkins, and Pedro Ronquillo Briceño, whose versions of events can be found in their correspondence and, chiefly, in England's *Colonial State Papers*.

Equally foundational has been the work of other authors, especially Lieutenant-Commander H. Derek Howse, who joined the HMS *Rodney* as a midshipman in 1937, went on to become one of the world's foremost authorities on maritime navigation, and then collaborated with UCLA cartographer Norman Thrower on *A Buccaneer's Atlas*, the first-ever publication of Ringrose's waggoner. Their meticulously researched annotation served as a compass in retelling Ringrose's story, if not a means of traveling back in time. And then there's Benerson Little, the historian responsible for *The Sea Rover's Practice: Pirate Tactics and Techniques* and four other books about pirates that are, in sum, the consummate piracy handbook. As an author of realistic pirate novels put it, "What would we do without Benerson Little?" Similarly integral to the reconstruction of the South Sea expedition were the raw data and wry commentary delivered by the English novelist, poet, and maritime historian John Masefield (1878–1967) in his collection of Dampier's journals, *Dampier's Voyages,* as well as his insights in *On the Spanish Main.*

Finally, it is hard to overstate the value of the British Library's Sloane Manuscript Collection, where the buccaneers' actual journals can be found, and England's National Archives, home to such documents as "Bazite Ringrose v Charles Toll and others, re. property in Charing Cross," the handwritten record of the minor 1683 Court of Chancery lawsuit that yielded fresh details about Ringrose, including that his father owned a shop called the Golden Sword and that rather than make and sell swords, Basil opted to go to sea to fight with them. Also of particular use was the Archives' currency converter, at nationalarchives.gov.uk/currency-converter/, which lets you input an amount of money and then learn its purchasing power in any given year between 1270 and 2017; for example, in 1680, £1,000 would get you either 185 horses, 240 cows, 1,666 stones of wool, 500 quarters of wheat, or the wages of a skilled tradesman for 11,111 days.

Bibliography

Adams, Simon. *The Unforgiving Rope: Murder and Hanging on Australia's Western Frontier.* Crawley, Western Australia: UWA Publishing, 2009.

Alexander VI. "Inter Caetera." Papal bull, May 4, 1493. Archives of the Indies at Seville, Patronato, 1-1-1, no. 3. Translation: https://en.wikisource.org/wiki/European_Treaties_bearing_on_the_History_of_the_United_States_and_its_Dependencies_to_1648/Document_05.

Anderson, Charles Loftus Grant. *Old Panama and Castilla del Oro.* Washington, DC: Press of the Sudwarth Company, 1911.

Anonymous [probably John Cox]. *The Voyages and Adventures of Capt. Barth. Sharp And Others in the South Sea, being a journal of the same.* Edited by Philip Ayres. London: P.A., Esq., 1684.

——— [probably Edward Povey]. "Bartholomew Sharp's Men." *Privateering and Piracy in the Colonial Period.* Edited by John Franklin Jameson. New York: Macmillan, 1923.

———. *The Gazetteer of the World, Prominence Being Given to Great Britain and Colonies, Indian Empire, United States of America.* Vol. 9. London: Thomas C. Jack, 1887.

Bancroft, Hubert Howe. *The Works of Hubert Howe Bancroft,* vol. 7, *History of Central America vol. II: 1530–1800.* San Francisco: A. L. Bancroft & Company, 1883.

Bassett, Fletcher S. *Legends and Superstitions of the Sea and of Sailors in All Lands and at All Times.* Chicago: Belford, Clarke & Company, 1885. Kindle.

Berry, B. Midi, and R. S. Schofield. "Age at Baptism in Pre-Industrial England." *Population Studies* 25, no. 3 (November 1971): 453–63.

Black, Clinton. *Pirates of the West Indies.* Cambridge, UK: Cambridge University Press, 1989.

Bowditch, Nathaniel. *The New American Practical Navigator.* Washington, DC: Government Printing Office, 1868.

Bown, Stephen J. *Scurvy: How a Surgeon, a Mariner, and a Gentleman Solved the Greatest Medical Mystery of the Age of Sail.* New York: Thomas Dunne Books, 2004.

Bradley, Peter T. *The Defence of Peru 1579–1700: Royal Reluctance and Colonial Self-Reliance.* Self-published, Lulu, 2009.

Brandon, Pepijn, Sabine Go, and Verstegen Wybren, eds. *Navigating History: Economy, Society, Knowledge, and Nature.* Library of Economic History 11. Leiden, Netherlands: Brill, 2018.

Breverton, Terry. *Admiral Sir Henry Morgan: King of the Buccaneers.* Gretna, LA: Pelican Publishing, 2005.

Brochu, Christopher A. "Phylogenetics, Taxonomy, and Historical Biogeography of Alligatoroidea." *Memoir (Society of Vertebrate Paleontology)* 6 (June 1999): 9–100.

Burkett, Josiah. *A Complete History of the Most Remarkable Transactions at Sea.* London: W.B., 1920.

Cary, Henry Nathaniel. *The slang of venery and its analogues.* Chicago, 1916.

Chamberlayne, John. *The Natural History of Coffee, Thee, Chocolate, Tobacco.* London: Christopher Wilkinson, 1682.

Climate-Data.org. https://en.climate-data.org/.

"Currency Converter: 1270–2017." National Archives, www.nationalarchives .gov.uk/currency-converter/#currency-result.

Curtler, W. H. R. *English Agriculture.* London: Clarendon Press, 1909.

Dampier, William. "The Campeachy Voyages." In *Dampier's Voyages,* vol. 2, edited by John Masefield. London: E. Grant Richards, 1906. First published by James Knapton, London, 1697.

———. "A New Voyage Round the World." In *Dampier's Voyages,* vol. 1, edited by John Masefield. London: E. Grant Richards, 1906. First published by James Knapton, London, 1697.

———. *A Voyage to New-Holland, &c. In the Year 1699.* London: James and John Knapton, 1729.

Darwin Correspondence Project. University of Cambridge. https://www.darwin project.ac.uk/.

Dick, William. *William Dick's South Sea Voyage: From Jamaica unto the Province of Darien, and South-Seas.* The Dampier Collection, vol. 13. N.p.: Tomes Maritime Press, 2018. First published in *Bucaniers of America: The Second Volume.* London: William Crooke, 1685.

Durston, Gregory. *The Admiralty Sessions, 1536–1834: Maritime Crime and the Silver Oar.* United Kingdom: Cambridge Scholars Publishing, 2017.

Emsley, Clive, Tim Hitchcock, and Robert Shoemaker. "History of the Old Bailey Courthouse: The Courtroom." *Old Bailey Proceedings Online,* April 17, 2011, https://www.oldbaileyonline.org/static/The-old-bailey.jsp#courtroom.

———. "Trial Procedures: How Trials Were Conducted at the Old Bailey." *Old Bailey Proceedings Online,* April 17, 2011, https://www.oldbaileyonline.org/ static/Trial-procedures.jsp.

Exquemelin, Alexander O. *The Buccaneers of America*. Overland Park, KS: Digireads, 2010. First published in Dutch as *De Americaensche Zee-Roovers* (Amsterdam: Jan ten Hoorn, 1678). Kindle.

Falconer, William. *An Universal Dictionary of the Marine*. Glasgow: Good Press, 2019. First published by T. Cadell, London, 1780. Kindle.

Fish, Shirley. *The Manila-Acapulco Galleons: The Treasure Ships of the Pacific*. Self-published, Author House, 2011.

Fortescue, J. W., ed. *Calendar of State Papers Colonial, America and West Indies,* vol. 11, *1681–1685*. London: Her Majesty's Stationery Office, 1898. Reproduced in *British History Online,* https://www.british-history.ac.uk/cal-state-papers/colo nial/america-west-indies/vol11.

Friedenberg, Zachary B. *Medicine Under Sail*. Annapolis, MD: Naval Institute Press, 2002.

Fuss, Norman. "You Say Huzzah! They Said Huzzay!" *Journal of the American Revolution,* April 22, 2014, https://allthingsliberty.com/2014/04/you-say-huzzah -they-said-huzzay/.

Gammon, Katharine. "The 10 Driest Places on Earth." *Live Science,* July 22, 2011, https://www.livescience.com/30627-10-driest-places-on-earth.html.

Garner, Richard L. "Long-Term Silver Mining Trends in Spanish America: A Comparative Analysis of Peru and Mexico." *American Historical Review* 93, no. 4 (1988): 898–935.

George, James, and Kenneth Rockwood. "Dehydration and Delirium — Not a Simple Relationship." *Journal of Gerontology: Medical Sciences* 59, no. 8 (August 2004): M811–12.

Gerhard, Peter. *Pirates on the West Coast of New Spain, 1575–1742*. Glendale, CA: A. H. Clark Company, 1960.

Ginger, John. *Handel's Trumpeter; the Diary of John Grano*. Hillsdale, NY: Pendragon Press, 1998.

Gisolfi, Carl V. "Water Requirements During Exercise in the Heat." In *Nutritional Needs in Hot Environments: Applications for Military Personnel in Field Operations,* edited by Bernadette M. Marriott. Washington, DC: National Academies Press, 1993.

Goodricke, Charles Alfred. *History of the Goodricke Family*. Aylesbury, UK: Hazell, Watson, and Viney, 1885.

Gosse, Philip. *The Pirates' Who's Who*. New York: Burt Franklin, 1924.

Hansen, Valerie, and Ken Curtis. *Voyages in World History,* vol. 2, *To 1500*. Boston: Cengage Learning, 2013.

Harding, Christopher. "'Hostis Humani Generis' — The Pirate as Outlaw in the Early Modern Law of the Sea." In *Pirates? The Politics of Plunder, 1550–1650,* edited by Claire Jowitt. London: Palgrave Macmillan, 2006.

Healey, Jonathan. "Just a Quick List of 17th Century Euphemisms for Being Drunk...." *The Social Historian,* August 30, 2016, https://thesocialhistorian .wordpress.com/2016/08/30/just-a-quick-list-of-17th-century-euphemisms -for-being-drunk/.

Helms, Mary W. *Ancient Panama: Chiefs in Search of Power.* Austin: University of Texas Press, 1979. Kindle.

"History of Court Dress." Courts and Tribunals Judiciary, https://www.judiciary .uk/about-the-judiciary/the-justice-system/history/.

Howe, James. *The Kuna Gathering: Contemporary Village Politic in Panama.* Tucson, AZ: Fenestra Books, 2002.

"Howler Monkeys." *National Geographic,* https://www.nationalgeographic.com/ani mals/mammals/facts/howler-monkeys.

Howse, Derek, and Norman J. W. Thrower, eds. *A Buccaneer's Atlas: Basil Ringrose's South Seas Waggoner.* Berkeley: University of California Press, 1992.

Hunt, James. "On the Negro's Place in Nature." *Journal of the Anthropological Society of London* 2 (1864): xv–lvi.

Jacobus de Voragine. *The Golden Legend; Readings on the Saints.* Princeton, NJ: Princeton University Press, 2012.

Jameson, John Franklin. *Privateering and Piracy in the Colonial Period.* New York: Macmillan, 1923.

Johnson, Charles. *A General History of the Robberies and Murders of the most notorious Pyrates.* London: T. Warner, 1724.

Joyce, Lilian Elwyn Elliot. Introduction to *A New Voyage and Description of the Isthmus of America* by Lionel Wafer, Edited by Lilian Elwyn Elliot Joyce. London: Hakluyt Society, 1934. First published by James Knapton, London, 1699.

Kehoe, Mark C. "Theriaca Londonensis (London Treacle)," in "The Sea Surgeon's Dispensatory, Page 21," *The Pirate Surgeon's Journals,* http://www.pirate surgeon.com/pages/surgeon_pages/dispensatory21.html#london_treacle.

Kemp, Peter. *The Oxford Companion to Ships and the Sea.* Oxford, UK: Oxford University Press, 1976.

Kemp, P. K., and Christopher Lloyd. *Brethren of the Coast: Buccaneers of the South Seas.* New York: St. Martin's Press, 1960.

Koerner, Brendan I. "Last Words: Why Are We So Sure That Death and Honesty Go Together?" *Legal Affairs,* November/December, 2002, https:// www.legalaffairs.org/issues/November-December2002/review_koerner _novdec2002.msp.

Konstam, Angus. *The Pirate Ship 1660–1730.* Oxford, UK: Osprey Publishing, 2003.

Kritzler, Edward. *Jewish Pirates of the Caribbean: How a Generation of Swashbuckling Jews Carved Out an Empire in the New World in Their Quest for Treasure, Religious Freedom — and Revenge.* New York: Doubleday, 2008.

Labat, Jean-Baptiste. *Voyage aux Isles de l'Amérique.* 2 vols. Paris: Editions Duchartre, 1931.

Lancaster, H. O. *Expectations of Life: A Study in the Demography, Statistics, and History of World Mortality.* Sydney: Springer Science and Business, 1990.

Langbein, John H. "The Prosecutorial Origins of Defence Counsel in the Eighteenth Century: The Appearance of Solicitors." *Cambridge Law Journal* 58, no. 2 (July 1999): 314–65.

Las Casas, Bartolome de. *A Short Account of the Destruction of the Indies.* Seville, 1552.

Lea, Henry Charles. *A History of the Inquisition of Spain.* Vol. 2. New York: Harper & Brothers, 1887.

Leslie, Charles. *A New History of Jamaica.* Cambridge, UK: Cambridge University Press, 2015. First published as *A New and Exact Account of Jamaica* (Edinburgh: R. Fleming, 1739).

Little, Benerson. *The Buccaneer's Realm: Pirate Life on the Spanish Main, 1674–1688.* Washington, DC: Potomac Books, 2007. Kindle.

———. "Eyewitness Images of Buccaneers and Their Vessels." *Mariner's Mirror* 98, no. 3 (August 2012): 313–28.

———. *The Golden Age of Piracy: The Truth Behind Pirate Myths.* New York: Skyhorse Publishing, 2006.

———. "Gunpowder Spots: Pirates & 'Tattoos.'" *Swordplay & Swashbucklers,* January 28, 2018, www.benersonlittle.blog/2017/08/16/gunpowder-spots-pirates-tattoos/.

———. *How History's Greatest Pirates Pillaged, Plundered, and Got Away with It: The Stories, Techniques, and Tactics of the Most Feared Sea Rovers from 1500–1800.* Beverly, MA: Fair Winds Press, 2010.

———. "The Myth of Sharp's Buccaneers, the Wreck of the *Santa María de la Consolación,* and Isla de Muerto." *Swordplay & Swashbucklers,* February 13, 2019, https://benersonlittle.blog/2019/02/13/the-myth-of-sharps-buccaneers-the-wreck-of-the-santa-maria-de-la-consolacion-and-isla-de-muerto/.

———. "Of Pirates & Wooden Legs." *Swordplay & Swashbucklers,* December 4, 2017, updated March 6, 2019, https://benersonlittle.blog/2017/12/04/of-pirates-wooden-legs/.

———. *The Sea Rover's Practice: Pirate Tactics and Techniques, 1630–1730.* Washington, DC: Potomac Books, 2005.

Lloyd, Christopher. "Bartholomew Sharp, Buccaneer." *Mariner's Mirror* 42, no. 4 (1956): 291–301.

Loveman, Kate. "The Introduction of Chocolate into England: Retailers, Researchers, and Consumers, 1640–1730." *Journal of Social History* 47, no. 1 (Fall 2013): 27–46.

Lunsford, Virginia. "A Model of Piracy: The Buccaneers of the Seventeenth-Century Caribbean." In *The Golden Age of Piracy: The Rise, Fall, and Enduring*

Popularity of Pirates, edited by David Head. Athens: University of Georgia Press, 2018.

Luscombe, Stephen. "Nevis: Brief History." *The British Empire: Where the Sun Never Sets,* www.britishempire.co.uk/maproom/nevis.htm.

Malt, Ronald A. "Lionel Wafer — Surgeon to the Buccaneers." *Journal of the History of Medicine and Allied Sciences* 14, no. 10 (October 1959): 459–74.

Mangas, Fernando Serrano. "El proceso de pirata Bartholomew Sharp." *Temas Americanistas* 4 (1984): 38–49.

Marley, David F. *Pirates of the Americas.* Vol. 1, *1650–1685.* Santa Barbara, CA: ABC Clio, 2010.

Masefield, John. *On the Spanish Main: Or, Some English forays on the Isthmus of Darien.* New York: Macmillan, 1906.

McKay, Rich. "Sunken Treasure Beckons Hunters." *Orlando Sentinel,* October 26, 2003, https://www.orlandosentinel.com/news/os-xpm-2003-10-26-03102 60412-story.html.

Morgan, Sam. "How to Use an Astrolabe." *Sciencing,* April 24, 2017, https://sciencing.com/use-astrolabe-4495712.html.

National Aeronautics and Space Administration Earth Observatory, https://earthobservatory.nasa.gov/.

National Aeronautics and Space Administration Eclipse Web Site, https://eclipse.gsfc.nasa.gov/.

National Oceanic and Atmospheric Administration. https://www.noaa.gov/.

New Zealand Maritime Museum. maritimemuseum.co.nz.

O'Conner, Patricia T., and Stewart Kellerman. "Hip Hip Hooray." *Grammarphobia,* March 5, 2012, https://www.grammarphobia.com/blog/2012/03/hooray.html.

O'Shea, J. G. "'Two Minutes with Venus, Two Years with Mercury' — Mercury as an Antisyphilitic Chemotherapeutic Agent." *Journal of the Royal Society of Medicine* 83, no. 6 (June 1990): 392–95.

Paré, Ambroise. *The Workes of that Famous Chirurgion Ambrose Parey.* London: R. Coates and W. Dugard, 1649.

"Pig Iron." International Iron Metallics Association, https://www.metallics.org/pig-iron.html.

Pratt, George, ed. *Papers Relating to the Ships and Voyages of the Company of Scotland Trading to Africa and the Indies, 1696–1707.* Edinburgh: University Press, 1924.

Prescott, William Hickling. *History of the Conquest of Peru.* Philadelphia: J.B. Lippincott & Company, 1843. Kindle.

Preston, Diana and Michael. *A Pirate of Exquisite Mind: Explorer, Naturalist, and Buccaneer: The Life of William Dampier.* New York: Walker & Company, 2004.

"The Procedure for the Trial of a Pirate." *American Journal of Legal History* 1, no. 3 (July 1957): 251–56.

Rediker, Marcus. *Between the Devil and the Deep Blue Sea: Merchant Seamen, Pirates and the Anglo-American Maritime World, 1700–1750.* Cambridge, UK: Cambridge University Press, 1987.

———. *Villains of All Nations: Atlantic Pirates in the Golden Age.* Boston: Beacon Press, 2004.

Ringrose, Basil. *Baz Ringrose's Journal into the South Seas.* The Dampier Collection, vol. 12. N.p.: Tomes Maritime Press, 2010. First published in *Bucaniers of America: The Second Volume.* London: William Crooke, 1685.

Ruffhead, Owen, ed. *The Statutes at Large,* volume 2, *From the First Year of King Edward the Fourth to the End of the Reign of Queen Elizabeth.* London: Basket, Woodfall, and Strahan, 1763.

———. *The Statutes at Large,* volume 6, *From the Ninth Year of the Reign of King George the Second to the Twenty-fifth Year of the Reign of King George the Second.* London: Eyre & Strahan, 1786. Reprinted in an edition edited by Charles Runnington. London: Eyre & Strahan, 1786.

Sainsbury, W. Noel, ed. *Calendar of State Papers Colonial, America and West Indies,* vol. 5, *1661–1668.* London: Her Majesty's Stationery Office, 1889. Reproduced in *British History Online,* https://www.british-history.ac.uk/cal-state-papers/colonial/america-west-indies/vol7.

———. *Calendar of State Papers Colonial, America and West Indies,* vol. 7, *1669–1674.* London: Her Majesty's Stationery Office, 1889. Reproduced in *British History Online,* https://www.british-history.ac.uk/cal-state-papers/colonial/america-west-indies/vol7.

Sainsbury, W. Noel, and J. W. Fortescue, eds. *Calendar of State Papers Colonial, America and West Indies,* vol. 10, *1677–1680.* London: Her Majesty's Stationery Office, 1898. Reproduced in *British History Online,* http://www.british-history.ac.uk/cal-state-papers/colonial/america-west-indies/vol10.

Schön, M. A., "The Anatomy of the Resonating Mechanism in Howling Monkeys." *Folia Primatologica* 15 (1971): 117–32.

Sellegren, Kim R., MD. "An Early History of Lower Limb Amputations and Prostheses." *Iowa Orthopeadic Journal* 2 (1982): 13–27.

Senior, William. *Doctors Commons and the Old Court of Admiralty.* London: Longman Green and Company, 1922.

Sepúlveda, Juan Ginés de. "Democrates Alter, Or, on the Just Causes for War Against the Indians" (1544). From *Boletín de la Real Academia de la Historia* 21 (October 1892). Originally translated for *Introduction to Contemporary Civilization in the West* (New York: Columbia University Press, 1946, 1954, 1961), www.columbia.edu/acis/ets/CCREAD/sepulved.htm.

Sharp, Bartholomew. *Captain Sharp's Journey Over the Isthmus of Darien and Expedition into the South Seas: The Journal of his Expedition, Written by Himself.* The Dampier Collection, vol. 14. N.p.: Tomes Maritime Press, 2010. First published in *A Collection of Original Voyages,* edited by William Hacke (London: James Knapton, 1699).

Sheridan, Richard. *Sugar and Slavery: An Economic History of the British West Indies, 1623–1775.* Kingston, Jamaica: Canoe Press, 1974.

"Shipbuilding: 800–1800: Discover How Many Trees It Took to Build One 18th Century Warship." Royal Museums Greenwich, www.rmg.co.uk/stories/topics/shipbuilding-800-1800.

"Silvagenitus." In *International Cloud Atlas.* World Meteorological Organization, https://cloudatlas.wmo.int/en/silvagenitus.html.

Simon, Rebecca. "Pirate Executions in Early Modern London." *English Legal History,* July 9, 2014, https://englishlegalhistory.wordpress.com/2014/07/09/pirate-executions-in-early-modern-london/.

Stevenson, Robert Louis. *Treasure Island.* London: Cassell and Company, 1883.

Steward, David J. *The Sea and Their Graves: An Archaeology of Death and Remembrance in Maritime Culture.* Gainesville: University Press of Florida, 2011.

Talty, Stephan. *Empire of Blue Water: Captain Morgan's Great Pirate Army, the Epic Battle for the Americas, and the Catastrophe That Ended the Outlaws' Bloody Reign.* New York: Three Rivers Press, 2007.

Tanner, Joseph Robson, ed. *A Descriptive Catalogue of the Naval Manuscripts in the Pepysian Library at Magdalene College, Cambridge.* Vol. 1. Cambridge, UK: Naval Records Society, 1903.

Thomas, Graham A. *The Pirate King: The Incredible Story of the Real Captain Morgan.* New York: Skyhorse Publishing, 2015.

Thomas, Hugh. *Rivers of Gold: The Rise of the Spanish Empire, from Columbus to Magellan.* United Kingdom: Random House Publishing Group, 2013.

Tiffin, Helen, Bill Ashcroft, and Gareth Griffiths. *The Post-colonial Studies Reader.* United Kingdom: Routledge, 2006.

Vallar, Cindy. "Notorious Pirate Havens — Part 4: Port Royal." *Pirates and Privateers: The History of Maritime Piracy,* www.cindyvallar.com/havens4.html.

Verrill, A. Hyatt. *The Real Story of the Pirate.* New York: D. Appleton and Company, 1923.

Vivian, Evelyn Charles. *Peru: Physical Features, Natural Resources, Means of Communication, Manufactures and Industrial Development.* New York: D. Appleton & Co., 1914.

Wafer, Lionel. *Wafer's New Voyage and Description of the Isthmus of Darien.* The Dampier Collection, vol. 10. N.p.: Tomes Maritime Press, 2010. First published by James Knapton, London, 1699.

W. D. [probably William Dick]. "A brief account of Captain Sharp and companions; their voyage from Jamaica unto the province of Darien and South Sea; with the robberies and assaults they committed therefore the space of three years, till their return for England in the year 1682. Given by one of the Bucaniers who was present at those transactions." In Alexandre Exquemelin, *Bucaniers of America: or, A true account of the most remarkable assaults committed of late years upon the coasts of the West-Indies, by bucaniers of Jamica and Tortuga, both English and French*. London: William Crooke, 1684.

Westergaard, Waldemar. *The Danish West Indies Under Company Rule (1671–1754)*. New York: Macmillan, 1917.

White, Jerry. *London in the Eighteenth Century: A Great and Monstrous Thing*. New York: Random House, 2012.

———. *Mansions of Misery: A Biography of the Marshalsea Debtors' Prison*. London: Bodley Head, 2016. Kindle.

Whitenton, Brian. "The Difference Between Pirates, Privateers and Buccaneers Pt. 1." *Mariners' Blog,* Mariners' Museum and Park, September 20, 2012, https://blog.marinersmuseum.org/2012/09/the-difference-between-pirates -privateers-and-buccaneers-pt-1/.

———. "The Difference Between Pirates, Privateers and Buccaneers Pt. 2." *Mariners' Blog,* Mariners' Museum and Park, October 4, 2012, https://blog .marinersmuseum.org/2012/10/the-difference-between-pirates-privateers -and-buccaneers-pt-2/.

"A wicked time in 17th century Jamaica." *Antiques Trader Gazette,* October 15, 2015. www.antiquestradegazette.com/news/2012/a-wicked-time-in-17th-century -jamaica/ (2012).

Wonderopolis. "Why Do Pirates Say 'Arrr!'?," www.wonderopolis.org/wonder/ why-do-pirates-say-arrr.

Wood, Michael. *Conquistadors*. Oakland: University of California Press, 2001.

Woodall, John. *The Surgions Mate: The First Compendium on Naval Medicine, Surgery and Drug Therapy (London 1617)*. Edited by Irmgard Müller. Classic Texts in the Sciences. Cham, Switzerland: Birkhäuser, 2016. First published by Laurence Lisle, London, 1617.

World Register of Marine Species. http://www.marinespecies.org/.

Yeomans, Donald K. "Great Comets in History." NASA Jet Propulsion Laboratory, April 2007, https://ssd.jpl.nasa.gov/sb/great_comets.html.

Zahedieh, Nuala. "Trade, Plunder, and Economic Development in Early English Jamaica, 1655–89." *Economic History Review* 39, no. 2 (May 1986): 205–22.

Notes

1. The Princess

3   Indigenous Kuna people and their orthography: They are known today as the Guna, and throughout history have often been called the Kuna as well as the Cuna. Their language is known as Kuna. Most now live in the San Blas Islands, also known as the Guna Yala.

3   Journals of European soldiers and adventurers: Those whose descriptions are incorporated are Basil Ringrose, Lionel Wafer, and Edward Povey (see the bibliography for specifics). Note that the initial capitalizations of many of the nouns — per the seventeenth-century trend of capitalizing significant words — have been modified here for readability's sake. Otherwise all quotations are reprinted with their original spellings.

3   "naturally inferior" and explanation of Spanish position on enslaving Indigenous peoples: Sepúlveda, *Democrates Alter.*

4   Treatment of the enslaved Natives by Spaniards: Las Casas, *A Short Account of the Destruction of the Indies,* 15.

4   "Even if the snows of the Andes": Wood, *Conquistadors,* 18.

4   "gentleman" with "the unique distinction of acting like a human being": Anderson, *Old Panama and Castilla del Oro,* 120.

4   A year after Bastidas's arrival in Panama: Anderson, 120–21.

4   Panama's Indigenous peoples (fifteenth-century overview): Howe, *The Kuna Gathering,* 9.

4   April 3, 1680: All dates are per the Julian calendar, which England used until adopting the "new style" Gregorian calendar, in 1752, when Wednesday, September 2, was followed by Thursday, September 14, syncing the English with the rest of the Western world.

4   Golden Island: Today it is known as Isla Seletupa, and the San Blas Islands are the Guna Yala, *yala* being the Kuna word for "land."

5   chief paramount: Helms, *Ancient Panama,* loc. 768, Kindle.

5   Eight-year-old Kuna boys: Wafer, *Wafer's New Voyage and Description of the Isthmus of Darien,* 104.

6   366 buccaneers: The day before, the fleet had had 477 buccaneers, but two French crews — one with twenty-five men led by Captain Jean Rose, the other with eighty-six men captained by Jean de Bernanos — were unwilling to cross the Darien and departed for other pirating opportunities.

6   *buccaneers* definition: According to Lunsford, in "A Model of Piracy," "The term is often but erroneously utilized to refer to pirates in general. In actuality, the Buccaneers were a specific group of marauders: a motley yet ferocious brotherhood based in the seventeenth-century Caribbean and based on the islands of Tortuga and Jamaica."

6   "open a door into the South Seas": Dampier, "A New Voyage Round the World," 201. Note that, for the most part, the chroniclers use "South Sea" and "South Seas" interchangeably, but, on occasion, South Sea (singular) refers only to the portion of the Pacific flanking the western coasts of South and Central America.

6   The last company of buccaneers to raid Panama: Exquemelin, *The Buccaneers of America,* 115.

7   the twenty-seven-year-old: Parish registry record of the christening of "Basill Ringrose" on January 28, 1653, in London's Church of St. Martin-in-the-Fields, in Howse and Thrower, *A Buccaneer's Atlas,* 28.

7   "The men here go naked": Ringrose, *Baz Ringrose's Journal into the South Seas,* 14. The original journal is at the British Library (Sloane Manuscript 3820). Note that in many of the cited works from the late seventeenth century, most nouns were capitalized — that has been modified herein for readability. Otherwise, quotations are reprinted with grammatical and syntactical warts and all intact, save for the odd extraneous comma or semicolon that would have impeded comprehension.

7   "They wear an ornament in their noses": Ringrose, 15.

7   "fairer than the fairest of Europe": Ringrose, 15.

8   "much like that of a white horse": Wafer, 89–90.

8   "No less than an hundred years of age": Sharp, *Captain Sharp's Journey Over the Isthmus of Darien and Expedition into the South Seas,* 16.

8   a gallon of beer or a pint of rum per day: Tanner, *A Descriptive Catalogue of the Naval Manuscripts in the Pepysian Library at Magdalene College, Cambridge,* 165–67.

9   eighteen thousand to twenty thousand pounds of gold: Wafer, 23–24.

9   pirate crews were democracies: Rediker, *Villains of All Nations,* 70.

9   Andreas elevated the pirates to the status of "privateers": For a slew of reasons, not least of which was the fact that England did not recognize the

sovereignty of the Kuna, the buccaneers would have a very difficult time with this argument in a court of law. But, as the reader will see, they tried.

9   The etymology of the term *buccaneer* and other facets of the buccaneers' origin story come from Lunsford.

9   adapted from Brazil's Indigenous Tupi peoples: Little, *The Buccaneer's Realm,* loc. 898, Kindle.

9   "to hang around with lowlives": Whitenton, "The Difference Between Pirates, Privateers and Buccaneers."

10   four million pieces of eight: 1680 gold rate per MeasuringWorth Foundation, www.measuringworth.com/calculators/ukcompare.

10   "pc. of 8/8" as shorthand for "pieces of eight": Jameson, *Privateering and Piracy in the Colonial Period,* 400.

10   a plantation worker or a sailor earned just a hundred pieces of eight in a year: Curtler, *English Agriculture,* 749.

11   his own plantation: According to Zahedieh, "Trade, Plunder, and Economic Development in Early English Jamaica," the cost of a one-hundred-acre plantation in Jamaica was £3,620; a piece of eight was worth around £0.25.

11   "That which often spurs men": from pages 1–2 of John Cox's diary, published in *The Voyages and Adventures of Capt. Barth. Sharp And Others in the South Sea.*

2. The Golden Swordsman

12   the christening of "Basill Ringrose": Howse and Thrower, *A Buccaneer's Atlas,* 28.

13   Richard Ringrose was listed as "poore": Howse and Thrower, 28.

13   the Golden Sword location and layout: "Deed of assignment, 13 Feb 1670/71," document LR 1/62 in folio 181 of the Office of the Auditors of Land Revenue and predecessors: Enrolment Books — at the National Archives in London.

13   "very plentifully furnished and provided with all manner and sorts of swords": "Bazite Ringrose v Charles Toll and others, re. property in Charing Cross," Office of the Auditors of Land Revenue and predecessors: Enrolment Books, at the National Archives, C 7/600/50.

13   *supercargo* definition: Falconer, *An Universal Dictionary of the Marine,* loc. 6888–90, Kindle.

14   In 1677, the couple had a son, Jonathan: he was baptized November 15, 1677, per the parish register of Church of St. Martin-in-the-Fields, held at the City of Westminster Archives.

14   children were typically baptized within eight days of their births: Berry and Schofield, "Age at Baptism in Pre-Industrial England."

14   Goodith's pregnancy would qualify as the longest in history: The current record was established in 1945 at Los Angeles's Methodist Hospital, when Beula Hunter gave birth to a daughter, Penny Diana, after 375 days of expecting ("Medicine: Prodigious Pregnancy," *Time,* March 5, 1945).

15   Portobelo expedition: Dampier, "A New Voyage Round the World," 26.

15   Bartholomew Sharp background information: Gosse, *The Pirates' Who's Who,* 71.

15   Sawkins had escaped from jail in Port Royal: Black, *Pirates of the West Indies,* 42.

16   "A merry life and a short one": According to Johnson, *A General History of the Robberies and Murders of the most notorious Pyrates,* 141, this motto originated with the Welsh pirate Bartholomew Roberts (1682–1722).

3. The Gap

18   The spelling of Edmond Cooke's first name is recorded in official documents as both "Edmund" and "Edmond" and his last as "Cook" and "Cooke," but in his own 1675 petition to the Privy Council, it's "Edmond Cooke."

18   coarse shirts, baggy linen or canvas breeches: Little, "Eyewitness Images of Buccaneers and Their Vessels."

19   "desired me once to get out of his cheek one of these imprinted pictures": Wafer, *Wafer's New Voyage and Description of the Isthmus of Darien,* 92.

19   typical of the era were initials, crosses: Little, "Gunpowder Spots: Pirates & 'Tattoos.'"

20   any man who failed to keep his weapons clean: Little, *The Sea Rover's Practice,* 64.

20   "no man, on the loss of life": Anonymous [Edward Povey], "Bartholomew Sharp's Men," 94.

20   three or four doughboys and other details of the provisions: Ringrose, *Baz Ringrose's Journal into the South Seas,* 17.

20   pelican beak (used as tobacco pouches): Dampier, *A Voyage to New-Holland, &c. In the Year 1699,* 337.

20   *league* etymology: Etymologeek, https://etymologeek.com/eng/league/5596 7075.

21   an albatross flying overhead: Bassett, *Legends and Superstitions of the Sea and of Sailors in All Lands and at All Times,* loc. 10246, Kindle; banana-free ship: "Top 20 Sailing Superstitions," New Zealand Maritime Museum, www .maritimemuseum.co.nz/collections/top-20-sailing-superstitions.

21   howler monkeys: National Geographic, "Howler Monkeys," https://www .nationalgeographic.com/animals/mammals/group/howler-monkeys/.

21 a cavernous larynx: Schön, "The Anatomy of the Resonating Mechanism in Howling Monkeys."

22 "in smell and colour like a lovely pleasant apple": Wafer, 60.

22 "blistered him all over": Wafer, 60.

23 "general rule" that "when we find any fruits": Dampier, "A New Voyage Round the World," 70.

23 disease's primary cause was sin: Friedenberg, *Medicine Under Sail,* 15.

23 "I perceived a strange giddiness": Wafer, 25.

23 a tropical phenomenon known as silvagenitus: "Silvagenitus, *International Cloud Atlas,* https://cloudatlas.wmo.int/en/silvagenitus.html.

23 "On this hill wee could finde no water": Anonymous [Edward Povey], 94.

24 "a peace concluded between the Spaniards and the Indians": Ringrose, 13.

24 The fate of John Gret and related details: Dampier, "A New Voyage Round the World," section 7.

25 "Wee all dranck and refreshed ourselves bravely": Anonymous [Edward Povey], 94.

25 "perpendicular" and details about the hill: Ringrose, 19.

4. Golden-Cap

27 Caimans: Brochu, "Phylogenetics, Taxonomy, and Historical Biogeography of Alligatoroidea."

27 they had never learned to swim: Steward, *The Sea and Their Graves,* 46.

28 "walled up with sticks, and daub'd over with Earth" and other Kuna village descriptions: Wafer, *Wafer's New Voyage and Description of the Isthmus of Darien,* 99–100.

28 "They will exactly imitate the Indians' voices": Wafer, 76–77.

28 *bohío*: Helms, *Ancient Panama,* loc. 283, Kindle.

28 450 feet long and 240 feet wide, other Kuna palace details: Helms, 215.

29 Bonete de Oro: Ringrose, *Baz Ringrose's Journal into the South Seas,* 28.

30 *Marriageable*: Ringrose, 21.

30 "some of our peopple by signes would ask": Anonymous [Edward Povey], "Bartholomew Sharp's Men," 95.

30 "The inhabitants for the most part are very handsome": Sharp, *Captain Sharp's Journey Over the Isthmus of Darien and Expedition into the South Seas,* 7–8.

30 chicha co-pah: Wafer, 101–2.

30 "very free, airy, and brisk": Ringrose, 21.

30 "if a man debauches a virgin": Wafer, 106.

31 "an hundred and fifty indians in our company": Sharp, 8.

31 "words" and other details of the Coxon-Harris contretemps: Sharp, 10.

31 Santa Marta in 1677, the Gulf of Honduras in 1679, and subsequent Coxon raids: Masefield, *Dampier's Voyages,* 531.

32 discretion as well as valor and other Peter Harris biographical information: Ringrose, 53.

32 December of 1679: Marley, *Pirates of the Americas,* 135.

32 The Darien's average low temperature in April: Temperatures used herein incorporate current temperature data minus approximately two degrees Fahrenheit per NOAA/NCEI estimates that yearly global land and ocean temperatures have increased at an average rate of 0.08 degrees Celsius (0.14 degrees Fahrenheit) per decade since 1880 (the year temperature records began). For more information, see National Centers for Environmental Information, "Global Climate Report — Annual 2020," National Oceanic and Atmospheric Administration, https://www.ncdc.noaa.gov/sotc/global/202013.

33 "I interposed, and brought him to be quiet": Sharp, 10.

33 "The wood is very red": Wafer, 56.

33 "the least touch of a cannoe against a stump or rock": Anonymous [Edward Povey], 95.

34 "For at the distance of almost every stone's cast": Ringrose, 22.

34 "the Indians had thus divided us": Anonymous [John Cox], *The Voyages and Adventures of Capt. Barth. Sharp And Others in the South Sea,* 7.

34 "a clear river and a pleasant day's passage" and other excerpts from Sharp's journal entries covering the river trip: Sharp, 10–11.

35 "canoes laden with warre, and plantaines": Sharp, 15.

5. The Forlorn

36 Attacking at daybreak (and ideal timing of buccaneer surprise attacks): Little, *The Buccaneer's Realm,* chapter 18.

36 "Thus we rowed with all haste imaginable": Ringrose, *Baz Ringrose's Journal into the South Seas,* 24.

36 "belt of tygers teeth" and details of Andreas's and Golden-Cap's attire: Anonymous [John Cox], *The Voyages and Adventures of Capt. Barth. Sharp And Others in the South Sea,* 37–38.

36 Kuna belief that animal body parts could supplement the wearer's own traits: per archaeologist and anthropologist Erland Nordenskiöld, cited in Helms, *Ancient Panama,* loc. 1351–56, Kindle.

36 Gold restricted to Kuna elite, symbolic of their power: Helms, loc. 1506, Kindle.

36 Body paint also represented rank: Helms, loc. 355, Kindle.

36 red, it was believed, imbued them with magic: archaeologist and anthropologist Erland Nordenskiöld, cited in Helms, loc. 1696, Kindle.

37 "a distinguishing mark of honour": Wafer, *Wafer's New Voyage and Description of the Isthmus of Darien*, 89.

37 "The country all about here is woody and low": Wafer, 46–47.

38 a cardinal rule of buccaneer surprise attacks: Little, *The Buccaneer's Realm*, chapter 18.

38 one man firing while his partner reloaded: Little, *The Sea Rover's Practice*, 194.

38 "a man of undaunted courage": W. D. [William Dick], "A brief account of Captain Sharp and companions," 45.

39 each of the defenders needed to reload his musket (reloading procedure, time required): Little, *The Sea Rover's Practice*, 61–62.

40 scaling the wall (strategy for breaching the garrison): Little, *The Sea Rover's Practice*, 60.

40 fifty pieces of eight "to him that in any battle should signalize himself": Exquemelin, *The Buccaneers of America*, 106.

41 an innovation that eliminated the ramrod: Jean-Baptiste Labat, *Voyage aux Isles de l'Amérique*, 1: 290–91, cited in Little, *The Sea Rover's Practice*, 60.

41 "We found and redeemed the eldest daughter" and Ringrose's additional reporting of the reunion: Ringrose, 27.

42 "neither riches to speak of, nor yet as much victuals": Sharp, *Captain Sharp's Journey Over the Isthmus of Darien and Expedition into the South Seas*, 19.

42 fourteen pieces of eight and price of a cow in 1680: "Currency Converter: 1270–2017."

43 standard pirate practice to strip victims: Little, *The Sea Rover's Practice*, 196.

43 "Our great expectations of taking a huge booty of gold": Ringrose, 27.

44 "Having no chymist to refine the ore": Anonymous [John Cox], *The Voyages and Adventures of Capt. Barth. Sharp And Others in the South Sea*, 10.

44 "treasure enough to satisfy our hungry appetite for gold and riches": Ringrose, 28.

44 181 tons of gold and sixteen thousand tons of silver: Richard L. Garner, "Long-Term Silver Mining Trends in Spanish America."

6. The Second-Largest City in the Western Hemisphere

46 "Dispatching a large naval vessel after a pirate ship": Rediker, *Villains of All Nations*, 28.

46 "gathered as easily as pears from a tree": Exquemelin, *The Buccaneers of America*, 68.

47 "no prey, no pay" and details of typical statutes: Exquemelin, 40–41.

47 five hundred pieces of eight or five slaves to each man who lost a left arm and other details of injury compensation: Exquemelin, 41.

48 "out of the desire they had to see that place taken and sacked": Ringrose, *Baz Ringrose's Journal into the South Seas,* 28.

48 1677 antipiracy act: Sainsbury and Fortescue, *Calendar of State Papers Colonial, America and West Indies,* vol. 10, *1677–1680,* no. 313.

48 "severall English merchants, who trading into the West Indies": Sainsbury, *Calendar of State Papers Colonial, America and West Indies,* vol. 7, *1669–1674,* no. 1320.

49 "by the authority of Almighty God": Alexander VI, "Inter Caetera."

49 a snuffbox with a likeness of King Charles II and other details of Morgan's avoidance of a trial: Breverton, *Admiral Sir Henry Morgan,* 82.

50 "Nothing but a diamond can cut a diamond": Henry Morgan to Sir Leoline Jenkins, August 22, 1681, Fortescue, *Calendar of State Papers Colonial, America and West Indies,* vol. 11, *1681–1685,* no. 208.

51 dinner with Sir Henry Morgan, Jamaica's acting governor: Thomas, *The Pirate King,* chapter 26.

52 by day's end, they were all dead: Talty, *Empire of Blue Water,* 271–72.

52 "ravenous vermin": Lord Carlisle's 1680 report to the Lords of Trade and Plantations: Sainsbury and Fortescue, *1677–1680,* 531.

52 "Nothing can be more fatal to the prosperity of this colony": Henry Morgan to Lord Sunderland, Sainsbury and Fortescue, *1677–1680,* 1425a.

52 "the utmost rigour of the law" and warrants for the pirates' apprehension: Sainsbury and Fortescue, *1677–1680,* 1420, 1425.

7. A Natural Pirate

53 Both died while he was still a boy and other details of Dampier's family history: Preston, *A Pirate of Exquisite Mind,* 23.

53 evidently at King's Bruton: https://www.kingsbruton.com/about-us/history-of-king-s.

53 "inclination for the sea": Dampier, "The Campeachy Voyages," 109.

54 "weary of staying ashore": Dampier, "The Campeachy Voyages," 108.

54 if they were to mutiny over their meals and fail: Rediker, *Villains of All Nations,* 71.

54 "I was clearly out of my element there": Dampier, "The Campeachy Voyages," 114.

55 "necklace of pearls of extraordinary size": Little, *The Golden Age of Piracy,* 15.

56 "proud lazy stalking gait": Ned Ward, *A Trip to Jamaica* (London: 1698), in Little, *The Buccaneer's Realm,* loc. 1414, Kindle.

56 myriad taverns and punch houses: Vallar, "Notorious Pirate Havens."

56 Unconscionable Nan, Salt-Beef Peg, and other famous strumpets: Rediker, *Between the Devil and the Deep Blue Sea,* 71.

56 126–40 gallons: Ruffhead, *The Statutes at Large,* 2: 496.

56 Exquemelin's onetime master: "My own master would buy, on like occasions, a whole pipe of wine, and, placing it in the street, would force every one that passed by to drink with him; threatening also to pistol them, in case they would not do it"; Exquemelin, *The Buccaneers of America,* 48.

57 he simply wasn't drawn to rum houses: John Masefield, introduction to Dampier, "The Campeachy Voyages," 11.

57 £100 per ton in Europe for logwood: Anonymous, *The Gazetteer of the World,* 9:830.

57 wheat sold for just £8: This means that for £100, one could buy fifty quarters of wheat, a quantity weighing around five hundred pounds each. Four quarters, or one ton, would therefore cost £8. See "Currency Converter: 1270–2017."

57 "a great prospect of getting money here": Dampier, "The Campeachy Voyages," 19.

58 guinea worms: Preston, chapter 2.

58 *avocado, barbecue,* and *cashew*: Preston, 7.

58 "Some it keeps sleepy, some merry": Adams, *The Unforgiving Rope,* 3.

58 The storm that one day meteorologists would consider a landmark: Preston, 43.

59 story of a pirate who was captured and brought before Alexander: Augustine, *The City of God,* in Rediker, *Villains of All Nations,* 170.

59 "was forced to range about": Dampier, "The Campeachy Voyages," 222.

59 a parrot was nevertheless a New World status symbol: Little, *The Buccaneer's Realm,* loc. 5117, Kindle.

60 a relative of the Duchess of Grafton: What little biographical information there is about Judith Dampier comes from Dampier himself, in "A New Voyage Round the World," 417.

8. An Easy Canoe Ride

62 "barbarous cruelty": Ringrose, *Baz Ringrose's Journal into the South Seas,* 27.

63 "we should leave him to the mercy of the Indians": Ringrose, 29.

65 "We were forced to lay by until highwater came" and subsequent quotations from Ringrose during his voyage from Santa Maria to the South Sea: Ringrose, chapters 4 and 5.

66 Pirates made it their business to thoroughly question all prisoners: Dampier, "A New Voyage Round the World," 58–59.

67   three miles wide, the outer limit of human eyesight: James Roland, "How Far Can We See and Why?," *Healthline,* May 23, 2019, https://www .healthline.com/health/how-far-can-the-human-eye-see.

68   "to lighten his canoe": Sharp, *Captain Sharp's Journey Over the Isthmus of Darien and Expedition into the South Seas,* 25.

68   "certainly perished": Sharp, 27.

68   "in exceedingly great danger": Sharp, 27.

68   "it being a certain truth that those who are born to be hang'd": Anonymous [John Cox], *The Voyages and Adventures of Capt. Barth. Sharp And Others in the South Sea,* 11.

9. Castaways

69   "Much trouble and toil" and Ringrose's subsequent narration of his travails at the entrance to the South Sea: Ringrose, *Baz Ringrose's Journal into the South Seas,* chapters 4 and 5.

70   "a mere mill-pond": According to the online *Collins English Dictionary,* a mill-pond, in British English, is either "a pool formed by damming a stream to provide water to turn a millwheel" or "any expanse of calm water."

76   *tormenta de toca*: Lea, *A History of the Inquisition of Spain,* 2:20.

10. Surprizal

80   "The King of All Fruit": Dampier, "A New Voyage Round the World," 321.

80   *huzza* etymology: O'Conner and Kellerman, "Hip Hip Hooray."

80   curses (commonly *damn*): Kyle Dalton, "Swear Like a Sailor," *British Tars 1740–1790,* December 27, 2017, www.britishtars.com/2017/12/swear-like -sailor.html.

80   as opposed to *argh*: Wonderopolis, "Why Do Pirates Say 'Arrr!'?"

81   its beacon, a stack of wood sitting at the ready: Masefield, *On the Spanish Main,* 157.

81   placing captives' thumbs or genitals in vises: Little, *The Buccaneer's Realm,* loc. 3860, Kindle.

81   holding just about any of their body parts to a fire: Exquemelin, *The Buccaneers of America,* 91.

82   *bark* definition: According to Falconer, *An Universal Dictionary of the Marine,* loc. 907–8, Kindle, *bark* is "a general name given to small ships: it is however peculiarly appropriated by seamen to those which carry three masts without a mizen top-sail."

83   "as softly as if they had been seeking manatee": Dampier, 263, in Little, *The Sea Rover's Practice,* 169.

83   board the barque amidships: Little, 173.

83   secure the doors, ports, and hatches: Little, 174.

83   Boarding axes came in especially handy: Little, 171.

83   Fists also came into play in close combat and other close-quarters tactics: Little, 158.

84   The crewmen on watch were indeed surprised and details of boarding the barque off Plantan Key: Anonymous [Edward Povey], "Bartholomew Sharp's Men," 98.

84   "to fight and curb certain Indians and negroes": Ringrose, *Baz Ringrose's Journal into the South Seas,* 43.

84   "something lesser than the former" and subsequent details of pursuing a Spanish barque: Ringrose, 43.

85   "In about nine days march we arrived at Santa Maria": Dampier, 29.

85   "The shell, rind or cod, is soft": Dampier, 321.

85   Peter Harris swooped in and details of Captain Harris's capture of the barque: Anonymous [Edward Povey], 99.

86   "man-of-war's tender": Falconer, loc. 7031.

87   "extraordinary sweet": Dampier, 222.

87   a garrison of 1,500 troops: Verrill, *The Real Story of the Pirate,* 173.

88   The company was now down by 137 men: Sharp reported 130, but as Ringrose's numbers by and large have been corroborated by his shipmates' accounts, they are used herein except where noted.

88   "or rather to murder and slay [them]": Ringrose, 45.

88   "We rowed all night long": Ringrose, 45.

11. The Dragon

89   "one of the finest objects that I did ever see": Dampier, "A New Voyage Round the World," 199.

89   "rubbish, and a few houses of poor people": Wafer, *Wafer's New Voyage and Description of the Isthmus of Darien,* 49.

90   New Panama, with a population of eight thousand: The figure comes from Clio Infra, a project subsidized by the Netherlands Organisation for Scientific Research, at https://clio-infra.eu/Countries/Panama.html.

90   whether the wall surrounding the city was made of silver and gold: Bancroft, *The Works of Hubert Howe Bancroft,* 517–18.

90   "according to the intelligence they had received" and Ringrose's subsequent description of the Panama Bay sea battle and its participants: Ringrose, *Baz Ringrose's Journal into the South Seas,* chapter 7.

93   "We made a resolution rather than drown in the sea": Anonymous [John Cox], *The Voyages and Adventures of Capt. Barth. Sharp and Others in the South Sea,* 13.

93   steady northwesterly wind: Masefield, *On the Spanish Main,* 161.

12. The Extreamest Hazard of Fire and Sword

94 Temperature in the city of Panama in April: See Weather Spark, https://weatherspark.com/m/19385/4/Average-Weather-in-April-in-Panam%C3%A1-Panama.

94 warships, each built from a thousand full-grown oaks: "Shipbuilding: 800–1800."

94 Don Diego de Carabaxal: The last name, as recorded by Ringrose, is likely a variation of Carabajal — which, according to the *Jewish Encyclopedia,* was the name of a family of Maranos (Jews of the Iberian Peninsula) living in Mexico at the end of the sixteenth and beginning of the seventeenth centuries. See https://www.jewishencyclopedia.com/articles/4015-carabajal.

95 Birding: Cox, 13.

96 injured or killed by shrapnel: Little, "Of Pirates & Wooden Legs."

98 Peralta's reputation for bravery and resourcefulness: Masefield, *On the Spanish Main,* 134.

100 Definition of *brigantine*: Falconer, *An Universal Dictionary of the Marine,* loc. 1365–69, Kindle. Falconer adds that "amongst English seamen, this vessel is distinguished by having her main-sail set nearly in the plane of her keel; whereas the main-sails of larger ships are hung athwart, or at right angles with the ship's length, and fastened to a yard which hangs parallel to the deck: but in a brig, the foremost edge of the main-sail is fastened in different places to hoops which encircle the main-mast, and slide up and down it as the sail is hoisted or lowered: it is extended by a gaff above, and by a boom below."

100 "I presently, with seven men" and the ensuing Pearl Islands episode: Sharp, *Captain Sharp's Journey Over the Isthmus of Darien and Expedition into the South Seas,* 34–37.

101 "dancing the cushion dance" and other seventeenth-century euphemisms: Cary, *The slang of venery and its analogues.*

13. Blood Ran Down the Decks in Whole Streams

105 It was clear to the surgeons: There is no record of which of them were in Panama and which were with Sharp, who at that moment was in the Pearl Islands — "in serious repose," as he put it.

107 bleed to death in as few as four minutes: "Exsanguination Time from Damage to Major Arteries," Biology Stack Exchange, January 14, 2017, https://biology.stackexchange.com/questions/55220/exsanguination -time-from-damage-to-major-arteries.

105–107 Amputation procedure: Sellegren, "An Early History of Lower Limb Amputations and Prostheses."

108   Accidental explosions of gunpowder: Friedenberg, *Medicine Under Sail,* 22.

111   *La Santísima Trinidad:* Howse and Thrower, *A Buccaneer's Atlas,* 10.

112   *Nemo moriturus praesumitur mentiri:* Koerner, "Last Words."

14. Mutiny

113   "We quenched the fire with all speed": Ringrose, *Baz Ringrose's Journal into the South Seas,* 52.

114   officers' cabins typically included mattresses, bed linens, and chamber pots: Fish, *The Manila-Acapulco Galleons,* 389.

114   "Had we gone ashore, instead of fighting": Ringrose, 55.

115   "much dissatisfied with some reflections": Ringrose, 57.

115   "We ought justly to attribute to him the greatest honour": Ringrose, 64.

115   "itt fester'd": Anonymous [Edward Povey], "Bartholomew Sharp's Men," 100.

115   "a brave and stout souldier, and a valiant Englishman": Ringrose, 53.

115   "in disgrace amongst our men": Anonymous [John Cox], *The Voyages and Adventures of Capt. Barth. Sharp and Others in the South Sea,* 14.

115   deep-cleft shipworm: World Register of Marine Species.

115   "We found worms of three quarters of an inch in length": Ringrose, 56.

116   "shewed himself more like a coward than one of our profession": Dick, *William Dick's South Sea Voyage,* 39–40.

116   "our vessels with gold": Dick, 41.

117   "Thus we disengaged from the pretended service": Dick, 41.

117   "The King desired we would not be less vigorous": Ringrose, 57.

15. The Muzzles of Our Guns

121   "Thay fierd their gunns off from Pennamau": Anonymous [Edward Povey], "Bartholomew Sharp's Men," 100.

121   Typical surgeon's salary: Exquemelin, *The Buccaneers of America,* 40.

122   Syphilis treatment: O'Shea, "'Two Minutes with Venus, Two Years with Mercury'"; Vallar, "Notorious Pirate Havens."

122   Spaniards paying two hundred pieces of eight per prisoner: Ringrose, *Baz Ringrose's Journal into the South Seas,* 59.

123   Pirates' views of slaves: Little, *The Buccaneer's Realm,* loc. 1916, Kindle.

123   *Strike* definition: Falconer, *An Universal Dictionary of the Marine,* loc. 6037, Kindle.

123   "1400 jars of wine and brandy on board" and subsequent details of the *San Pedro* plunder: Sharp, *Captain Sharp's Journey Over the Isthmus of Darien and Expedition into the South Seas,* 46.

124   Two hundred pieces of eight as share of Morgan's 1671 expedition: Exquemelin, 129.

124 1680 prices for horses and cows: "Currency Converter: 1270–2017."

124 "an exceedingly pleasant island": Sharp, 52.

124 Introduction of *avocado* to the English language: *Oxford English Dictionary,* second edition (1989), article "avocado", n.2. "The *Avogato Pear-tree* is as big as most pear-trees, and is commonly pretty high; the skin or bark black, and pretty smooth; the leaves large, of an oval shape, and the fruit as big as a large lemon": Dampier, "A New Voyage Round the World," 223.

125 "We came to assist the King of Darien" and subsequent details of the exchange between Sawkins and the governor of Panama: Ringrose, 60.

125 Lucas Fernandez y Piedrahita: Marley, *Pirates of the Americas,* 135.

126 "a certain Frenchman": Ringrose, 207.

126 "meete him on shoare with a hundred men to try their manhoods": Anonymous [Edward Povey], 102.

127 "Our men were so importunate for fresh victuals": Ringrose, 61.

127 "Among privateers": Dampier, 169.

128 "Our peopple, being headstronge, would have meate to eate first": Anonymous [Edward Povey], 101.

16. Swallowed by the Sea

129 Method of cruising along the coast undetected: Little, *The Sea Rover's Practice,* 49.

129 Doldrums definition: "What Are the Doldrums?," National Ocean Service, https://oceanservice.noaa.gov/facts/doldrums.html.

130 "Being arrived there, we lay by": Ringrose, *Baz Ringrose's Journal into the South Seas,* 61.

130 Speed of icebergs, pedestrians: The Measure of Things, Blue Bulb Projects, bluebulbprojects.com/MeasureOfThings.

132 Sail sizes and weights: USS Constitution Museum, https://ussconstitution museum.org/2016/07/29/sails/.

132 Prohibition of drinking belowdecks: Johnson, *A General History of the Robberies and Murders of the most notorious Pyrates,* 211.

133 *hostis humani generis*: Harding, "'Hostis Humani Generis'."

133 "We met with very bad weather": Sharp, *Captain Sharp's Journey Over the Isthmus of Darien and Expedition into the South Seas,* 57.

133 Wave metrics: "The Weight of a Wave," *SurferToday,* surfertoday.com/surfing/the-weight-of-a-wave.

134 Pressure systems: NASA Earth Observatory, https://earthobservatory.nasa.gov/images/10588/low-pressure-system-over-northwestern-pacific.

134 "Fire shot out of their great guns": Dampier, "A New Voyage Round the World," 442.

134   "split all to pieces": Sharp, 57.

135   "We lost two of our barks": Ringrose, 61.

135   And the second barque? "Lost": Sharp, 56

135   "Nothing remarkable happened": Dick, *William Dick's South Sea Voyage*, 43.

135   Sailing superstitions: "Top 20 Sailing Superstitions," New Zealand Maritime Museum, www.maritimemuseum.co.nz/collections/top-20-sailing -superstitions.

136   "We had the good luck": Sharp, 58.

17. As Valiant and Courageous as Any Could Be

137–138   Ringrose map including Silva: Howse and Thrower, *A Buccaneer's Atlas*, 115.

138   Implication of whistling at sea: Bassett, *Legends and Superstitions of the Sea and of Sailors in All Lands and at All Times*, loc. 3310–3315.

138   "a man whom nothing on earth": Anonymous [John Cox], *The Voyages and Adventures of Capt. Barth. Sharp and Others in the South Sea*, 16.

139   "Follow me": This was originally written as "Follow me and doe not lye behind, for if I doe amise You will all fair the worse for itt," in Anonymous [Edward Povey], "Bartholomew Sharp's Men," 102.

140   "comeing downe so fast uppon us": Anonymous [Edward Povey], 102.

141   Definition of *pitch*: Falconer, *An Universal Dictionary of the Marine*, loc. 5178, Kindle.

141   "as valiant and couragious as any could be": Ringrose, *Baz Ringrose's Journal into the South Seas*, 65.

141–42   "prosecute the design Captain Sawkins had undertaken": Ringrose, 65.

142   "determined to be buried in those seas": Dick, *William Dick's South Sea Voyage*, 49.

142   "totally desirous in my mind to quit those hazardous adventures": Ringrose, 66.

142   Buccaneers remaining on Isla de Coiba: The number was somewhere between 134 and 140 buccaneers. The former, derived from the documented attrition since Golden Island, does not take into account new recruits, whereas the latter is the usually reliable Ringrose's count.

143   "Determining to rule over such unruly company no longer": Ringrose, 67.

143   "promised to do great things for us" and subsequent Captain Moreno details: Ringrose, 68.

144   Chocolate believed to be an aphrodisiac: Chamberlayne, *The Natural History of Coffee, Thee, Chocolate, Tobacco*, 18.

144   Chocolate's status and history in England: Loveman, "The Introduction of Chocolate into England."

144   "cacao-nut, whereof chocolate is made": Ringrose, 68.

144 "worthy consort": Dampier, "A New Voyage Round the World," 90.

145 "That night we had such thunder and lightning": Ringrose, 68.

145 "Heaven and Earth would meet": Wafer, *Wafer's New Voyage and Description of the Isthmus of Darien,* 14.

145 lightning data: "Supercharged Thunderstorm Reaches a Record 1.3 Billion Volts," *Nature,* March 22, 2019, https://www.nature.com/articles/d41586-019-00934-z.

145 Elevation of Isla de Coiba: "Elevation of Coiba Island, Panama," Worldwide Elevation Map Finder, https://elevation.maplogs.com/poi/coiba_island _panama.321836.html.

18. Snake-Haired Sisters

146 Astrolable details: Morgan, "How to Use an Astrolabe."

147 thirty-two miles south of Isla de Coiba: Ringrose determined that the ships were at latitude 06°30′ (latitude is measured in degrees from 0 to 90 and minutes from 0 to 60; each minute equals one nautical mile). He knew that Isla de Coiba lay two nautical miles north of the seventh parallel, at 07°02′.

147 "discovering the longitude": Hansen and Curtis, *Voyages in World History,* 596.

148 "lay tumbling in the calm": Ringrose, *Baz Ringrose's Journal into the South Seas,* 72.

148 "to send advice of our coming" and the subsequent account of the buccaneers' decision to go to Gorgona: Ringrose, 74.

149 "inferno" and the rank soil: Prescott, *History of the Conquest of Peru,* loc. 2316, Kindle.

150 "Our bullets rebounded from their bodies" and additional details of the buccaneers' stay on Gorgona: Ringrose, 74–79.

150 "It takes [sloths] eight or nine minutes": Dampier, "The Campeachy Voyages," 162.

151 Veritable jungles of weeds and the cost of not careening in terms of speed: Konstam, *The Pirate Ship 1660–1730,* 5.

151 seventeenth-century cure-all: Paré, *The Workes of that Famous Chirurgion Ambrose Parey,* 28.

152 London treacle: Kehoe, "Theriaca Londonensis."

152 Spaniards who lived on the neighboring island, Gorgonilla: Sharp, *Captain Sharp's Journey Over the Isthmus of Darien and Expedition into the South Seas,* 67.

153 "a place called Arica": Ringrose, 78–79.

154 Rain could kill a land raid: Little, *The Sea Rover's Practice,* 192.

156 "in an enimies cuntry and unknowne seas": Anonymous [Edward Povey], "Bartholomew Sharp's Men," 104.

156 "This loss occasioned sundry distractions in our minds": Dick, *William Dick's South Sea Voyage,* 52.

158 "we had lost [Cox] in the obscurity of the night": Ringrose, 81.

158 "These creatures here are so little fearful" and subsequent Isla de la Plata details: Ringrose, 93.

158 "Their fat is yellow": Dampier, "A New Voyage Round the World," 131.

158 "fit for new adventures": Anonymous [John Cox], *The Voyages and Adventures of Capt. Barth. Sharp and Others in the South Sea,* 22.

19. The Merry Blades

159 "We were forced to lye by": Ringrose, *Baz Ringrose's Journal into the South Seas,* 94.

160 *Shot-plugs* definition: Falconer, *An Universal Dictionary of the Marine,* loc. 2687, Kindle.

161 *Boatswain* definition: Falconer, loc. 1163.

161 Wafer's job and details of surgeons' preparations for the battle and subsequent role during the fight: Friedenberg, *Medicine Under Sail,* 17–22.

161 the *Trinity* had swivel guns: The *Trinity* cannon count included seven "small guns" (likely swivel cannon) when Peralta sailed her away from Panama during the Morgan raid in 1671. See Anderson, *Old Panama and Castilla del Oro,* 429; also per Exquemelin, *The Buccaneers of America,* 123: "The strength of this galleon was inconsiderable, having only seven guns, and ten or twelve muskets."

161 no cannons: Dick lamented this on another occasion, when sizing the *Trinity* up against a trio of prospective opponents with eight, twelve, and sixteen guns: "We had not so much as one gun, for all our vessel was of four-hundred ton or more" (Dick, *William Dick's South Sea Voyage,* 73).

161 "Let's jump on board, and cut them to pieces": Johnson, *A General History of the Robberies and Murders of the most notorious Pyrates,* 31.

162 the carpenter bolted or lashed shut all the hatches and other preparations for shipboard combat: Little, *The Sea Rover's Practice,* chapter 14.

164 a former governor of Guayaquil and other Argandona biographical information: Dick, 57.

165 "Gentlemen, I am now your prisoner at war" and subsequent examination of Argandona: Ringrose, 101–2.

166 one of the two commanders, Morris Connoway: Anonymous [Edward Povey], "Bartholomew Sharp's Men," 107.

167 *Patache* is typically a term for a swift two-masted vessel often employed as a tender, but in this case, Ringrose recorded it as the name of the vessel bound for Arica "to fetch the King's plate."

167 "Such cruelties though I abhorred": Ringrose, 103.

168 the story of French buccaneer captain François l'Olonais: Exquemelin, 64.

20. Water, Water

170 *Pilot* definition: Falconer, *An Universal Dictionary of the Marine*, loc. 5155, Kindle.

170 the deliberation over whether to chase after an unidentified sail: Little, *The Sea Rover's Practice*, 105.

171 "These animals gave to the Indians": Ringrose, *Baz Ringrose's Journal into the South Seas*, 105.

171 "Their insupportable cruelties to these poor natives": Howse and Thrower, *A Buccaneer's Atlas*, 94.

171 Such evasive action was standard operating procedure: Little, 110.

172 Merchantman captain's countermeasures: Little, 123.

172 sailing away from the wind, as though her holds were empty: Little, 124.

173 eleventh parallel data: "Earth Radius by Latitude Calculator," Rechner Online, https://rechneronline.de/earth-radius/.

173–74 Almanac details: Howse and Thrower, 38. Data for the September 12, 1680 (September 22, 1680 Gregorian), annular eclipse can be found at "Besselian Elements — Annular Solar Eclipse of 1680 September 22," NASA Eclipse Web Site, https://eclipse.gsfc.nasa.gov/SEsearch/SEdata .php?Ecl=+16800922.

174 four pints per day: Presumably, as the rations were adjusted in half-pint increments, and the subsequent adjustment left each man with three and a half pints per day.

174 average sedentary adult male requires five pints (2.4 liters): "Maintaining Proper Hydration," National Council on Strength and Fitness, https:// www.ncsf.org/pdf/ceu/maintaining_proper_hydration.pdf.

174 highs in the midsixties and weather for the South Seas in the vicinity of Arica: "Average Weather in September in Arica (Arica y Parinacota), Chile," Weather & Climate, https://weather-and-climate.com/Arica -September-averages-fahrenheit.

175 "one cake of boyled bread": Ringrose, 117.

175 primary symptom is dry mouth and dehydration in its early stages: "Dry Mouth," NHS Inform, https://www.nhsinform.scot/illnesses-and-conditions/ mouth/dry-mouth.

175   the occasional "chew stick" twig and pirate oral hygiene: "Pirate Dentistry," Main Street Children's Dentistry and Orthodontics, https://www.mainstreetsmiles.com/pirate-dentistry/.

175   "The Rime of the Ancient Mariner": Samuel Taylor Coleridge, "The Rime of the Ancient Mariner (Text of 1834)," Poetry Foundation, https://www.poetryfoundation.org/poems/43997/the-rime-of-the-ancient-mariner-text-of-1834.

175–76   To measure distance traveled: Bowditch, *The New American Practical Navigator*, 126. Attached to the cord Cox used, by two strands, was a "logship," a buoyant slab of wood shaped like a slice of pie and weighted on its curved side. When Cox dropped the logship overboard from the stern of the moving ship, it caught the water, causing the cord to unspool; the two strands meanwhile held the logship upright so as to present a consistently flat surface to the water. After waiting thirty seconds, which he measured with a half-minute sandglass, Cox retrieved the cord and counted the number of knots that had unspooled. Since forty-four feet is 1/120th of mile and thirty seconds is 1/120th of an hour, the total number of knots gave him the *Trinity*'s speed in knots per hour. For additional logship details, see Masefield, *Dampier's Voyages*, 310 (footnote 2).

176   "three or four glasses": Ringrose, 118.

176   the spate of symptoms: "What Is Dehydration? What Causes It?," WebMD, May 20, 2021, https://www.webmd.com/a-to-z-guides/dehydration-adults#1.

176   "We spied floating upon the sea" and subsequent details of the return leg of the voyage to Arica: Ringrose, 119.

178   "There was nothing occurred but bare sailing": Sharp, *Captain Sharp's Journey Over the Isthmus of Darien and Expedition into the South Seas*, 81.

178   "many days infinite hunger and thirst": Dick, *William Dick's South Sea Voyage*, 59.

179   Acute confusion bordering on delirium: George and Rockwood, "Dehydration and Delirium — Not a Simple Relationship."

21. Ransom

180   "to our great sorrow and vexation" and subsequent details of the buccaneers' Arica approach: Ringrose, *Baz Ringrose's Journal into the South Seas*, 124.

181   the Spaniards' intent had been to intimidate and other details of Spanish ships firing cannons: Anonymous [Edward Povey], "Bartholomew Sharp's Men," 109.

181   "giving over this enterprize": Ringrose, 125.

181   "water was worth 30 pieces of eight": Anonymous [John Cox], *The Voyages and Adventures of Capt. Barth. Sharp and Others in the South Sea*, 33.

182   "No whit discouraged": Sharp, *Captain Sharp's Journey Over the Isthmus of Darien and Expedition into the South Seas*, 84.

182   "With little resistance they yielded": Sharp, 84.

183   "refreshed and feasted": Dick, *William Dick's South Sea Voyage*, 61.

183   the ideal site for growing olives: Vivian, *Peru*, 148.

185   "The enemy came riding at full speed toward us" and Cox's subsequent description of the scene at the shore: Anonymous [John Cox], 35–36.

22. Eighty-Five Stout Fellows

186   The diagnosis was easy and scurvy symptoms: Friedenberg, *Medicine Under Sail*, 44.

186   *scurf* definition: *The Free Dictionary by Farlex*, https://medical-dictionary.thefreedictionary.com/scurfy.

186   when sailors started going to sea for months at a time: Friedenberg, 42.

186   scurvy killed more sailors than storms: Bown, *Scurvy*, 20.

187   "to prevent the disease, as also to helpe when it comes": Woodall, *The Surgions Mate*, 162.

187   a prescribed midjourney daily ration of lime juice: Friedenberg, 48.

188   sopping hammock he might share with a drowned rat: Masefield, *On the Spanish Main*, 217.

188   "The natives say that the best remedy they can find": Dampier, "A New Voyage Round the World," 293.

188   a gale sprang up and subsequent commentary on the journey from Hilo to Arica: Ringrose, *Baz Ringrose's Journal into the South Seas*, chapter 14.

189   the appearance of the Great Comet of 1680: Yeomans, "Great Comets in History."

190   "Deriving courage from their advantage in numbers" and subsequent details of the fight on landing at La Serena: Anonymous [John Cox], *The Voyages and Adventures of Capt. Barth. Sharp and Others in the South Sea*, 40.

192   "to be well to live" and "to have a piece of bread and cheese in your head": Healey, "Just a Quick List of 17th Century Euphemisms for Being Drunk…"

193   In Spanish cities, churches made good bases: Little, *The Sea Rover's Practice*, 200.

193   "such sociable enemies and so good-natured victors" and the subsequent invitation: Anonymous [John Cox], 42.

194   "Our fancies being filled with the expectation of so much money": Anonymous [John Cox], 43.

196　"began to pink some of their jackets": Anonymous [John Cox], 45.

23. Robinson Crusoe

197　"plot our destruction in earnest": Ringrose, *Baz Ringrose's Journal into the South Seas*, 147.

198　"a heap of rocks": Ringrose, 153–54.

198　Goats had been brought there a century earlier: Dampier, "A New Voyage Round the World," 115.

199　"we were forced to kill them": Ringrose, 155.

199　"part savannahs, part wood land": Dampier, 115.

199　a massive creature, about twelve to fourteen feet long: Dampier, 118.

199　"His mouth is like that of a hare": Wafer, *Wafer's New Voyage and Description of the Isthmus of Darien*, 128–29.

201　The killing of such a bird and other seabird-related superstitions: Bassett, *Legends and Superstitions of the Sea and of Sailors in All Lands and at All Times*, loc. 2974–76, Kindle.

202　"This fewd was carried on so fiercely": Anonymous [John Cox], *The Voyages and Adventures of Capt. Barth. Sharp and Others in the South Sea*, 49.

202　"dissembling New England man": Sharp, *Captain Sharp's Journey Over the Isthmus of Darien and Expedition into the South Seas*, 97.

202–3　his master had "oft times buggered him": Ringrose, 161.

203　"if any person in the fleet shall commit the unnatural and detestable sin of buggery": Ruffhead, *The Statutes at Large*, 6:434.

203　"Searching his writing": Ringrose, 161.

203　a surprising number of buccaneers were Christians, and more than a few were Jewish: In addition to Watling, crewman Richard Gopson, as will be seen, was something of a Bible thumper. For information about Jewish buccaneers, see Kritzler, *Jewish Pirates of the Caribbean*.

205　the Miskito "had no names among themselves": Dampier, 114.

206　William the Striker: For the entire story, see Dampier, 112–14.

207　"run for it": Dick, *William Dick's South Sea Voyage*, 74.

24. The Very Illustrious and Royal City of Saint Mark of Arica

208　"two old white men": Ringrose, *Baz Ringrose's Journal into the South Seas*, 170.

209　"Gentlemen, I am clear of the blood of this old man": Ringrose, 172.

210　"All of these things pleased us mighty well": Ringrose, 173.

210　"bear up the helm" definition: Falconer, *An Universal Dictionary of the Marine*, loc. 961, Kindle.

210　He would have Arica, he swore: Anonymous [John Cox], *The Voyages and Adventures of Capt. Barth. Sharp and Others in the South Sea*, 54.

211   cast-iron balls packed with slow-burning gunpowder and other pirate grenades: Little, *The Sea Rover's Practice*, 73.

211   "the day that is consecrated in our English kalendar": Ringrose, 174.

213   "We saw from thence no men nor forces": Ringrose, 174.

214   Rodríguez agreed to pay eighteen thousand pieces of eight: Bradley, *The Defence of Peru*, 177.

215   five pieces of eight to each man: Little, 195.

215   they failed to explode and explanations for grenade failure: Masefield, *On the Spanish Main*, 174.

217   "The enemy made several retreats": Ringrose, 175.

217   "But our rage increasing with our wounds": Ringrose, 175.

217   a battle postmortem written by an anonymous Ariqueño: Bradley, 193.

217   "men that never give it themselves": Anonymous [John Cox], 57.

217   "Gentlemen, I know you are men come to seek a fortune": Anonymous [Edward Povey], "Bartholomew Sharp's Men," 114.

218   "We placed some of these prisoners": Dick, *William Dick's South Sea Voyage*, 76.

219   "numbers and vigour increasing every moment" and subsequent details of the second battle for the fort: Ringrose, 176–77.

219   muscle cramps, diminished reaction time, and dangerous balance deficits: Gisolfi, "Water Requirements During Exercise in the Heat."

220   "in the reins": *American Heritage Dictionary of the English Language*, 5th ed., in Wordnik, wordnik.com/words/reins.

220   "So many of our party being almost choked for water": Anonymous [Edward Povey], 115.

221   When Henry Morgan's ship the *Oxford* caught fire: Talty, *Empire of Blue Water*, 144–45.

223   "Valiente soldados, buina valienta soldados": Anonymous [Edward Povey], 115.

25. The Itch

224   "I hope it will not be esteemed a vanity": Sharp, *Captain Sharp's Journey Over the Isthmus of Darien and Expedition into the South Seas*, 105.

224   "send out the three ships we had seen in the harbour": Ringrose, *Baz Ringrose's Journal into the South Seas*, 180.

224   Traditionally, such a declaration marked the end point of a pirate cruise: Masefield, *On the Spanish Main*, 86.

226   "knockt on the head": Anonymous [John Cox], *The Voyages and Adventures of Capt. Barth. Sharp and Others in the South Sea*, 70.

226   "the abler and more experienced men": Dampier, "A New Voyage Round the World," 31.

226   "the meaner sort": Dampier, 31.

227 "doe the uttmost of his power to gett money enough": Anonymous [Edward Povey], "Bartholomew Sharp's Men," 118.

227 "altogether dissatisfied with Sharp's former conduct": Dampier, 31.

228 "This was a great weakning to our party": Anonymous [John Cox], 75.

228 fifty-four to sixty men remaining: based on recorded attrition since Golden Island, there were fifty-four buccaneers aboard the *Trinity*; based on Ringrose's last count, the number is sixty.

228 "did fully resolve": Ringrose, 192.

26. Expect to Be Shot to Death

231 "If any man faultred in the journey": Dampier, "A New Voyage Round the World," 34.

231 a Caribbean native of St. Christopher: Dampier, 92.

231 Cook had been forced to abandon his ship: Dampier, 530.

231 "very intelligent" and "sensible": Dampier, 92.

232 "vessels for carrying water": Dampier, 33. Masefield, in his commentary, notes that the word *bumkins* is derived from *butt-kin,* a little butt or tub.

237 "gave us the slip" and subsequent narration of the Darien trek in April of 1681: Dampier, 43–54.

239 "I made hard shift to jog on": Wafer, 8.

239 "allowed him a slave to carry his things...": Dampier, 46.

239 "thereby left me deprived of the wherewithal to dress my sore...": Wafer, 8.

240 "extraordinary hard rain": Dampier, 47.

240 "I got over": Wafer, 8.

27. The Pyre

242 "Our company and forces": Dick, *William Dick's South Sea Voyage,* 83–84.

242 "The greatest part of our attempts on land": Ringrose, *Baz Ringrose's Journal into the South Seas,* 211.

242 "fit up" the ship: Konstam, *The Pirate Ship 1660–1730,* 14.

243 other "necessaries," as he put it: Sharp, *Captain Sharp's Journey Over the Isthmus of Darien and Expedition into the South Seas,* 113.

243 Modifications to the *Trinity*: The carpenters shortened the mainmast by six feet and the foremast by five feet. They also built and installed new crosstrees and trestle trees for both, per Cox, and "cut off her upper deck, and sunk her quarter deck; she was six foot ten inches high, between decks, and we left her something more than four foot in the waste."

243 "we had one Mr. Ringrose with us": Anonymous [John Cox], *The Voyages and Adventures of Capt. Barth. Sharp and Others in the South Sea,* 80.

245 "was so deeply laden": Ringrose, 214.

245 "Our great ship got up with her": Ringrose, 214.

245 "many disappointments": Dick, 83.

246 Born in Scotland to itinerant parents in 1660 and subsequent Wafer biographical information: Gosse, *The Pirates' Who's Who*, 251–52.

246 reputation in London as a "gentleman" and a "trusted shipmaster": Joyce, introduction to *A New Voyage and Description of the Isthmus of America*, xiv.

247 job interview with a pair of buccaneers: Wafer, *Wafer's New Voyage and Description of the Isthmus of Darien*, 6.

247 when pirates decided to liberate the entire crew: Malt, "Lionel Wafer — Surgeon to the Buccaneers."

247 "took me along with them": Wafer, 7.

247 "not able to trudge it further": Wafer, 8.

248 "Some of them look'd on us very scurvily": Wafer, 9.

249 "perfectly cured": Wafer, 9.

249 "seem'd resolved to revenge on us": Wafer, 9.

28. Bloodletting

251 The story, as reported by the *Orlando Sentinel*: McKay, "Sunken Treasure Beckons Hunters."

252 "it appears like a dead man": Dampier, "A New Voyage Round the World," 171.

252 "This day our pilot told us": Ringrose, *Baz Ringrose's Journal into the South Seas*, 224.

253 Spanish records from the time of the *Consolación* wreck: Little, "The Myth of Sharp's Buccaneers, the Wreck of the *Santa María de la Consolación*, and Isla de Muerto."

253 To make the case that the buccaneers nevertheless engaged: Treasure hunter Joel Ruth's claims of a cover-up in a March 6, 2021, phone conversation as well as a series of March 2021 emails with the author.

253 "In the year 1681 Capt Sharpe gave chace to a ship": William Hacke map in British Library's Sloane Manuscript collection, file 44.

254 "nothing but swamps, having great rains": Wafer, *Wafer's New Voyage and Description of the Isthmus of Darien*, 12.

254 no provisions save a handful of dry corn: Wafer, 53.

254 "to such of the company as were dispos'd…": Wafer, 8.

255 The compasses were pretty things: Dampier, 50.

255 They guided themselves by the sun: Wafer, 114.

256 "hunger and weariness had brought us": Wafer, 13.

257 "hissing or shrieking of snakes": Wafer, 53.

259   They were not at all put off by his sudden appearance: Wafer, 18.

259   "At our first landing in this country": Dampier, 54.

259   "large commendations of the kindness and generosity": Wafer 18.

260   the confluence of two rivers: Helms, *Ancient Panama,* loc. 3386, Kindle.

261   "a better way," a way of letting blood: Wafer, 22.

261   "But this rash attempt": Wafer, 22.

262   "Thus I was carried from plantation to plantation": Wafer, 22.

262   "as big as a man's head": Wafer, 59.

262   "I lived thus some months among the Indians": Wafer, 22.

262   "I plainly perceiv'd he intended to keep me in this country": Wafer, 24.

29. A Warm Deck

263   "one of the greatest adventures of this whole voyage": Dick, *William Dick's South Sea Voyage,* 91.

264   "the Spaniard began to fire": Anonymous [John Cox], *The Voyages and Adventures of Capt. Barth. Sharp and Others in the South Sea,* 88.

264   "about the number of forty, more or less": Ringrose, *Baz Ringrose's Journal into the South Seas,* 18.

264   "the beautifullest woman that I ever did see": Ringrose, 218.

264   "the beautifullest creature that my eyes ever beheld": Sharp, *Captain Sharp's Journey Over the Isthmus of Darien and Expedition into the South Seas,* 124.

265   "670 piggs of metal": Anonymous [John Cox], 88.

265   The term *pigs*: "Pig Iron," International Iron Metallics Association, https://www.metallics.org/pig-iron.html.

265   "Thus we parted with the richest booty": Dick, 92–93.

265   "But by good luck I saved it": From Sharp's original journal, cut from the published version but reprinted in Lloyd, "Bartholomew Sharp, Buccaneer."

265   It contained 315 pages: *Santo Rosario* pilot Francisco Bernardo's testimony, cited in Mangas, "El proceso de pirata Bartholomew Sharp."

266   eight buccaneer crews: Dampier, "A New Voyage Round the World," 57.

266   losing several of his seventy-man party: Dampier, 531.

30. The Horn

268   "We have got nothing" and subsequent journal entry: Anonymous [John Cox], *The Voyages and Adventures of Capt. Barth. Sharp and Others in the South Sea,* 89.

269   "What we got in the day by the help of the wind": Ringrose, *Baz Ringrose's Journal into the South Seas,* 221.

269   Sword and pistol procedure: Little, *The Buccaneer's Realm,* loc. 1006, Kindle.

269 "Our quarter-master, James Chappel, and myself fought": Ringrose, 222.

270 "all in drink" and subsequent details of the slave revolt: Ringrose, 222.

271 *Boot-topping* definition: Falconer, *An Universal Dictionary of the Marine,* loc. 1197, Kindle.

271 "very merry all the while": Ringrose, 222.

272 "This preposterous firing": Ringrose, 227.

272 "All our hopes of doing any farther good": Ringrose, 230.

274 around midnight, when the wind barreled in: Ringrose, 240.

274 pintel and *gooseneck* definitions: Falconer, loc. 3443–44.

274 "Great was now our extremity" and subsequent details of the Duke of York's Islands: Ringrose, 240–48.

275 "The De'ill himself can't hold to a bargain": Bassett, *Legends and Superstitions of the Sea and of Sailors in All Lands and at All Times,* loc. 2024–27, Kindle.

276 seventeenth-century mariners returning from the Pacific often sailed west: Little, *The Sea Rover's Practice,* 217.

277 "islands of ice": Sharp, *Captain Sharp's Journey Over the Isthmus of Darien and Expedition into the South Seas,* 128.

277 "such a way as peradventure never any mortals came before us": Dick, *William Dick's South Sea Voyage,* 106.

31. Landfall

278 Several of them simply couldn't bear the cold: Ringrose, *Baz Ringrose's Journal into the South Seas,* 254.

278 "We were now kept to a very short allowance": Ringrose, 254.

279 "much easier passage from the North Sea": Dick, *William Dick's South Sea Voyage,* 106.

279 "Yet none we could see": Ringrose, 254.

280 causing them to quarrel: Anonymous [Edward Povey], "Bartholomew Sharp's Men," 129.

280 "Things came to an understanding" and "All was husht up": Anonymous [Edward Povey], 130.

281 the then average price for a horse: "Currency Converter: 1270–2017."

281 Cox purchased the spaniel from the quartermaster: Anonymous [John Cox], *The Voyages and Adventures of Capt. Barth. Sharp and Others in the South Sea,* 109.

281 "rather that my men might not mutiny": Sharp, *Captain Sharp's Journey Over the Isthmus of Darien and Expedition into the South Seas,* 130.

282 "good hopes we should e'er long see land": Ringrose, 272.

282 they began to look out in earnest for land: Ringrose, 274.

282–83   "I cannot easily express the infinite joy": Ringrose, 276.

283   the buccaneers feared that once the *Richmond* received: Dick, 107.

283   Siboney People: Tiffin, *The Post-Colonial Studies Reader*, 281.

284   37,500 enslaved Africans: Sheridan, *Sugar and Slavery*, 123.

284   Colonel Christopher Codrington II: Sheridan, 193.

284   gentry and common people alike: Ringrose, 279.

285   "Thus I myself and thirteen more": Ringrose, 279.

285   Nevis sugar production history: Luscombe, "Nevis."

285   "I arrived on the 30th of January at Nevis": Sharp, 132.

285   "Some came into England, others went to Jamaica": Anonymous [John Cox], 114.

285   "Thus we dispersed": Dick, 107.

285   "the shipp was so crewell leakey": Anonymous [Edward Povey], 132.

286   The residents of St. Thomas's reception of the *Trinity*: Letter from Governor Esmit, May 17, 1682, in Westergaard, *The Danish West Indies Under Company Rule (1671–1754)*, 48.

286   "Thus the good shipp Trinity": Anonymous [Edward Povey], 133.

286   "since been found guilty and condemned": Henry Morgan to Sir Leoline Jenkins, March 8, 1682, in Fortescue, *Calendar of State Papers Colonial, America and West Indies*, vol. 11, *1681–1685*, no. 431.

287   "Thiss being what I can think on att present": Anonymous [Edward Povey], 133.

32. The Silver Oar

288   Opening scene of *Treasure Island*: Robert Louis Stevenson, *Treasure Island* (Mineola, NY: Dover, 1993), 1.

288   Rear Admiral John Benbow: Benbow pursued Sharp to St. Thomas in 1699 per Burkett, *A Complete History of the Most Remarkable Transactions at Sea*, 579.

288   a stout man of fifty-two: Per the 1678 or 1679 portrait by Herman Hendrik de Quiter at the Herzog Anton Ulrich Museum, Braunschweig, Germany.

289   destroyed twenty-five ships and murdered more than two hundred Spaniards: Gerhard, *Pirates on the West Coast of New Spain, 1575–1742*, 251.

289   "he had lived a wicked course of life abroad" and subsequent remarks by Sharp's landlord: Howse and Thrower, 27.

290   a mix of seamen and debtors: White, *Mansions of Misery*, loc. 715, Kindle.

290   mounds of filthy hay and other details of the Marshalsea: White, *London in the Eighteenth Century*, 446.

291   option of paying rent for superior accommodations: Ginger, *Handel's Trumpeter*, 166.

291   lawn the inmates called the Park: White, *Mansions of Misery*, 996–1002.

292   "with all the privacy": Conway to Jenkins, quoted in Howse and Thrower, 27.

292   Sharp's value in the production of the copy of the *derrotero*: Howse and Thrower, 28.

292   "[H]is Majesty will acquaint you with the reason": Howse and Thrower, 27.

293   petit jury: After a grand jury found that there was "true bill" (adequate evidence to justify a prosecution), the case proceeded to the twelve-man petit jury hearing all the cases during the Admiralty court session.

294   in some courtrooms, a mirrored reflector: Emsley, Hitchcock, and Shoemaker, "History of the Old Bailey Courthouse."

294   "a plain and honest defence" and other pre-1696 rules for defendants' legal representation or lack thereof: Langbein, "The Prosecutorial Origins of Defence Counsel in the Eighteenth Century."

295   "to burn the [frigate]": Sainsbury, *Calendar of State Papers Colonial, America and West Indies*, vol. 5, *1661–1668*, and vol. 7, *1669–1674*, 313–26.

295   rich scarlet robe with a starched ruff: "History of Court Dress," Courts and Tribunals Judiciary, https://www.judiciary.uk/about-the-judiciary/the-justice-system/history/.

296   "You stand here accused of pyracy and robbery" and other pirate trial procedures: "The Procedure for the Trial of a Pirate."

296   "piratically and feloniously stealing": Howse and Thrower, 285.

296   "How say you, are you guilty of the pyracy": "The Procedure for the Trial of a Pirate."

297   "40 lb. weight of sea bread worth 50 shillings" and subsequent charges: Howse and Thrower, 284.

297   Domingo Fernández and Jacinto de Urbina: Mangas, "El proceso de pirata Bartholomew Sharp."

297   Calderón's relation of the *Santo Rosario* crewmen's initial encounter with the *Trinity*: Jameson, *Privateering and Piracy in the Colonial Period*, 235.

298   Urbina, who had been aboard the *Trinity*: Mangas.

298   it was incumbent upon Sharp, Cox, and Dick and general information regarding protocol for defendants: Emsley, Hitchcock, and Shoemaker, "Trial Procedures."

298   "Everyone knew that those kings did not know how to write": Pedro Ronquillo to S. M., December 28, 1682, cited in Mangas.

298   "in their own defence" and subsequent Sharp testimony: National Archives, High Court of Admiralty records, HCA 1/51, folios 183, 187d.

299   "two or three villains of our own company": Dick, *William Dick's South Sea Voyage*, 113–14.

299 "Negroes and blackamoors": Paul L. Hughes and James F. Larkin, eds., *Tudor Royal Proclamations*, vol. 3, *The Later Tudors (1588–1603)* (New Haven, CT: Yale University Press, 1969), 221–22 (circa January of 1601).

299 "those kinde of people should be sente forth of the land": Open letter by Elizabeth I to the mayors of England, 11 July 1596 (PC 2/21 f. 304), National Archives PC 2/21, f. 304 (July 11, 1596). See https://www.nationalarchives.gov.uk/education/resources/elizabeth-monarchy/open-letter-by-elizabeth-i/.

299 the *Encyclopaedia Britannica*'s "Negro" entry: Hunt, "On the Negro's Place in Nature."

299 the sailors had not been baptized: Pedro Ronquillo to S. M., cited in Mangas.

299 "We are already insured of the business": Mangas.

300 With an eye toward getting litigants back to sea: Durston, *The Admiralty Sessions, 1536–1834*, 99.

300 "Session of Oyer and Terminer": Howse and Thrower, 285.

300 "a fair trial": Dick, 113.

300 "did not meddle with matters relating to law": Howse and Thrower, 28.

301 Spain's secretary of state expressed astonishment: Howse and Thrower, 28.

301 "how uncontrollable the verdict of juries are": Howse and Thrower, 28.

301 "the damage is so great as to deserve an interposition": Letter from Sir Leoline Jenkins to Henry Goodricke, National Archives Public Records Office, PRO, SP 94/67, 147.

301 the Spaniards seized Goodricke: Goodricke, *History of the Goodricke Family*, 54.

33. The Sequel

302 The most drastic such edit: Howse and Thrower, *A Buccaneer's Atlas*, 11. In addition, Ringrose in his journal called Sawkins "a man as stoute as could bee and beloved above any that ever wee had amongst us and he well deserved, for wee may attribute but the greatest honour to him in our fighte at Panama" (Howse and Thrower, 11).

303 "To the high and mighty monarch Charles the Second": "South Sea Waggoner," British Library, https://www.bl.uk/collection-items/south-sea-waggoner.

304 the *Bonetta*, a sleek fifty-seven-ton sloop of war: Kemp and Lloyd, *Brethren of the Coast*, 60

304 "he was soon reduced low": Dick, *William Dick's South Sea Voyage*, 115.

304 "no commander should carry him into those parts": Dick, 115.

304 one merchant captain after the next refused him: Dick, 115–17.

305 "he clapt aboard, seized, and made himself master thereof": Dick, 116.

306 Ringrose's original choice: Lloyd, "Bartholomew Sharp, Buccaneer."

306 "He had no mind to this voyage": Dampier, "A New Voyage Round the World," 286.

306 "fought with his sword in the most desperate engagements": Howse and Thrower, 29–30.

307 "the Spanish Seas as [the Spaniards] proudly call them": Howse and Thrower, 130.

308 "some troubles," as he put it: Masefield, appendix to *The Voyages of Captain William Dampier,* vol. I, 537.

308 1,158 pieces of eight, 162 pounds of plate, and one and a half ounces of gold toward: Malt, "Lionel Wafer — Surgeon to the Buccaneers," 471.

308 1693 founding of the College of William and Mary: Malt, 471–72.

309 the Company of Scotland Trading: Pratt, *Papers Relating to the Ships and Voyages of the Company of Scotland Trading to Africa and the Indies, 1696–1707,* xi.

309 lobby the English government to try another Darien colony: Pratt, 54.

309 British Bencoolen, Sumatra: Dampier, 500–501.

309 "richly detailed account of people, places, things": This quotation is part of an evaluation of "A New Voyage Round the World" in the journal of Edward Stanly, the captain who succeeded Sharp (see Lloyd, "Bartholomew Sharp, Buccaneer").

309 a great influence on Darwin himself: "Books on the Beagle," Darwin Correspondence Project, University of Cambridge, darwinproject.ac.uk/people/about-darwin/what-darwin-read/books-beagle.

310 the English Admiralty's expedition to explore New Holland: Preston, *A Pirate of Exquisite Mind,* chapter 13.

311 "They were stript, and cut and mangl'd": Dampier, 285–86.

311 He certainly had not lived long: At the time, Englishmen who had survived childhood disease could expect to live an average of 62.4 years, according to the life expectancy data in H. O. Lancaster, *Expectations of Life: A Study in the Demography, Statistics, and History of World Mortality* (New York: Springer-Verlag, 1990), 8.

Illustration Credits

Page 5: An English pirate. From Howard Pyle, *Howard Pyle's Book of Pirates* (New York: Harper & Brothers, 1921), 13, via Wikimedia Commons.

Page 29: Kuna smoking tobacco. From Lionel Wafer, *A New Voyage and Description of the Isthmus of Panama* (Cleveland: The Burrows Brothers Company, 1903), 108, via Google Books.

Page 50: Portrait of Henry Morgan. From A. O. Exquemelin, *Bucaniers of America, Part II* (London: William Crooke, 1684), 60.

Page 55: Port Royal. From John Masefield, *On the Spanish Main* (London: Methuen & Co., 1906), 132, via Project Gutenberg.

Page 60: Portrait of William Dampier. "William Dampier," by J. Horsburgh, from Christian Isobel Johnstone, *Lives and Voyages of Drake, Cavendish, and Dampier* (Edinburgh: Oliver & Boyd, Tweedale Court, 1837), 181, via Google Books.

Page 77: An "examination." From Howard Pyle, *Howard Pyle's Book of Pirates* (New York: Harper & Brothers, 1921), 37, via Wikimedia Commons.

Page 86: Ship raid. From Howard Pyle, *Howard Pyle's Book of Pirates* (New York: Harper & Brothers, 1921), 211, via Wikimedia Commons.

Page 95: Burning ship. "Burning of the Gaspee" from Howard Pyle, *Howard Pyle's Book of the American Spirit: The Romance of American History* (United Kingdom: Harper & Brothers, 1923), 197, via Google Books.

Page 99: Naval battle. "Morgan's attack of Maracaibo," from F. Whymper, *The Sea: Its Stirring Story of Adventure, Peril, & Heroism, Volume III* (London: Cassell, Peter, Galpin & Co., 1877), 40, via Project Gutenberg.

Page 106: Surgeon's instruments. "Fold out chart of instruments," from John Woodall, *The Surgions Mate* (London: Laurence Lisle, 1617), via Wikimedia Commons.

Page 109: Surrender. "And again my captain took the biggest," by Howard Pyle, *Harper's Magazine*, January 1895, 331, via Google Books.

Page 136: Squid. Pen and wash drawing by malacologist Pierre Dénys de Montfort, 1801, from the descriptions of French sailors reportedly attacked by such a creature off the coast of Angola, via Wikimedia.

Page 153: Crewmen waiting to hear the captain's plan. From Howard Pyle, *Howard Pyle's Book of Pirates* (New York: Harper & Brothers, 1921), 13, via Wikimedia Commons.

Page 157: Francis Drake's crew seizing the silver that may still lie on Isla de la Plata. "Thomas Moon began to Lay about him with his Sword," from Howard Pyle, *Howard Pyle's Book of the American Spirit: The Romance of American History* (United Kingdom: Harper & Brothers, 1923), 4, via Google Books.

Page 165: Plotting in a tavern. "He Led Jack up to a Man Who Sat upon a Barrel," from Howard Pyle, *Howard Pyle's Book of Pirates* (United Kingdom: Harper and Brothers, 1921), 136, via Project Gutenberg.

Page 195: A ship is "fired." "The Burning Ship," from Howard Pyle, *Howard Pyle's Book of Pirates* (New York: Harper & Brothers, 1921), 236, via Project Gutenberg.

Page 198: Alexander Selkirk on Más a Tierra. From William Lee, *Daniel Defoe: His Life and Recently Discovered Writings: Extending from 1716 to 1729, Vol. III*, 388, via Google Books.

Page 206: The rescue of William the Striker. Copperplate-engraving by Robert Pollard after the drawing by Hubert-Francois Gravelot, in John Hamilton Moore, *A New and Complete Collection of Voyages and Travels* (London: Alexander Hogg, 1790), 55.

Page 210: Arica. "Rada de Arica," from François Coreal, *Voyages de François Coreal aux des Occidentales* (Paris: Jean-Baptiste Coignard, 1720), via Wikimedia Commons.

Page 244: Map of the Golfo Dulce. From Basil Ringrose, *The South Sea Waggoner shewing the making & bearing of all the coasts from California to the Streights of Le Maire done from the Spanish originall by Basil Ringrose* (1682), 32, courtesy of the National Maritime Museum, Greenwich, London, via Wikimedia Commons.

Page 248: A recruitment. "Brownejohns Wharf" illustration by Howard Pyle, in John Austin, "Old New York Taverns by John Austin Stevens," *Harper's Magazine*, May 1890, 847, via Google Books.

Page 253: Chief Lacenta and other Kuna. From Lionel Wafer, *A New Voyage and Description of the Isthmus of Panama* (Cleveland: The Burrows Brothers Company, 1903), 136, via Google Books.

Page 261: The bloodletting of one of Lacenta's wives. From Lionel Wafer, *A New Voyage and Description of the Isthmus of Panama* (Cleveland: The Burrows Brothers Company, 1903), 55, via Google Books.

Page 270: Sword fight. "Why don't you end it?" by Howard Pyle, from Johnston, Mary, *To Have and to Hold* (Cambridge, MA: Riverside Press, 1900).

Page 276: Rocky seas. Illustration by E. Duncan, in Samuel Taylor Coleridge, *The Rime of the Ancient Mariner* (University of California, D. Appleton, 1857), 10, via Google Books.

Page 291: King Charles II of England. "Portrait of Charles II of England" by Lambert van den Bos Schauplatz des Krieges, 1675, via Wikimedia Commons.

Page 294: Seventeenth-century trial. Engraving by CG Lewis of Sir George Hayter's painting "The Trial of William Lord Russell," 1683, from *The Art Journal*, Volume 41, 1879, 180.

Page 296: Pirates at Execution Dock in London. Seventeenth-century engraving, artist unknown, via Wikimedia Commons.

Page 303: Map from Sharp's waggoner. From William Hack and Bartholomew Sharpe, *Waggoner of the South Seas* (1682), courtesy of Philadelphia Free Library, Rare Book Department.

Index

About the Author

Keith Thomson is the author of several novels, including *Pirates of Pensacola* and the *New York Times* bestseller *Once a Spy*. The former Columbia history major also writes nonfiction for the *New York Times*, *Garden & Gun*, and the *Huffington Post* on a range of topics including national security and piracy. He lives in Birmingham, Alabama.